GOD'S WORD

TO THE NATIONS

New Evangelical Translation

Proverbs

Spreading and teaching through the Spirit's Holy Word
the message of our loving, heavenly Father
who gave His Son to save sinful human beings.

NET Publishing

Cleveland

ISBN 1-880189-03-8

NET Publishing
Division of God's Word To The Nations Bible Society
P.O. Box 26343
22050 Mastick Road
Cleveland, OH 44126
1-800-937-9050

Contents

Abbreviations and Codes

General abbreviations

BDB	Brown, Driver, Briggs, *Hebrew and English Lexicon of the Old Testament*
c.	around, about, approximately
cf.	compare, confer
ch., chs.	chapter, chapters
e.g.	for example
Eng	English
etc.	and so forth
GWNBS	God's Word To The Nations Bible Society
Gk	Greek
Heb	Hebrew
Holladay	Holladay, *A Concise Hebrew and Aramaic Lexicon of the Old Testament*
i.e.	that is
lit.	literally
LXX	Septuagint, Gk translation of Heb OT
MT	Masoretic Text
MSS	manuscripts
NET	*New Evangelical Translation*
NT	New Testament
note(s)	footnote(s)
OT	Old Testament
p., pp.	page, pages
pl.	plural
sing.	singular
v., vv.	verse, verses

General codes

[...]	full brackets:	enclose word(s)/terms used to aid Eng communication
⌞ ... ⌟	half brackets:	enclose word(s) added to text that help the Eng meaning track more intelligibly or smoothly
italics	italics:	indicate words directly quoted from the OT in the NT

Footnote indicators

Eng equivalent difficult = It is difficult or nearly impossible to communicate the meaning of a given Heb word/phrase/sentence into Eng with a suitable, modern Eng equivalent, even though the Heb meaning is clear.

Heb meaning uncertain = Our understanding of a given Heb word/phrase/sentence has become clouded by lack of information. One or more reasons have contributed to this dilemma through the ages.

Lit. (Literally) = This indicated NET translation is a faithful rendering of the original Hebrew by being "literal to the original meaning," rather than being "literal to form," i.e., literalistic (word-for-word). In this way the NET strives to achieve *naturalness* in its English style.

Alphabetical Listing of the Books of the Bible
Old and New Testaments

The NET uses the following abbreviations for the books of the Old and New Testaments. NT books are indicated by *italics*.

1 Chr	1 Chronicles	Hos	Hosea
1 Cor	*1 Corinthians*	Is	Isaiah
1 Jn	*1 John*	*Jas*	*James*
1 Kgs	1 Kings	Jer	Jeremiah
1 Pet	*1 Peter*	*Jn*	*John*
1 Sam	1 Samuel	Job	Job
1 Thess	*1 Thessalonians*	Joel	Joel
1 Tim	*1 Timothy*	Jonah	Jonah
2 Chr	2 Chronicles	Josh	Joshua
2 Cor	*2 Corinthians*	*Jude*	*Jude*
2 Jn	*2 John*	Judg	Judges
2 Kgs	2 Kings	Lam	Lamentations
2 Pet	*2 Peter*	Lev	Leviticus
2 Sam	2 Samuel	*Lk*	*Luke*
2 Thess	*2 Thessalonians*	Mal	Malachi
2 Tim	*2 Timothy*	*Matt*	*Matthew*
3 Jn	*3 John*	Mic	Micah
Acts	*Acts*	*Mk*	*Mark*
Amos	Amos	Nah	Nahum
Col	*Colossians*	Neh	Nehemiah
Dan	Daniel	Num	Numbers
Deut	Deuteronomy	Obad	Obadiah
Eccl	Ecclesiastes	*Phil*	*Philippians*
Eph	*Ephesians*	*Phlm*	*Philemon*
Esther	Esther	Prov	Proverbs
Ex	Exodus	Ps	Psalms
Ezek	Ezekiel	*Rev*	*Revelation*
Ezra	Ezra	*Rom*	*Romans*
Gal	*Galatians*	Ruth	Ruth
Gen	Genesis	S of S	Song of Solomon
Hab	Habakkuk	*Tit*	*Titus*
Hag	Haggai	Zech	Zechariah
Heb	*Hebrews*	Zeph	Zephaniah

To the Reader

Can there be a more pertinent writing for the people of today's society than the book of *Proverbs*? People everywhere are searching for answers to current dilemmas. Many claim to have the answers, but so often their answers are so short-range, only lasting until the next riot or war, the next car payment or default, the next sexual encounter or divorce, the next earthquake or disaster.

In the midst of it all comes *Proverbs*. This God-inspired book deals with issue after burning issue. Its answers are God's answers—*timely, long-range,* even *eternal.* Those who will apply the "wisdom sayings" of *Proverbs* to their own lives will benefit beyond comparison.

Proverbs deals with moral responsibility, honesty, and justice—and evaluates these virtues in terms of the "fear of the LORD." This *fear of the LORD* builds godly *wisdom, knowledge,* and *understanding* (1:5-7). This is done on the basis of God's spiritual savvy and His everyday, common sense application. In short, *Proverbs* is concerned with *human conduct*: one's relationship to God and also one's responsibility toward other human beings.

Proverbs is ageless. Its ageless value lies in its ability to deal with the totality (i.e., root and substance) of any given topic. Yet, its application speaks to *moral particulars of today*:

- the obligation and benefit of repaying debts (applicable to the S & L bailouts, inside traders, bankruptcy claims, lasting friendships, good feelings);

- the value of and need for telling the truth (having reference to being "as good as your word," making deals with an old-fashioned handshake, absence of guilt feelings, political double-talk, media bias, scientific half-truths and industrial denials [evolutionistic theory, pollution, etc.]);

- the dishonesty of justifying immorality as "art-form" (the pressing need to evaluate pornography, much of MTV and audio recordings, many movies and TV segments as well as "900"-number advertisings);

- the wisdom of living your faith on God's terms (as pertaining to Sunday worship, daily Bible reading and spiritual growth, helping the poor through sacrifice);

- the trap of becoming obsessed with get-rich schemes (lottery and gambling);

- the responsibility to voice God's truths in relation to "political footballs" (the issues of abortion, homosexuality, gay and lesbian rights);

■ the importance of analyzing and dealing with modern marriage and family life as it pertains to promises (lifelong commitments, divorce, remarriage), sexual matters (faithfulness, premarital sex, live-ins, extramarital affairs), encouragement (compliments, sharing of obligations at home, family activities).

Because of this *pertinence to the lives of today's people*, God's Word To The Nations Bible Society (GWNBS) and its team of translation specialists are pleased to present you with *Proverbs* in the New Evangelical Translation (NET). For persons and nations in conflict and those who desire to end conflict by using the *absolutes* of God's ethics (6:16-19), we have chosen *Proverbs* as the *first* NET OT book to be translated.

We pray that you will benefit both spiritually and physically from this timely word spoken by Him who is KNOWLEDGE, WISDOM, and UNDERSTANDING, our all-wise God—Father, Son, and Holy Spirit (see diagram on p. 15). May *Proverbs* bring much spiritual and earthly value into your private and public life. We have divided this *Proverbs* booklet into three parts for your benefit: (1) introductory and background matter; (2) the Biblical text; (3) study information, containing sections entitled STUDIES IN *PROVERBS*, AN ABRIDGED CONCORDANCE, and PARALLELING *PROVERBS* TO THE NEW TESTAMENT.

About *Proverbs*

During his lifetime, as 1 Kgs. 4:32 states, Solomon spoke over three thousand (3,000) proverbs. The content of the book of *Proverbs* implies that he also gathered and compiled the "wise sayings" of others into his overall body of "wisdom literature" (30:1; 31:1). Visits by others to his throne room would have provided opportunity for Solomon to hear the *wisdom* that God had given to others (1 Kgs. 4:29-34). Later, from this collection of Solomonic "wisdom," the men of Hezekiah "copied," that is, *copied out, selected*, and *arranged* a number of these wise sayings into the Biblical book of *Proverbs* (25:1). Thus Solomon was the author and initial compiler of everything that eventually formed the *content* of *Proverbs*.

This understanding of Solomonic authorship is intricately involved in the arrangement of the book, as edited in its final form by "the men of King Hezekiah" (25:1). This arrangement may be viewed as follows:

Title (1:1); Purpose (1:2-6); Theme (1:7; cf. 9:10)
A. "Knowledge, Wisdom, and Understanding" Call Out (1:8–9:18)
B. The Proverbs of Solomon (10:1–22:16)
C. The Words of the Wise (22:17–24:34)
D. The Proverbs of Solomon Copied Out by the "Men of Hezekiah"
     (25:1–29:27)
E. The Words of Agur (30:1-33)
F. The Counsel of Lemuel's Mother (31:1-9)
G. A Wife with Strength of Character (31:10-31)

Proverbs has a general title (1:1) which both indicates its author and serves as a caption for the whole book. From this title unfolds the *purpose* of *Proverbs* (1:2-6) as well as its *theme* or, what we might call the underlying heartbeat of its content, namely, "the *fear of the* LORD is the beginning of knowledge" (1:7). This theme appears in its *extended* form in 9:10:

The *fear of the* LORD is the beginning of wisdom, and
the knowledge of the Holy One is understanding.

This *fear*-woven purpose is then developed into *seven* (7) self-contained units (A-G, above). The first four units flow from the hand of Solomon himself, while the remaining three are selections from Solomon's collection of "wisdom" material. This collection, which is alluded to in Prov. 25:1, is the body of literature from which the whole book emanates. (The three major elements of *Proverbs'* extended theme—"wisdom, fear, LORD"—are dealt with in Studies 1, 2, 3, 4, 5, and 13 on pages 69, 74, 77, 80, 83, and 109, respectively.)

a. Arrangement

Unit A [1:8–9:18] consists of *ten* appeals [discourses] fashioned in terms of a father-son/teacher-pupil relationship. Chapters 8 and 9 form an *epilog* to this first part. Within this epilog stands the vital section on "wisdom" and "the understanding of wisdom" (8:22-31). It portrays "the *eternity* of wisdom" most vividly in triple trilogies. The passage points directly and unmistakably to "Christ, in whom are hidden all the treasures of wisdom and knowledge" (Col. 2:3). He is the very "Word" of God who "was in the beginning with God" (Jn. 1:1,2). Thus, in the OT the pre-incarnate Christ speaks a *wisdom* for all to hear. *Unit B* [10:1-22:16] begins with the statement: "The proverbs of Solomon," recalling the complete title of 1:1. In this unit two discernible groups of trilogies exemplify the wise son (10:1–12:28; 13:1–15:19; 15:20–17:24) and the foolish son (17:25–19:12; 19:13-25; 19:26–22:16). Throughout this entire unit, there is, contrary to the opinion of many, a unique clustering or grouping of proverbs, based on subject matter. These are clearly indicated in the NET. *Unit C* [22:17–24:34] consists of about *thirty* sayings with an appendix listing *five* more (cf. Study 14, p. 115). This section is composed of "the words of the wise" (22:17). However, the introductory words to this unit (22:17-21) speak of these "words" as being imparted by an individual whose identity does not need to be stated because it is none other than Solomon himself. Some scholars speak of an *anonymous* author for this unit. But that disrupts the unity of the book since the next unit, *Unit D* [25:1–29:27], states that its contents are "also" the words of Solomon, drawn from Solomon's own collection (25:1).

Since such is the case, it may be concluded that Solomon's collection, upon which Hezekiah's men relied, also contained "the words of Agur," *Unit E* [30:1-33], "the sayings of King Lemuel's mother," *Unit F* [31:1-9], and King Lemuel's mother's poem about "a wife with strength of character," *Unit G* [31:10-31]. This final unit is an "acrostic poem" (cf. Study 12, p. 105), perhaps inspired by Ps. 145, the acrostic masterpiece of King David, Solomon's father.

b. Authorship

To emphasize once more, Solomon—who ruled from 971-931 B.C. (Whitcomb) or 985-945 B.C. (Faulstich) and was reputed for his genius (1 Kgs. 3:10-13; 4:29-34; 10:1-10)—composed a body of "wisdom literature" from which King Hezekiah's men (716-686 B.C.) transcribed and put together the present book called *Proverbs* (25:1). Selections attributed to Agur and Lemuel apparently stem from that same Solomonic collection. They are homogeneous with the book itself and, since nothing indicates the contrary, it's logical to conclude that Solomon's gift of brilliance, coupled with humility, did not exclude collecting and using the observations of other wise men. In chapter 31 a final tribute to the overall theme of *wisdom* is seen in terms of the practical way by which "a wife with strength of character" cares for her home in the *fear of the LORD*.

This understanding of the Solomonic authorship of *Proverbs* is consistent with the structure of the book itself. To assume numerous unknown redactors, editors, wisdom schools, and circles of wise men, who leaning on Solomon's "alleged" wisdom formulated the book under his name, is pure speculation.

It is significant to note that *all* chapters of *Proverbs* are referred to in the NT. There are well over one hundred references to *Proverbs*, either by quote or allusion (see PARALLELING *PROVERBS* TO THE NEW TESTA-MENT on p. 131).

Part 2

By way of definition—*Proverbs* and "proverbs"

Proverbs is a book full of the obvious—"proverbs." Yet the meaning of these Biblical proverbs at times is anything but *obvious*. Many do not even realize what a *proverb* is, let alone understand the meanings of various proverbs within the book of *Proverbs*. Therefore, it is worth describing this literary phenomenon.

The All Nations English Dictionary (1990) defines a "proverb" as "A short well-known saying usually in popular language." Some examples from *Proverbs* are:

> Trust the LORD with all your heart,
>   and do not rely on your own understanding. (3:5)

> The fear of the LORD is the beginning of wisdom, and
> the knowledge of the Holy One is understanding. (9:10)

> Better to have a dish of vegetables where there is love
>   than juicy steaks where there is hate. (15:17)

> A lazy person puts his fork in his food;
> he doesn't even bring it back to his mouth. (19:24)

> Like golden apples in silver settings,
>   so is a word spoken at the right time. (25:11)

> Without wood a fire goes out, and
> without gossip a quarrel dies down. (26:20)

a. Structured with "brevity"

Generally, the very nature of a *proverb* implies a saying that is *short* and *brief*. At times though, *proverbial thought* can be very *lengthy*, extending over an entire discourse (cf. Prov. 1:8–9:18). Pithy *proverbs* can be found within the larger sections. One such shorter proverb within a longer discourse is Prov. 9:10, as printed above. Here the Hebrew text has only *seven* (7) words, compared with our English which has *nineteen* (19) words. The old King

James Version (KJV), the standard for literal translations, uses *eighteen* (18) words to translate the seven Hebrew words. If the English translation were as terse as the Hebrew text, Prov. 9:10 would read:

> Fear LORD beginning wisdom,
> knowledge Holy understanding.

English almost always requires many more words for a smooth, intelligible *Proverbs* text than does the Hebrew. This imbalance occurs time after time. Yet, when compared with the general wisdom of modern books, political rhetoric, and media commentary, these translated proverbs in today's English Bibles are still very *short*.

It's quite a challenge to be faithful to the terseness of Hebrew and at the same time to the requirements of fluid, understandable English, as Prov. 9:10 demonstrates. This *sparseness* of words in the Bible's proverbial sayings should both surprise and alert the reader. As a result, one can appreciate how difficult it is to pick up the intended meaning of the Hebrew, let alone to decide how to put such Hebrew thoughts into flowing, meaningful English. For this reason few books of the OT are as difficult to translate as is *Proverbs*. In reference to *Proverbs* the 1988 French *Ecumenical Translation of the Bible* (TOB) comments: "The modern translator is confronted with innumerable difficulties."

Also, the NET translators wish to remind readers that languages such as Hebrew and Greek may use certain nouns or verbs in one line of poetry but not repeat them in other lines—though they assume the reader will "fill in the ellipses" by repeating the nouns or verbs from line to line as needed for sake of clarity or communication. NET *Proverbs* has followed this assumption and, therefore, has *not* indicated *filled-in ellipses* with "half-bracket indicators," contrary to the general NET NT pattern. However, half-brackets are frequently employed where—for sake of flow and clarity—other words are added beyond those of the Hebrew text.

b. Made well known through "teaching"

According to the definition above, a *saying*—if it is to qualify as a "proverb"—must also be *well known*. To accomplish this, a *saying* must be "taught" to many people and, in turn, be acknowledged by many of them as a "wise" truth. *The Random House College Dictionary* (1988) implicitly identifies *wisdom* with *teaching* when it defines a Biblical "proverb" as "a profound saying, maxim, or oracular utterance, requiring interpretation."

This is illustrated by 1 Kgs. 4:29-34 which talks about Solomon's proverbs. We are told that Solomon's "wisdom" was famous throughout the surrounding nations; many people, even kings, came to hear his vast wisdom. In particular, this 1 Kgs. 4 passage reports that Solomon spoke three thousand proverbs. The book of *Proverbs* contains only about a third of them.

In Solomon's time and even many years later, these proverbs were held in high esteem and were regularly applied to everyday life. Today, however, the advice of *Proverbs* is widely ignored, even by many Christians. This is unfortunate since *Proverbs* formerly played such a great part in shaping the values of Judeo/Christian thinking and the societies they permeated. The disregard for *Proverbs* and other parts of Scripture has led to widespread moral decay.

(1) "Obscurity" recognized

Beyond this, *Proverbs* continues to become even more obscure. Its contents no longer seem to qualify as *proverbs* since they are no longer *well known*. Yet, they remain God's proverbs. People cannot existentially wish them away. God's truth does not change simply because people ignore or deny it. Consequently, we need to deal with this problem of *obscurity*.

Just why have so many of the Biblical proverbs grown so obscure? In addition to the general indifference and opposition to God's Word, there are several answers: (1) the *wisdom* of *Proverbs* is not always readily apparent in this day and age; (2) the "images" used in *Proverbs* are not the type of images that we normally use in our daily conversations, and as a result many of them tend to be confusing and misleading; (3) many people have become so "busy" that they avoid those time-consuming sections of Scripture which demand any serious, deep, and contemplative thinking. However, the understanding of *proverbial thinking* demands time to meditate, evaluate, filter, apply, and experience.

(2) "Imagery" resolved

In general *proverbs* are meant to be taught, and their teaching is most effective when they are presented in popular language. Their fullest meaning unfolds through *teaching*. Thus the structure of the dialog in the book of *Proverbs*! A father-son relationship is presented in a teacher-pupil setting. Prov. 1:8,9 illustrates this father-son relationship:

> Listen, my son, to your father's discipline
> and do not neglect your mother's teaching,
> > because they are a graceful garland on your head
> > and a golden chain around your neck.

Like many proverbs, these verses employ *imagery*. But it's not our everyday kind of imagery. When "discipline" and "teaching" are identified as a "graceful garland on your head" and "a golden chain around your neck," they can seem confusing. We do not express ourselves in these terms. We might expect "mind" and "heart" instead of "head" and "neck." The wording is hard to *swallow* ("neck"), just as it has been hard for children of all ages to swallow what their parents, as well as their heavenly Father, wish to drill into their heads, hang around their necks, and dangle over their hearts. With the term "graceful," we can visualize a father saying in the language of his teenager, "I'm going to lay it on you easy this time." This level of everyday, secular understanding can be comprehended even by those who have no spiritual relationship with the LORD.

But to fully appreciate the two verses above, a person needs several minutes of explanation and a childhood of experience to comprehend what the Hebrew wishes to convey. Moreover, the highest level of meaning can only become apparent when both the *LORD* and the *"fear* of the LORD" enter the heart as *"Teacher* and *teacher,"* respectively. As the NT so ably states: "…we speak about them [the things of God] in words not taught by human wisdom but taught by the Spirit, explaining the things of the Spirit to those who have the Spirit" (1 Cor. 2:13).

For example, only God's people can receive the fuller meaning and benefit of the imagery above. To be personal, the "graceful garland on your head" and the "golden chain around your neck" imagery should remind you the Christian reader that God's grace ("undeserved love") penetrates your mind ("head") through the Word as the "fear of the LORD" comes to be precious like gold, like a golden chain that dangles down from your head and neck to channel the LORD's truth and protection into your heart, that part of your body over which a necklace or chain often hangs. You can catch such imagery through the eyes of faith.

Not only are the images of *Proverbs* different from our way of *thinking,* they are also different from our way of *talking.* We usually do not make comparisons to "garlands" and "golden chains." But that's not the worst of it. The ancient Hebrews employed the words "heart/lips/tongue/mouth" in different ways than we do. In and of themselves, comparable to "golden chains," these are common, easy-to-understand words. Yet, they are made quite challenging to the English reader by the way Hebrew sometimes combines them with other words. Take, for example, 10:18-21:

> Whoever conceals hatred has lying lips, and
> whoever spreads slander is a fool.
>> Sin is unavoidable when there is much talk,
>> but whoever seals his lips is wise.
>> The tongue of the righteous is pure silver;
>> the heart of the wicked is worthless.
> The lips of the righteous feed many,
> but stubborn fools die because they have no sense.

Like many other proverbs, this set of short sayings uses *familiar* words clothed in some *unfamiliar* expressions. To most English readers their meanings are difficult to understand, communicating little or nothing at times. Yet, these proverbs are able to break through the barriers of language and communicate much to the people of today! A contradiction? Not really when such communication is opened up by the Holy Spirit in His Word and transmitted through the teaching ministries of His servants of the Word! Spiritually and physically, *Proverbs* continues to yield its richness and to benefit those who will take time to read and consider.

Part 3
Surprises and blessings

And so, welcome to *Proverbs*! May the LORD move you to read and contemplate His teachings in *Proverbs*. A wealth of surprises and blessings awaits your inner being and outward life. This short booklet can become well known to you through diligent reading, contemplation, and application to your life. Hint: Read through chapters 1–9 in just a few sittings. (This is the most complex section; return to it later after you learn to handle *Proverbs* a bit better; it is precious.) Handle chapters 10:1–31:9 differently than you handle the rest of the Bible. Do *not* read a chapter a day. Rather, read five or so proverbs daily and chew on them throughout the day. You'll sense which ones need application to your life at a certain time. Prov. 31:10-31 should be read as a unit.

Blessings on your journey into your new world of *Proverbs*. We are confident that *Proverbs* will become one of your favorite books of Scripture.

NOTES: This NET edition of *Proverbs* has been produced under the auspices of God's Word To The Nations Bible Society (GWNBS). The purpose of this Christian organization is: (1) to reach and teach people in the world who do not know or embrace the Christian message, including those who read or wish to learn to read American English, and (2) to further educate people who already endorse Christianity, including those who read or wish to learn to read American English.

To ultimately achieve this purpose, GWNBS has a specific, *short-range goal*—produce an easy-to-read, easy-to-listen-to, and easy-to-understand Bible translation. One part of this purpose has been realized. *The New Testament* portion of the New Evangelical Translation (NET) is now in print. The other portion of the short-range objective, namely, to complete the entire Old Testament text, is now becoming more of a reality with the publishing of *Proverbs*. Our present motto: "Go for the Old!" If you are interested in more information on any phase of the NET work, please contact us. You are invited to become part of the GWNBS team; your concerns and suggestions are welcome.

About six months after the publication of *Proverbs*, GWNBS will produce an accompanying booklet. It will group the Biblical proverbs according to *topics*. You will find this most beneficial in further exploring the riches of *Proverbs*.

In the months to come the NET texts of *Genesis, Ruth/Song of Solomon/ Esther, Psalms, Haggai/Zechariah/Malachi,* and others will appear in serial form.

Outline of *Proverbs*

Proverbs

PROVERBS

1ST CHAPTER

Title (1:1); Purpose (1:2-6); Theme (1:7; cf. 9:10)

1 The proverbs of Solomon son of David, king of Israel,
2   ⸤given⸥ in order
            to grasp wisdom[a] and discipline,
            to understand deep thoughts,
3   to acquire the discipline of wise behavior
                — righteousness and justice[b] and fairness —
4   to give insight to gullible people,[c]
            to give knowledge and foresight to the young —
5   a wise person will listen and continue to learn,
                and an understanding person will gain direction
6   to understand a proverb and a clever saying,
            to understand the words of the wise and their riddles.

7 The fear of the LORD[d] is the beginning of knowledge;
        wisdom and discipline are despised by stubborn fools.[e]

SPECIAL NOTE: The entire book of *Proverbs* is set in poetic style. Indentations of the various lines have been placed with precision to permit *visual* perception of parallel thoughts. For this reason the NET refuses to split units of thought from one page to another since this would interrupt unified *visual* tracking. This method has created a very educational format but also has forced several pages to remain unfilled since the beginning of units often had to be pushed to a new page because the whole unit would not fit on a former page. Also, connectives, such as, "and" or "but" are often moved back to the end of previous lines to permit identical words in parallel lines to line up *visually*. See POETIC STRUCTURES THAT CONVEY TEXTUAL MEANINGS on p. 105.

1 *a-* 2 Heb: "*hokmah*" (also at v. 7); see "WISDOM" IN *PROVERBS* on p. 69 and HEBREW TERMS FOR "WISDOM" on p. 74.

b- 3 Heb: "*mishpat*" (also "justice" at 2:8; 8:20); "*mishpat*" is translated "just" at 2:9; see *MISHPAT* on p. 100.

c- 4 "The gullible/gullible people" also at vv. 22,32; 7:7; 8:5; see THE "FOOL" IN *PROVERBS* on p. 91.

d- 7 Phrase also at v. 29; see THE "FEAR" OF THE LORD on p. 77; also for "LORD," see GOD: HIS DESIGNATIONS AND NAMES on p. 80.

e- 7 Cf. "stubborn fool" with "fool," "godless fool," "mocker," and "the gullible/gullible person" throughout *Proverbs*; see THE "FOOL" IN *PROVERBS* on p. 91.

A. "Knowledge, Wisdom, and Understanding" Call Out (1:8–9:18)
1. Ten urgent appeals (1:8–7:27)
a. First appeal (1:8-33)

8 Listen, my son, to your father's discipline
and do not neglect your mother's teaching,*f*
9   because they are a graceful garland on your head
and a ˌgoldenˌ chain around your neck.

10 My son, if sinners lure you, do not go along!
11 If they say,
"Come with us;
let's set an ambush to commit murder;
let's hide to ambush the innocent just for fun;
12   we'll swallow them alive like the grave,*g*
like those in good health who go down to the pit.*h*
13   We'll find all kinds of valuable possessions;
we'll fill our homes with stolen goods!
14   Join up with us;
we'll split the loot equally!"*i*

15 My son, do not follow them in their way;
do not even set foot on their path,
16   because they rush to do evil
and *hurry to shed blood*,
17   for it does no good to spread a net
within the sight of any bird.
18 But these men set an ambush for their own murder;
they go into hiding only to lose their lives.
19 This is what happens to*j* everyone
who is greedy for unjust gain;
it takes away his life.

20 Wisdom*k* sings her song in the streets;
in the public squares she raises her voice;
21 at the corners of noisy streets she calls out;
at the entrances to the city*l* she speaks her words:

---

16 Rom 3:15

---

f- 8 Heb: "*torah*"; see TORAH AND *MITZWAH* on p. 96.
g- 12 Heb: "*sheol*"; see DEATH AND *SHEOL* on p. 103.
h- 12 Heb: "*bor*"; see DEATH AND *SHEOL* on p. 103.
i- 14 Lit.: "Throw in your lot with us;
we will all have just one purse."
j- 19 Lit.: "So are the ways of."
k- 20 Heb: "*hokmah*"; see GENDER AND HEBREW GENDER on p. 109.
l- 21 Lit.: "at the opening of the gates in the city."

22   "How long will you gullible people love being so gullible, and
      how long will you mockers[m] delight in your mocking, and
      how long will you fools[n] hate knowledge?

23   "Turn to me when I warn you—
            I will generously pour out my spirit for you;
            I will make my words known to you.

24   "Since I called
                  (and you refused to listen),
            since *I stretched out my hands* to you
                  (but no one pays attention)
25   and *you ignored all my advice*
                  and you did not want me to warn you, ⸤therefore,⸥
26   I too will laugh at your calamity;
                        I will make fun of you
                              when panic strikes you,
27   when panic strikes you like a violent storm, and
                              when calamity strikes you like a tornado,
                              when trouble
                              and anguish come upon you.

28   "They will call to me at that time, but I will not answer;
            they will look for me, but they will not find me,
29   because they hated knowledge
                  and did not choose the fear of the LORD.
30   They refused my advice;
            they despised my every warning.
31   They will eat the fruit of their lifestyle and
            they will be stuffed with their own schemes.

32   "Because of their turning away, the gullible kill themselves;
            and because of their indifference, fools destroy themselves;
33   but whoever listens to me will live without worry
                  and will be free from the dread of disaster."

2ND CHAPTER

b. Second appeal (2:1-22)

1   My son,

---

24 Rom 10:21   25 Lk 7:30   28 Jn 7:34

---

m- 22 "Mocker(s)" also at vv. 3:34; 9:7,8; see THE "FOOL" IN *PROVERBS* on p. 91.
n- 22 "Fools" also at vv. 32; 3:35; 8:5; see THE "FOOL" IN *PROVERBS* on p. 91.

if you take my words ⌊to heart⌋,
and treasure my commands[a] within you,

2   paying close attention to wisdom,[b]
letting your mind[c] reach for understanding

3   (if indeed you call out for insight;
if you ask aloud for understanding);

4 if you search for it [wisdom] as if it were money
and hunt for it as if it were *hidden treasure* —

5   then you will understand the fear of the LORD[d]
and you will find the knowledge of God,[e]

6   for *the LORD gives wisdom*,
from His mouth come knowledge and understanding;

7   and He has reserved[f] priceless wisdom for upright people;
He is a Shield for those who walk in integrity

8   in order to guard those on paths of justice
and to watch over the way of His godly ones;

9   then you will understand
what is right and just and fair —
every good course ⌊in life⌋.

10 For wisdom will come into your heart[g]
and knowledge will be pleasant to your soul;

11   foresight will protect you;
understanding will guard you.

12   ⌊Wisdom will⌋ save you[h]
from the way of evil,
from the man who speaks devious things,

13   from those who abandon the paths of righteousness
to walk the ways of darkness,

14   from those who enjoy doing evil,
from those who rejoice in the deviousness of evil;

15   their paths are crooked,
and their ways are devious.

---

4 Matt 13:44; Col 2:3   6 Jas 1:5

---

2   *a-* 1 Heb: "*mitzwah*"; see *TORAH* AND *MITZWAH* on p. 96.
     b- 2 Heb: "*hokmah*" (also at vv. 6,10); see "WISDOM" IN *PROVERBS* on p. 69.
     c- 2 Heb: "*leb*"; see *LEB*: "HEART" AND "MIND" on p. 95.
     d- 5 See THE "FEAR" OF THE LORD on p. 77.
     e- 5 Heb: "*Elohim*" (also at v. 17; 3:4); see GOD: HIS DESIGNATIONS AND NAMES on p. 80.
     f- 7 Or "and understanding; He reserves" (lines 6b and 7a).
     g- 10 Heb: "*leb*"; see *LEB*: "HEART" AND "MIND" on p. 95.
     h- 12 Eng transition difficult; lit.: "For wisdom will come into your heart (v. 10)...to save you"
         (v. 12). Note how the thought is extended from v. 10 to v. 12 (also to v. 16).

16   ⌊Wisdom will⌋ also save you[i]
            from the adulterous woman,
            from the loose woman[j] with her smooth talk,

17   who leaves the closest friend of her youth [her husband][k] and
            who forgets the covenant[l] with her God.

18   For her house sinks down to death,
            and her ways lead to the souls of those who died.[m]

19   None who have sex with her come back
            nor do they ever reach the paths of life.

20   Therefore, walk in the way of good people
       and stay on the paths of the righteous,

21   *for the upright will live in the land*
       and the people of integrity will remain in it,

22   but the wicked will be cut off from the land
            and the treacherous will be torn from[n] it.

3RD CHAPTER

c. Third appeal (3:1-35)

1 My son, do not forget my teaching,[a]
   and keep my commands[b] in mind,[c]

2   because they will bring you
            long life, good years,[d] and peace.

3   Do not let mercy and truth leave you:
                  fasten them around your neck;
            write them on the tablet of your heart.[e]

4   Then *you will find favor and much success*
            in the sight of God and mankind.

---

21 Matt 5:5   3 2 Cor 3:3   4 Lk 2:52; 2 Cor 8:21

---

i- 16   Eng transition difficult; lit.: "For wisdom will come into your heart (v. 10)...also to save you"
        (v. 16). Note how the thought is extended from v. 10 to v. 16 (also to v. 12).
j- 16   Lit.: "foreign woman," meaning a prostitute from another nation (also at 5:20; 6:24; 7:5).
k- 17   Read Jer. 3:1-5: "Friend," implying "Husband," refers to "God" in a context which deals with
        both physical adultery and the spiritual adultery of unbelief. Cf. also Hos. 1–3; Jer. 2,3; Ps.
        55:12-14; Is. 54:5-8.
l- 17   Here the word "covenant" refers primarily to the Ten Commandments, in particular to Ex.
        20:14: "You are not to commit adultery." Read Deut. 4:23,31; 2 Kg. 17:38. Cf. also Ezek.
        16:8; Mal. 2:14.
m- 18   See 9:18.
n- 22   Heb meaning uncertain. If Hebrew root is "nsch," the meaning is "will be torn from"; if
        "schh," then "will be swept away."
3 a- 1 Heb: "torah"; see *TORAH AND MITZWAH* on p. 96.
  b- 1 Heb: "mitzwah"; see *TORAH AND MITZWAH* on p. 96.
  c- 1 Heb: "leb"; see *LEB: "HEART" AND "MIND"* on p. 95.
  d- 2 Lit.: "length of days and years of life" (also at 9:11).
  e- 3 Heb: "leb" (also at v. 5); see *LEB: "HEART" AND "MIND"* on p. 95.

5   Trust the LORD*f* with all your heart,
         and do not rely on your own understanding.
6   In all your ways acknowledge [give credit to] Him,
         and He will make your paths smooth.*g*
7   *Do not consider yourself wise;*
         *fear the LORD*h* and turn away from evil.*
8   ⌐Then⌐ your body will have healing
         and your bones will have nourishment.*i*

9   Honor the LORD with your wealth
         and with *the first and best part of all your income.j*
10   Then your barns will be filled with plenty,
         and your vats will overflow with fresh wine.

11   *Do not reject the discipline of the LORD, my son,*
     nor resent His warning,
12   *because the LORD warns the one He loves,*
         even as a father warns a son in whom he delights.k

13   Blessed is the one who finds wisdom*l*
     and the one who obtains understanding —
14   for the profit ⌐gained⌐ from ⌐wisdom⌐ is greater than
         the profit ⌐gained⌐ from silver;
     its yield is better than fine gold.
15   ⌐Wisdom⌐ is more precious than jewels,*m*
         and all your desires cannot equal it.
16   Long life is in ⌐wisdom's⌐ right hand;
     in ⌐wisdom's⌐ left hand are riches and honor.
17   ⌐Wisdom's⌐ ways are pleasant ways
         and all its paths lead to peace.
18   ⌐Wisdom⌐ is *a tree of life*
         for those who take firm hold of it [wisdom],
         and *those who cling* to it *are blessed.*

---

7 *Matt 10:28; Lk 12:5; Acts 10:2,22,35; 13:16,26; Rom 12:16; 1 Pet 2:17; Rev 14:7*
9 *Mk 12:41-44; Lk 21:1-4; 1 Cor 16:2*   **11, 12** *Heb 12:5,6; Rev 3:19*   **18** *Rev 1:3; 2:7; 22:2,7,14,19*

---

f- 5 Heb: "*YHWH*"; used some 6,800 times of God on the pages of the OT; used often in *Proverbs* in
     the phrase "the fear of the LORD"; some of its more significant occurrences in Proverbs 1–9
     appear here and at 1:7; 5:21; 6:16; 8:22; 9:10; see GOD: HIS DESIGNATIONS AND NAMES
     on p. 80.
g- 6 Or "straight."
h- 7 See THE "FEAR" OF THE LORD on p. 77.
i- 8 Meaning that you will be healthy inside and out.
j- 9 Lit.: "harvest" (also at 15:6).
k- 12 See Heb. 12:5,6 in the NET NT. *Hebrews* quotes the LXX word for word, rather than the MT.
l- 13 Heb: "*hokmah*"; see "WISDOM" IN *PROVERBS* on p. 69.
m- 15 Lit.: "than pieces of coral."

19 By Wisdom[n] the LORD laid the foundation of the earth and
  by Understanding He established the heavens.
20 By His Knowledge the deep waters were divided
   and the skies dropped dew.

21 My son, do not lose sight of these things:
   Use priceless wisdom and foresight,
22   then they will mean life for you
     and they will grace your neck;
23   then you will go safely on your way,
     and you will not stub your foot.
24   When you lie down, you will not be afraid;
    as you lie there, your sleep will be sweet.

25   Do not be afraid of sudden terror
   nor of the destruction of the wicked when it comes,
26   for the LORD will be your confidence
    and He will keep your foot from getting caught.

27   *Do not hold back any good thing*
    from those who are entitled to it
     when it is in your power to do so.
28   When you have it with you, do not tell your neighbor:

    "Go away!
    Come back tomorrow ˌandˌ
    I'll give you something then."

29   Do not plan to do wrong against your neighbor
    while he is sitting there with you, suspecting nothing.
30   Do not quarrel with a man for no reason
    if he has done you no harm.
31   Do not envy a violent man,
    and do not choose any of his ways,
32   for the devious person is disgusting to the LORD;
    His intimate advice is with the upright.

33 The curse of the LORD is on the house of the wicked,
   but He blesses the home of the righteous.
34 *When He mocks the mockers,*
   He is gracious to the humble.
35 The wise will inherit honor,
   but fools will bear disgrace.

---

27 *Rom 16:1,2; 1 Tim 5:18; Jas 5:4* **34** *Jas 4:6; 1 Pet 5:5*

---

n- 19 Heb: *"hokmah"*; see HEBREW TERMS FOR "WISDOM" on p. 74.

4TH CHAPTER

d. Fourth appeal (4:1-9)

1 Sons, listen to ⸢your⸣ father's discipline,
and pay attention in order to gain understanding,
2   for I have taught you well;
        do not abandon my teaching.*a*
3 Once I also was a son to my father,
        a tender and only child of my mother.
4 He used to teach me and say to me:

        "Let your heart*b* cling to my words;
        keep my commands*c* so that you may live:
5   Acquire wisdom!*d*
            Acquire understanding!
        Do not forget and
        do not turn away from the words that I have spoken;
6   do not abandon ⸢wisdom⸣
                and it will watch over you;
            love ⸢wisdom⸣
                and it will protect you!

7   "The beginning is wisdom:
            Acquire wisdom!
        And with all that you have:
            Acquire understanding!
8   Cherish ⸢wisdom⸣ and it will raise you up:
                it will bring you honor when you embrace it;
9   it will give you a graceful garland for your head;
                it will hand you a beautiful crown."

e. Fifth appeal (4:10-19)

10 Listen, my son, and accept my words,
        and they will multiply the years of your life.
11   I have taught you the way of wisdom;
        I have guided you along upright paths.

---

4 *a-* 2 Heb: "*torah*"; see *TORAH* AND *MITZWAH* on p. 96.
   b- 4 Heb: "*leb*" (also at v. 23; 5:12); see *LEB*: "HEART" AND "MIND" on p. 95.
   c- 4 Heb: "*mitzwah*"; see *TORAH* AND *MITZWAH* on p. 96.
   d- 5 Heb: "*hokmah*" (also at vv. 7,11); see "WISDOM" IN *PROVERBS* on p. 69.

12 When you walk, your stride will not be hampered;
        even if you run, you will not stumble.
13 Cling to discipline;
        do not relax your grip on it;
            keep it because it is your life.
14 Do not stray onto the path of the wicked
        nor walk in the way of evil people.
15 Avoid it;
        do not walk near it;
            turn away from it;
                and keep on walking!
16   For the wicked cannot sleep
            unless they do wrong,
        and they are robbed of their sleep
            unless they make someone stumble,
17   for they eat food ˻obtained˼ through wrongdoing
                and drink wine ˻obtained˼ through violence.

18 But the path of the righteous is like the light of dawn
        that becomes brighter and brighter
            until it reaches midday.
19 *The way of the wicked is like deep darkness;*
    they do not know what makes them stumble.

f. Sixth appeal (4:20-27)

20 My son, pay attention to my words;
    open your ears to what I say:
21   Do not lose sight of these things;
            keep them deep within your heart,
22   because they are life to those who find them,
                and they heal the whole body.
23   More than anything else, guard your heart,
            because the source of your life ˻flows˼ from it. *e*
24   Remove dishonesty from your mouth
            and put deceptive speech far away from your lips;
25   let your eyes look straight ahead
            and your sight be focused in front of you.
26   Carefully walk a straight path
            and all your ways will be secure;
27   do not lean to the right or to the left;
            walk away from evil!

---

19 Jn 12:35

---

e- 23 Lit.: "from it," referring to "your heart"; or "from them," referring to "my words" (v. 20).

5TH CHAPTER

g. Seventh appeal (5:1-23)

1 My son, pay attention to my wisdom;[a]
open your ears to my understanding
2 　　so that you may act with foresight
　　and speak with insight.

3 　　For the lips of an adulterous woman drip with honey,
　　and her kiss[b] is smoother than oil,
4 　　　　but in the end she is as bitter as wormwood,[c]
　　　　as sharp as a two-edged sword.
5 　　Her feet descend to death;
　　her steps lead straight to hell.[d]
6 　　　　She doesn't even think about the path of life;
　　　　her steps wander and she doesn't realize it.

7 But now, sons, listen to me,
and do not turn away from what I say to you:

8 　　Keep far away from her
　　and do not even go near her door:
9 　　　　either you will surrender your reputation to others
　　　　　　and ⌊the rest of⌋ your years to some cruel person;
10 　　　　or strangers will benefit from your strength,
　　　　　　and you will have to work hard in a pagan's house.[e]

11 　　Then you will groan when your end comes,
　　when your body and flesh are consumed,
　　and you will say,

12 　　　　"Oh, how I hated discipline
　　　　and how my heart despised correction;
13 　　　　　　I didn't listen to what my teachers said to me
　　　　　　　　nor did I keep my ear open to my instructors;
14 　　　　　　I almost reached total ruin
　　　　　　　　in the assembly[f] and in the congregation!"

15 　　Drink water out of your own cistern
　　and running water from your own well.
16 　　　　Why should water flow out of your spring?
　　　　Why should your streams flow into the streets?
17 　　They should be yours alone,
　　　　so do not share them with strangers.

---

5 a- 1 Heb: "hokmah"; see "WISDOM" IN *PROVERBS* on p. 69.
　b- 3 Lit.: "her palate."
　c- 4 A bitter, poisonous plant. See Rev. 8:11 for the effects that wormwood has on humans.
　d- 5 Heb: "sheol"; see DEATH AND *SHEOL* on p. 103.
　e- 10 Lit.: "in a foreigner's house."
　f- 14 As in "legislative assembly," the group that made religious decisions pertaining to censure.

18   Let your own fountain be blessed
             and enjoy the girl you married when you were young,
19   a loving doe and a graceful deer.*g*
       Always let her breasts satisfy you;
       always be intoxicated with her love.
20   Why should you, my son,
             be intoxicated with an adulterous woman
             and fondle a loose woman's breast?

21   *For a man's ways are clearly seen by the* L<small>ORD</small>,
       and He surveys all his actions;
22   the wicked person will be trapped by his own wrongs,
       and he will be caught in the ropes of his own sin;
23   he will die for his lack of discipline
             and stumble around because of his great stupidity.

6TH CHAPTER

h. Eighth appeal (6:1-19)

1 My son, if you guarantee a loan for your neighbor
or pledge yourself for a stranger with a handshake,*a*
2   you are trapped by the words of your own mouth,
       caught by your own promise.

3   Now do this, my son, so that you may free yourself,
       because you have fallen into your neighbor's hands:

           Go,
           humble yourself
           and pester your neighbor;
4   give no sleep to your eyes
           nor slumber to your eyelids;
5   free yourself like a gazelle from the hand of the hunter
           and like a bird from the hand of the hunter.*b*

6 Consider the ant, you lazy bum;
       watch its ways and become wise:
7 Although it has no overseer, officer, or ruler,
8   in summertime it stores its food supply,
       at harvest time it gathers its food.

---

21 Heb 4:13

g- 19 Lit.: "graceful goat."
6 a- 1 Refers to the act of co-signing for a loan. Cf. 17:18; 20:16; 22:26 (also 11:15; 27:13).
   b- 5 Lit.: "hand of the fowler."

9   How long will you lie there, you lazy bum?
    When will you get up from your sleep?
10   "Just a little sleep,
           just a little slumber,
           just a little nap."*c*
11 So your poverty will come ⌊upon you⌋ like a drifter,
    and your need will come ⌊upon you⌋ like a bandit.

12 A good-for-nothing scoundrel is a man who has a dishonest mouth:
13   he winks his eye,
           makes a signal with his foot,*d*
           points with his fingers.
14   With a twisted mind*e* he is devising evil all the time;
       he spreads conflict.
15   *That is why disaster will come on him suddenly;*
       in a moment he will be crushed beyond recovery.

16 There are six things that the LORD hates,
    even seven that are disgusting to Him:
17   arrogant eyes,
           a lying tongue,
           and *hands that kill innocent people;f*

18   a mind devising wicked plans,
           feet that are quick to do wrong,
19   a dishonest witness spitting out lies,
           and a person who spreads conflict among brothers.

i. Ninth appeal (6:20-35)

20 My son, keep the command*g* of your father
    and do not disregard the teaching*h* of your mother:
21   fasten them on your heart*i* forever;
           hang them around your neck.
22 When you walk around, they will lead you;
           when you lie down, they will watch over you;
           and when you wake up, they will talk to you,

---

15 2 Pet 2:1   *17* Matt 23:35; Jas 5:6

---

c- 10 Lit.: "a little folding the hands to lie down."
d- 13 Lit.: "scrapes with his foot."
e- 14 Heb: "*leb*" (also at v. 18); see *LEB*: "HEART" AND "MIND" on p. 95.
f- 17 Lit.: "hands that shed innocent blood."
g- 20 Heb: "*mitzwah*" (also at v. 23); see *TORAH* AND *MITZWAH* on p. 96.
h- 20 Heb: "*torah*" (also at v. 23); see *TORAH* AND *MITZWAH* on p. 96.
i- 21 Heb: "*leb*" (also at v. 25); see *LEB*: "HEART" AND "MIND" on p. 95.

23   for the command is a lamp
and the teaching is a light,
and the warnings from discipline are the path of life[j]
24   to keep you from an evil woman
and from the smooth talk of a loose woman.

25   *Do not desire her beauty in your heart;*
do not let her catch you with her eyes.
26   A prostitute's price is ⸢only⸣ a loaf of bread,
but a married woman hunts for ⸢your⸣ very life itself.[k]
27   Can a man carry fire in his lap
without burning his clothes?
28   Or can anyone walk on red-hot coals
without burning his feet?

29   So it is with the man who has sex with his neighbor's wife;
none who touch her will escape punishment.
30   People do not despise a thief who is hungry
when he steals to satisfy his appetite;
31   but when he is caught,
he has to repay it seven times;
he must give up all the possessions in his house.

32   Whoever commits adultery with a woman has no sense;[l]
whoever does this destroys himself.[m]
33   The adulterous man will find disease and dishonor,
and his disgrace will not be blotted out,
34   because jealousy arouses a husband's fury
and the husband will show no mercy when he takes revenge.
35   No amount of money will change his mind,
and the largest bribe will not satisfy him.

7TH CHAPTER

j. Tenth appeal (7:1-27)

1   My son, keep my words
and treasure my commands[a] that are within you.
2   Keep my commands so that you may live,
and keep my teaching[b] just as you protect the pupil of your eye.

---

25 Matt 5:28

---

j- 23   Vv. 20-23 reflect Deut. 6:6-9.
k- 26   The consequences of adultery are spelled out in 7:21-23. See also Lev. 20:10; Deut. 22:22.
l- 32   Heb: "*leb*" (also "sense" at 7:7); see *LEB*: "HEART" AND "MIND" on p. 95.
m- 32   See 1 Cor. 6:16,17.
7   *a*- 1   Heb: "*mitzwah*" (also at v. 2); see *TORAH* AND *MITZWAH* on p. 96.
   b- 2   Heb: "*torah*"; see *TORAH* AND *MITZWAH* on p. 96.

3 Tie them on your fingers;
   write them on the tablet of your heart.^c

4 Say to wisdom,^d "You are my sister,"
  and give the name "My Relative"^e to understanding

5   in order to guard yourself from the adulterous woman,
    from the loose woman with her smooth talk.

6 From a window in my house I looked through my screen.

7 I was looking at the gullible people
  when I saw a young man without much sense among the youths.

8 He was crossing a street near her corner,
  and walking toward her house,

9   in the twilight,
  in the evening,
  in the dark hours of the night.

10 A woman meets him, dressed as a prostitute,
   with an ulterior motive!

11   She [her type] is loud and rebellious;
    her feet will not stay at home.

12   One moment she is out on the street,
  the next she is at the curb,^f
  on the prowl at every corner.

13 She grabs him and kisses him
  and brazenly says to him:

14   "I have some sacrificial meat;
   today I kept my vows.

15   That's why I came out to meet you,
   eagerly looking for you;
   and I've found you!

16   "I've made my bed,
   with colored sheets of Egyptian linen;

17   I've sprinkled my bed with myrrh, aloes, and cinnamon.

18   Come, let's drink our fill of love till morning;
   let's enjoy making love,

19   for my husband's not home;
   he's gone on a long trip;

20   he took lots of money with him;
   he won't be home for a couple of weeks!"^g

---

3 2 Cor 3:3

---

c- 3 Heb: "*leb*" (also "heart" at v. 25; "ulterior motive" at v. 10); see *LEB*: "HEART" AND "MIND"
    on p. 95.

d- 4 Heb: "*hokmah*"; see "WISDOM" IN *PROVERBS* on p. 69.

e- 4 See Ruth 2:1; 3:2 in regard to the term "relative."

f- 12 Lit.: "at the broad places."

g- 20 Lit.: "he won't be home until the full moon"; if Israel was following the lunar calendar, the
    meaning would be "he won't be home until the middle of the month," the time when the full
    moon appeared.

21 With all her seductive charms she persuades him;
with her smooth lips she makes him give in.
22   Immediately he follows her,
            like a steer on its way to be slaughtered,
            like a ram hobbling into captivity[h]
23   (until an arrow pierces his heart[i]),
            like a bird darting into a trap,
      he does not realize that it will cost him his life.

24 But now, sons, listen to me,
and pay attention to the words of my mouth:
25   Do not let your heart be turned to her ways;
      do not wander onto her paths,
26   because she has brought down many victims,
            and numerous are all those she has killed.
27   Her home is the way to hell,[j]
                  leading down to the darkest vaults of death.

8TH CHAPTER

2. Wisdom's sevenfold call (8:1–9:18)
a. Wisdom's "divine call" (8:1-11)

1 Does not wisdom[a] call out, and
does not understanding raise its voice?

2 ⌞Wisdom⌟ takes its stand on high ground,
by the wayside where the roads meet,
3 near the gates to the city;
at the entrance ⌞wisdom⌟ sings its song:

---

h- 22 Heb meaning of this line uncertain.
i- 23 Lit.: "liver."
j- 27 Heb: "*sheol*"; see DEATH AND *SHEOL* on p. 103.
8 *a*- 1 Heb: "*hokmah*" (also at vv. 11,12); see GENDER AND HEBREW GENDER on p. 109.

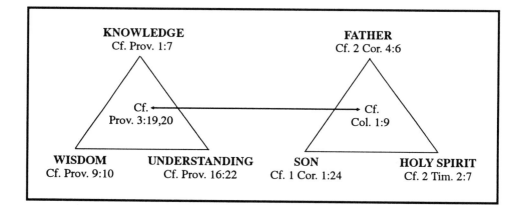

KNOWLEDGE
Cf. Prov. 1:7

FATHER
Cf. 2 Cor. 4:6

Cf.
Prov. 3:19,20

Cf.
Col. 1:9

WISDOM
Cf. Prov. 9:10

UNDERSTANDING
Cf. Prov. 16:22

SON
Cf. 1 Cor. 1:24

HOLY SPIRIT
Cf. 2 Tim. 2:7

4   "I am calling to you, men,
          and my appeal is to all people:
5   You gullible people, learn how to be sensible!
          You fools, get a heart*b* that has understanding. *c*

6   "Listen, for I am speaking about noble things,
          and my lips will say what is right;
7   my mouth expresses the truth,
          and wickedness is disgusting to my lips;
8   everything I say is just,
              and there is nothing *twisted or crooked* in it;
9   all of it is clear to a person who has understanding
                  and right to those who have acquired knowledge.
10   Take my discipline, not silver,
          and my knowledge rather than fine gold,
11   because wisdom is better than jewels, *d*
          and nothing you desire can equal it."

b. Wisdom's self-description (8:12-21)

12   "I, Wisdom, live with insight, and
          I acquire knowledge and foresight.
13   The fear of the LORD*e* is to hate evil;
              I hate pride, arrogance, evil behavior, and twisted speech.
14   Advice and priceless wisdom are Mine;
          I, Understanding, have strength.

15   "By Me kings reign,
          and rulers decree just laws.
16   By Me princes rule,
          so do nobles and all just judges.
17   I love those who love Me;
          those eagerly looking for Me will find Me.
18   I have riches and honor,
          lasting wealth and righteousness.
19   What I produce is better than gold, pure gold;
          what I yield is better than fine silver.
20   I walk *in the way of righteousness*, on the paths of justice,
21   to give an inheritance to those who love Me
              and to fill their treasuries."

---

8 Phil 2:15   20 Matt 21:32

---

b- 5 Heb: "*leb*"; see *LEB*: "HEART" AND "MIND" on p. 95.
c- 5 Eng equivalent difficult.
d- 11 Lit.: "than pieces of coral."
e- 13 See THE "FEAR" OF THE LORD on p. 77.

c. Wisdom's eternal existence (8:22-31)

22   "The Lord*f* already possessed Me*g*
        long ago, when His way began,
        before any of His works.
23   From everlasting
            I was appointed,*h*
                from the first,
                before the earth began.
24   Before there were oceans
            I was born,*i*
                before there were springs filled with water.
25   Before the mountains were settled in their places and
                before the hills
            I was born,*j*
26   when He had not yet made
                land or fields or the first dust of the world.

27   "When He set up the heavens
                I was there.
        When He traced the horizon on the surface of the ocean,
28   when He established the skies above,
        when He determined the currents in the ocean,*k*
29   when He set a limit for the sea
                so the waters would not overstep His command,
        when He traced the foundations of the earth — then
30   *I was beside Him* as a Master Craftsman.*l* And
            I was His delight day after day;
                rejoicing before Him all the time,
31   rejoicing in His inhabited world, and
                delighting in mankind."

---

22 Jn 1:1-18; Col 1:15,17; Rev 3:14   *23* Jn 17:5   *30* Jn 1:1-3

---

f- 22 Heb: "*YHWH*"; see GOD: HIS DESIGNATIONS AND NAMES on p. 80.
g- 22 On the basis of passages like this, NT Christians believe that Jesus is the "WISDOM" of God; traditionally these verses have been understood as referring to the divine essence of God the Son. Cf. Matt. 11:19; Jn. 1:1-18; 1 Cor. 1:24 (cf. also Matt. 23:34 with Lk. 11:49); see CHRIST, THE "WISDOM" OF GOD on p. 83.
h- 23 See Ps. 2:6 for the same word.
i- 24 Read in light of v. 22; this is *not* "personification" where an abstract idea (like "wisdom" in general) is merely presented as a person; rather, as the Christian church has taught, Prov. 8:22-31 equates "Wisdom" with the "Son of God" (cf. 1 Cor. 1:24). As such, "I was born" should be viewed as speaking about Christ's "eternal generation" (cf. Ps. 2:7; Heb. 1:5). The lines surrounding "I was born" here and at v. 25 are *qualifiers* that teach "Wisdom's" [Christ's] existence from eternity, namely, an existence "without beginning."
j- 25 See note at v. 24.
k- 28 Lit.: "when He strengthened the fountains [eyes, wells] of the ocean."
l- 30 Heb meaning of "Master Craftsman" uncertain.

d. Wisdom's warning (8:32-36)

32 "And now, sons, listen to Me:
    Blessed are those who keep My ways.
33   Listen to discipline and become wise.
    Do not leave My ways.
34   Blessed is the person who listens to Me,
      watching at My doors day after day,
      waiting by My doorposts.
35 For whoever finds Me finds life
    and obtains favor from the LORD.
36 For whoever sins against Me harms himself;
    all those who hate Me love death."

9TH CHAPTER

e. Wisdom's invitation (9:1-6)

1 Wisdom[a] has built her house;
    she has carved out her seven pillars;
2 she has *prepared her meat*;[b]
    she has mixed her wine; also,
    she has set her table;
3 she has sent out her servant girls;
    she calls from the highest places in the city:

4   "Whoever is gullible turn in here!"

To the one without sense,[c] she says:

5   "Come, eat my bread[d]
    and drink the wine I have mixed;
6   give up being gullible
    and live;
    and start traveling the road to understanding!"

f. Wisdom's effect (9:7-12)

7 *Whoever corrects a mocker receives abuse, and*
    whoever warns a wicked person gets hurt.
8   Do not warn a mocker or he will hate you;
    warn a wise person and he will love you.

---

32 Lk 11:28   *2 Matt 22:4*   *7 Matt 7:6*

---

9 *a-* 1 Heb: "*hokmah*"; see GENDER AND HEBREW GENDER on p. 109.
    b- 2 Lit.: "she has slaughtered her animals."
    c- 4 Heb: "*leb*" (also at v. 16); see *LEB*: "HEART" AND "MIND" on p. 95.
    d- 5 See Is. 55:1,2; Jn. 6:51,55.

9   Give ˌadviceˌ to a wise person
        and he will become even wiser;
    teach a righteous person
        and he will learn more.

10 The fear of the LORD[e] is the beginning of wisdom,[f] and
    the knowledge of the Holy One is understanding.

11 Because of me[g] you will live longer,
        and years will be added to your life.
12 If you are wise, your wisdom will help you;
    if you mock, you alone will be held responsible.

g. Wisdom's opponent (9:13-18)

13 The woman, Stupidity, is a loudmouth, gullible and ignorant;[h]
14 she sits at the doorway of her house,
    enthroned on the high ground of the city,
15 calling to those who pass by,
    those minding their own business:

16   "Whoever is gullible turn in here!"

    And she says to the one without sense:

17   "Stolen waters are sweet,
        and food eaten in secret is tasty."
18   But he does not know
        that the souls of those who died are there,
        that her guests are in the depths of hell.[i]

10TH CHAPTER

B. The Proverbs of Solomon (10:1–22:16)
1. Set 1: Description of a wise son (10:1–12:28)

1   The proverbs of Solomon:

A Wise Son

    A wise son makes his father happy,
        but a foolish son brings grief to his mother.

---

e- 10 See THE "FEAR" OF THE LORD on p. 77.
f- 10 Heb: "*hokmah*"; see HEBREW TERMS FOR "WISDOM" on p. 74.
g- 11 MT: "For by me"; LXX and other versions: "In this way."
h- 13 LXX: "and shameful"; Heb meaning of this verse uncertain.
i- 18 Heb: "*sheol*"; see DEATH AND *SHEOL* on p. 103.

The Triumph Of Righteousness

2 Treasures gained dishonestly profit no one,
    but righteousness rescues from death.
3 The LORD[a] will not allow the righteous person to starve,
    but He intentionally ignores the desires of the wicked.

Work Habits

4 Lazy hands bring poverty,
    but hardworking hands bring riches;
5   he who gathers in the summer is a wise son;
he who sleeps at harvest time brings shame.

Blessings Of Righteousness

6 Blessings cover the head of the righteous,
    but violence covers the mouth of the wicked.
7 Remembrance of the righteous is blessed,
    but the name of the wicked will rot away.

Pros And Cons Concerning The Mouth

8 The one who is truly wise[b] accepts commands,[c] but
the one who talks foolishly will be thrown down headfirst.
9   Whoever lives honestly will live securely, but
whoever lives dishonestly will be found out.
10   Whoever winks with his eye causes heartache, and
the one who talks foolishly will be thrown down headfirst.
11   The mouth of the righteous is *a fountain of life*, but
the mouth of the wicked conceals violence.
12   Hate starts quarrels, but
love covers every wrong.
13 Wisdom[d] is found on the lips of a person who has understanding,
    but a rod[e] is for the back of one without sense.[f]

---

11 Jn 4:14; Rev 7:17; 21:6   *12 Jas 5:20; 1 Pet 4:8*

10 *a-* 3 Heb: "*YHWH*"; see note at 3:5; some significant occurrences of "LORD" in chs. 10–31 are: 15:3; 16:9,33; 18:10,22; 20:12,27; 21:2; 22:2; 28:5; 29:26; 31:30; see GOD: HIS DESIGNATIONS AND NAMES on p. 80.
   b- 8 Lit.: "who is wise of heart"; see *LEB*: "HEART" AND "MIND" on p. 95.
   c- 8 Heb: "*mitzwah*"; see *TORAH* AND *MITZWAH* on p. 96.
   d- 13 Heb: "*hokmah*"; see notes on "*hokmah*" throughout chs. 1–9; some significant occurrences of "wisdom" in chs. 10–31 are: 14:33; 16:16; 18:4; 24:3; 28:26; 29:15; 31:26; see "WISDOM" IN *PROVERBS* on p. 69.
   e- 13 Heb refers to a discipline that is physical in nature (see also 13:24; 22:15; 23:13,14; 26:3; 29:15).
   f- 13 Heb: "*leb*" (also "sense" at v. 21; 11:12; 12:11; 15:21; 17:18; 19:8; 24:30); "*leb*" is translated "heart" at 10:20 (also see note "j") and "mind" at 12:8 (also see note "f"); see *LEB*: "HEART" AND "MIND" on p. 95.

14 Those who are wise store up knowledge,
     but by the mouth of a stubborn fool[g] ruin comes near.

Resources For Living

15 The rich person's wealth is ⌞his⌟ strong city;[h]
    poverty ruins the poor.
16   The reward of the righteous is life;
     the harvest of the wicked is sin.
17   Whoever practices discipline is on the way to life, but
     whoever ignores a warning strays.

Verbal Expression

18 Whoever conceals hatred has lying lips, and
   whoever spreads slander is a fool.[i]
19   Sin is unavoidable when there is much talk,
     but whoever seals his lips is wise.
20   The tongue of the righteous is pure silver;
    the heart[j] of the wicked is worthless.
21 The lips of the righteous feed many,
   but stubborn fools die because they have no sense.

Blessings And Riches Versus Human Efforts And Plans

22 It is the LORD's blessing that makes a person rich,
    and hard work adds nothing to it.
23 Like the laughter of a fool
    when he carries out an evil plan,
      so is wisdom to a person who has understanding.

The Righteous And The Wicked

24 That which the wicked dreads happens to him,
    but ⌞the LORD⌟ grants the desire of the righteous.

---

g- 14 Cf. "stubborn fools" at note "e" at 1:7; the other occurrences of "stubborn fool(s)" in chs. 10–31 are: v. 21; 11:29; 12:15,16; 14:3,9; 15:5; 16:22; 17:28; 20:3; 24:7; 27:3,22; 29:9; see THE "FOOL" IN *PROVERBS* on p. 91.

h- 15 The rich person's wealth is like having an insurance policy against poverty for times of recession (see also 18:11).

i- 18 Cf. "fool(s)" at note "n" at 1:22; the other occurrences of "fool(s)" in chs. 10–31 are: v. 23; 13:16,19,20; 14:7,8,16,24,33; 15:2,14; 17:10,12,16,21,24; 18:2,6,7; 19:1,10,29; 23:9; 26:1,3-12; 28:26; 29:11,20; see THE "FOOL" IN *PROVERBS* on p. 91.

j- 20 Heb: "*leb*"; see notes on "*leb*" throughout chs. 1–9; some significant occurrences of "*leb*" as "heart(s)" in chs. 10–31 are: 14:10,13,14,30,33; 15:13; 16:1; 17:3,22; 19:21; 22:15; 23:15; 27:9,19; 28:26; "*leb*" is translated "sense" at 10:13 (also see note "f"); "mind" at 12:8 (also see note "f"); "heartache" at 15:13; see *LEB*: "HEART" AND "MIND" on p. 95.

25   *When the storm has passed, the wicked person has vanished,*
       but the righteous person has an everlasting foundation. [k]
26   Like vinegar to the teeth and
     like smoke to the eyes,
       so the lazy person is to those who send him ˌon a missionˌ.
27   The fear of the LORD [l] lengthens ˌthe number ofˌ days,
       but the years of the wicked are shortened.
28   The hope of the righteous ˌleads toˌ joy,
       but the eager waiting of the wicked comes to nothing.
29   The way of the LORD is a fortress for the innocent
       but a ruin to those who are troublemakers.
30   The righteous will never be moved,
       but the wicked will not continue to live in the land.
31   The mouth of the righteous increases wisdom,
       but the devious tongue will be cut off.
32   The lips of the righteous announce good will,
       but the mouth of the wicked is devious.

11TH CHAPTER

Integrity

1   Dishonest scales are disgusting to the LORD,
       but accurate weights are pleasing to Him.
2   Pride comes,
         then comes shame,
             but wisdom remains with the humble.
3   Integrity guides the upright,
       but hypocrisy leads the treacherous to ruin.

The Value Of Righteousness

4   Riches are of no help on the Day of Fury, [a]
       but righteousness saves from death;
5   the righteousness of the innocent makes his road smooth,
       but the wicked falls by his own wickedness.
6   The upright are saved by their righteousness,
     but the treacherous are trapped by their own greed.

---

25 *Matt 7:25,27*

k- 25 Cf. Matt. 7:24-27.
l- 27 Phrase also at 14:26,27; 15:16,33; 16:6; 19:23; 22:4; 23:17; 24:21; 31:30; see THE "FEAR"
    OF THE LORD on p. 77.
11 a- 4 Or "day of fury"; notice that the Heb is sing.

7   At the death of the wicked person, hope vanishes;
        moreover, his confidence in strength vanishes.
8   A righteous person is rescued from trouble,
        and the wicked person takes his place;
9   with his talk a godless person can ruin his neighbor,
    but the righteous are rescued by knowledge.

Righteousness And A City's People

10 When the righteous prosper, a city is glad;
    when the wicked perish, there are songs of joy.
11   With the blessing of the upright a city is exalted,
        but by the words of the wicked it is torn down.

The Right Way To Act

12 A person who despises a neighbor has no sense, but
    a person who has understanding keeps quiet.
13   Whoever gossips gives away secrets, but
        whoever is trustworthy in spirit can keep a secret.
14 A nation will fall when there is no direction, but
    with many advisers there is victory.
15   Whoever guarantees a stranger's loan will get into trouble, but
        whoever hates the closing of a deal remains secure.
16 A gracious woman wins respect, but
    ruthless men gain riches.
17   *A merciful man benefits himself*, but
        a cruel man hurts himself.
18 A wicked person earns dishonest wages, but
    whoever spreads righteousness earns honest pay.
19   As righteousness leads to life,
        so whoever pursues evil finds his own death.

The Inner Nature

20 The devious in heart are disgusting to the LORD,
        but He is delighted with those whose ways are innocent.
21 Certainly an evil person will not go unpunished,
        but the descendants of the righteous will escape.
22 ⌊Like⌋ a gold ring in a pig's snout,
        ⌊so⌋ is a beautiful woman who lacks good taste.
23 The desire of the righteous ends only in good,
        but the hope of the wicked ends only in fury.

---

17 Matt 5:7

Generosity Compared With Selfishness

24 *One person spends freely and yet grows richer,*
    while another holds back what he owes and yet grows poorer.
25   A generous person will be made rich,
    and whoever satisfies others will himself be satisfied.*b*
26   People will curse the one who hoards grain,
but a blessing will be upon the head of the one who sells it.

Inheriting Rewards

27   Whoever eagerly seeks good searches for good will, but
whoever looks for evil finds it.
28   Whoever trusts in his riches will fall,
    but the righteous will flourish like a green leaf.
29   Whoever brings trouble upon his family inherits ˏonlyˎ wind, and
that stubborn fool becomes a slave to the wise in heart.
30   *The fruit of the righteous is a tree of life,*
    and *a winner of souls is wise.*
31   If the righteous person is rewarded on earth —
how much more the wicked and the sinner!

12TH CHAPTER

Character Determines Direction

1   Whoever loves discipline loves to learn,
    but whoever hates correction is a dumb animal.*a*
2   A good person *obtains favor from the LORD,*
    but the LORD condemns everyone who schemes.
3   A man cannot stand firm on a foundation of wickedness,
    but the root of the righteous cannot be moved.
4   A wife with strength of character is the crown of her husband,
    but the wife who disgraces him is like bone cancer.*b*

Righteous And Wicked Profiles

5   The thoughts of the righteous are just;*c*
the advice of the wicked is treacherous;

---

24 *2 Cor 9:6; Gal 6:7*   **30** *Phil 1:11; Jas 5:20; Rev 2:7; 22:2,14,19*   **2** *Lk 1:30*

---

b- 25 Or "and whoever gives someone a drink will also get a drink."
12 *a-* 1 See 30:2.
   b- 4 Lit.: "like a rotting in his bones" (see 14:30).
   c- 5 Heb: "*mishpat*" (also "just" at 21:3,7); see *MISHPAT* on p. 100.

6   the words of the wicked are a deadly ambush,[d] but
       the words[e] of the upright rescue.
7 Overthrow the wicked
       and they are no more,
            but the family of the righteous continues to stand.

Obvious Outcomes

8 A man is praised according to his insight,
       but whoever has a twisted mind[f] will be despised.
9 Better to be unimportant and have a slave[g]
       than to act important and have nothing to eat.
10 A righteous person cares ˌevenˌ about the life of his animals,
       but the compassion of the wicked person is ˌnothing butˌ cruelty!
11 Whoever works his land will have plenty to eat,
       but the one who chases rainbows[h] has no sense.
12 A wicked person delights in setting a trap for ˌotherˌ evil people,
       but the root of the righteous produces ˌfruitˌ.[i]
13 An evil person is trapped by his own sinful talk,
       but a righteous person escapes from trouble.
14 One man enjoys good things as a result of his speaking ability,
       and another person is paid according to what his hands have accomplished.

The Stubbornness Of A Fool

15 A stubborn fool considers his own way the right one,
       but a person who listens to advice is wise.
16 When a stubborn fool is irritated, he shows it immediately,
       but a sensible person hides the insult.

The Way Of Deceit

17 A truthful witness speaks honestly,
       but a lying witness speaks deceitfully.
18 Careless words stab like a sword,
       but the words of the wise bring healing.
19 The word of truth lasts forever,
       but lies last only a moment.
20 Deceit is in the heart of those who plan evil,
       but joy belongs to those who advise peace.

---

d- 6 Lit.: "are an ambush with bloodshed."
e- 6 Lit.: "mouth."
f- 8 Heb: "*leb*"; see notes on "*leb*" throughout chs. 1–9; another significant occurrence of "*leb*" as "mind" in chs. 10–31 is: 17:16; "*leb*" is translated "sense" at 10:13 (note "f"); "heart" at 10:20 (note "j"); "attitude" at 15:7; "understanding" at 15:32; "opinion" at 18:2; "disciplined life" at 23:12; "pay close attention" at 27:23; see *LEB*: "HEART" AND "MIND" on p. 95.
g- 9 Some MSS read: "have work."
h- 11 Lit.: "chases emptiness."
i- 12 Heb meaning of this verse uncertain.

General Advice And Observations

21 No ⌐lasting¬ harm comes to the righteous,
but the wicked have lots of trouble.
22   Lips that lie are disgusting to the LORD,
but honest ⌐people¬ are His delight.
23   A sensible person ⌐discreetly¬ hides knowledge,
but the foolish mind preaches stupidity.
24   Hardworking hands gain control,
but lazy hands do slave labor.
25   A man's anxiety[j] will weigh him down,
but an encouraging word makes him joyful.
26   A righteous person looks out for his neighbor,
but the path of the wicked leads others astray.
27   A lazy hunter does not catch[k] his prey,
but a hardworking person becomes wealthy.[l]
28 *On the road of righteousness* there is ⌐everlasting¬ life,
and along its path there is no ⌐eternal¬ death.

13TH CHAPTER

2. Set 2: Description of a wise son (13:1–15:19)

A Wise Son

1 A wise son listens to his father's discipline,
but a mocker[a] does not listen to scolding.

Using One's Mouth To Advantage

2 A man eats well as a result of his speaking ability,
but the appetite of the treacherous ⌐craves¬ violence.
3   Whoever controls his mouth protects his own life;
whoever has a big mouth[b] comes to ruin.

The Lazy And The Hardworking

4 A lazy person craves food and there is none,
but the appetite of hardworking people is satisfied.

---

28 *Matt 21:32*

---

j- 25 Lit.: "Anxiety in a man's heart/mind"; see *LEB*: "HEART" AND "MIND" on p. 95.
k- 27 Heb meaning of "catch" uncertain.
l- 27 Heb meaning of this line uncertain.
13 a- 1 Cf. "mocker(s)" at note "m" at 1:22; the other occurrences of "mocker(s)" in chs. 10–31 are:
14:6; 15:12; 19:25,29; 20:1; 21:11,24; 24:9; see THE "FOOL" IN *PROVERBS* on p. 91.
b- 3 Lit.: "whoever opens his lips wide."

Righteousness Versus Wickedness

5 A righteous person hates lying,
    but a wicked person behaves with shame and disgrace.
6 Righteousness protects the honest way of life,
    but wickedness negates a sacrifice for sin.

The Vanity Of Riches

7 One person pretends to be rich but has nothing;
another pretends to be poor but has great wealth.
8   A man's riches are the ransom for his life,
    but the poor person does not pay attention to threats.

Righteous And Evil Living

9 The light of the righteous beams brightly, [c]
    but *the lamp of the wicked will be snuffed out.*
10 Pride produces only quarreling,
    but those who take advice gain wisdom.
11 Wealth ⌐gained⌐ through injustice dwindles away,
    but whoever gathers little by little has plenty.

The Essence Of Life

12 Hope delayed makes one sick at heart,
    but a fulfilled longing is *a tree of life.*
13 Whoever despises ⌐God's⌐ word[d] will pay the penalty,
    but the one who fears ⌐His⌐ law[e] will be rewarded. [f]
14 The teaching[g] of the wise is *a fountain of life*
    to turn ⌐one⌐ away from the grasp of death.

Wise And Unwise Behavior

15 Good sense brings favor,
    but the way of the treacherous is always the same. [h]

---

9 Matt 25:8   *12* Rev 2:7; 22:2,14,19   *14* Jn 4:14; Rev 7:17; 21:6

c- 9 Lit.: "The light of the righteous rejoices."
d- 13 See 16:20.
e- 13 Heb: "*mitzwah*" (also at 19:16); see *TORAH* AND *MITZWAH* on p. 96.
f- 13 Cf. this verse and 19:16 with Lk. 6:23,35; 1 Cor. 3:8; Col. 3:24; Heb. 10:35; 2 Jn. 8.
g- 14 Heb: "*torah*"; the other occurrences of "*torah*" as "teaching" in chs. 10–31 are: 28:4 (twice),
    7,9; 29:18; "*torah*" is translated "instruction" at 31:26; see *TORAH* AND *MITZWAH* on
    p. 96.
h- 15 LXX: "is their disaster."

16 Any sensible person acts with knowledge,
    but a fool displays stupidity.
17 An undependable messenger gets into trouble,
    but a dependable envoy brings healing.
18 Poverty and shame come to the one who ignores discipline,
    but whoever pays attention to constructive criticism will be honored.

Associate With Wise People

19 A desire fulfilled is sweet to the soul,
    but turning from evil is disgusting to fools.
20 Whoever walks with the wise will be wise,
    but whoever associates with fools will suffer.

The Reward Of The Righteous

21 Disaster hunts down sinners,
    but the righteous are rewarded with good.
22 A good man leaves an inheritance to his grandchildren,
    but the wealth of a sinner is stored away for the righteous.

Concerning Society, Family, And Self

23 When poor people are able to plow, there is much food,
    but a person is swept away where there is no justice.[i]
24 He who refuses to spank[j] his son hates him,
    but he who loves his son disciplines him from early on.[k]
25 The righteous person eats to satisfy his appetite,
    but the belly of the wicked is always empty.

14TH CHAPTER

The Way Of The Wise

1 The wisest of women builds up her home,
    but a stupid one tears it down with her own hands.
2 Whoever lives right fears the LORD,
    but the person who is devious in his ways despises Him.
3 Because of a stubborn fool's words
    a whip is lifted against him,
        but the wise are protected by their speech.[a]

---

i- 23 Heb: "*mishpat*" (also "justice" at 17:23; 18:5; 19:28; 21:15; 28:5; 29:4,26); see *MISHPAT* on
    p. 100. Heb meaning of this verse uncertain.
j- 24 See note "e" at 10:13.
k- 24 See 3:12; Eph. 6:4; Heb. 12:5-11.
14 a- 3 Lit.: "but the lips of the wise protect them."

Strength Of Character

4　Where there are no cattle, the feeding trough is empty,
　　　but the strength of an ox produces plentiful harvests.
5　A *trustworthy witness* does not lie,
　　　but *a dishonest witness* breathes lies.
6　A mocker searches for wisdom without finding it,
　　　but knowledge comes easily to a person who has understanding.

Fools Compared With Sensible People

7　Stay away from a fool,
　　　because you will not receive knowledge from his lips.
8　The wisdom of a sensible person guides his way of life,
　　　but the stupidity of fools misleads them.
9　Stubborn fools make fun of guilt,
　　　but there is forgiveness among the upright.

The Essence Of Joy

10　The heart knows its own bitterness,
　　　and no stranger can share its joy.
11　The house of the wicked will be destroyed,
　　　but the tent of the upright will continue to expand.
12　There is a way that seems right to a man,
　　　but eventually it ends in death.
13　Even while laughing a heart can ache,
　　　and joy can end in grief.

Personality Patterns

14　A heart that turns ˻from God˺ becomes bored with its own ways,
　　　but a good man is satisfied with God's ways.
15　A gullible person[b] believes anything,
　　　but a sensible person watches his step.
16　A wise person is cautious and turns away from evil,
　　　but a fool is careless[c] and overconfident.
17　A short-tempered person acts stupid,
　　　and a man who plots evil is hated.
18　Gullible people are gifted with stupidity,
　　　but sensible people are crowned with knowledge.
19　Evil people will bow before good people
　　　and the wicked at the gates of the righteous.

---

5 Acts 6:13; Rev 1:5; 3:14　　　*12 Rom 6:21*

---

b- 15 Cf. "gullible person/people" at note "c" at 1:4; the other occurrences of "gullible person/
　　people" in chs. 10–31 are: v. 18; 19:25; 21:11; 22:3; 27:12; see THE "FOOL" IN
　　PROVERBS on p. 91.
c- 16 Heb meaning of "careless" uncertain.

Neighbors

20 A poor person is hated even by his neighbor,
       but a rich person is loved by many.
21 Whoever despises his neighbor sins,
       but *blessed is the one who is kind to the humble*.

General Advice And Observations

22 Don't the ones who stray plan evil,
       while the ones who are merciful and faithful plan good?
23   In hard work there is always something gained,
       but idle talk leads only to poverty.
24 The crown of the wise is their wealth;
       the stupidity of fools is just that — stupidity!
25   An honest witness saves lives,
       but one who tells lies is dangerous.
26 In the fear of the LORD there is strong confidence,
       and His children will have a place of refuge.
27   The fear of the LORD is *a fountain of life*
       to turn ⌊one⌋ away from the grasp of death.
28 A large population is an honor for a king,
       but without people a ruler is ruined.

The Results Of Wise Living

29 A person of great understanding is *slow to become angry*,
       but a short temper is the height of stupidity.
30   A tranquil heart makes for a healthy body,
       but jealousy is ⌊like⌋ bone cancer. *d*
31 Whoever oppresses the poor insults his Maker,
       but whoever is kind to the needy honors Him.
32   A wicked person is thrown down by his own wrongdoing,
       but even in his death a righteous person has a refuge.
33 Wisdom finds rest in the heart of an understanding person;
       even fools recognize this. *e*

Righteous Ruling

34 Righteousness lifts up a nation,
       but sin is a disgrace in any society.
35 A king is delighted with *a servant who acts wisely*,
       but he is furious with one who acts shamefully.

---

21 Matt 5:7   *27* Jn 4:14; Rev 7:17; 21:6   *29* Jas 1:19   *35* Matt 24:45; Lk 12:42

---

d- 30 See 12:4.
e- 33 Heb meaning of this line uncertain.

15TH CHAPTER

Effective Words

1 A gentle answer turns away rage,
     but a harsh word stirs up anger.
2 The tongue of the wise gives good expression to knowledge,
     but the mouth of fools pours out a flood of stupidity.
3 *The eyes of the* Lord *are everywhere*,
     watching the evil and the good.
4 A soothing tongue is *a tree of life*,
     but a deceitful tongue breaks the spirit.
5 A stubborn fool despises his father's discipline,
     but whoever appreciates a warning shows good sense.
6 Great treasure is in the house of the righteous,
     but trouble comes along with the income[a] of the wicked.
7 The lips of the righteous spread knowledge,
     but a foolish attitude does not.

What The Lord Loves

8 A sacrifice brought by the wicked is disgusting to the Lord,
     but the prayer of the upright is His delight.
9 The way of the wicked is disgusting to the Lord,
     but He loves the one who pursues righteousness.

The Consequences Of Foolishness

10 Discipline is a terrible ⌊burden⌋ to
     anyone who leaves the ⌊right⌋ path;
     anyone who hates a warning will die.
11 If *Sheol* and *Abaddon*[b] lie open before the Lord—
     how much more the human heart!
12 A mocker does not appreciate a warning;
     he will not go to the wise.

The Joyful Heart

13 A joyful heart makes a cheerful face,
     but with a heartache comes depression.[c]
14 The mind of a person who has understanding searches for knowledge,
     but the mouth of fools feeds on stupidity.

---

3 Heb 4:13   *4 Rev 2:7; 22:2,14,19*   *11 Rev 9:11*

15 *a-* 6 Lit.: "harvest" (also at 3:9).
   b- 11 Meaning "Hell" ("*Sheol*") and "Decay" ("*Abaddon*"); for NT usage see Rev. 9:11; see DEATH AND *SHEOL* on p. 103.
   c- 13 Lit.: "comes a broken spirit"; see also 17:22; 18:14.

15 Every day is a terrible day for a miserable person,
        but a cheerful heart has a continual feast.

The Better Things

16 Better to have a little with the fear of the LORD
        than great treasure —
            and turmoil with it.
17 Better to have a dish of vegetables where there is love
        than juicy steaks where there is hate.

Differing Dispositions

18 A hothead stirs up a fight,
        but one who holds his temper calms disputes.
19 The path of a lazy man is like a thorny hedge,
        but the road of the upright is an ˷open˷ highway.

3. Set 3: Description of a wise son (15:20–17:24)

A Wise Son

20 A wise son makes his father happy,
        but a foolish child[d] despises its mother.

Fun And Delight

21 Stupidity is fun to the one without much sense,
        but a man who has understanding forges straight ahead.
22   Without advice plans go wrong,
            but with many advisers they succeed.
23   A man is delighted to hear an answer from his own mouth,
            and a timely word — oh, how good!

Destruction For The Wicked; Life For The Upright

24 The path of life for the wise leads upward
        in order to turn him away from hell[e] below.
25 The LORD tears down the house of the proud,
        but He protects the property[f] of the widow.
26 The thoughts of evil people are disgusting to the LORD,
        but pleasant words are pure[g] to Him.

---

d- 20 Lit.: "man."
e- 24 Heb: "*sheol*"; see DEATH AND *SHEOL* on p. 103.
f- 25 Lit.: "He firmly fixes the boundary."
g- 26 Meaning "ceremonially pure" as in the case of God-pleasing sacrifices.

27 Whoever is greedy for unjust gain brings trouble upon his family,
     but whoever hates bribes will live.

Comparing The Righteous And The Wicked

28 The heart of the righteous carefully considers how to answer,
      but the mouth of the wicked pours out a flood of evil things;
29   the LORD is far from the wicked,
     but He hears the prayer of the righteous.

Good Eyes And Ears

30 A twinkle in the eye delights the heart;
     good news refreshes the body.
31   The ear that listens to a life-giving warning
      will be at home among the wise.

Discipline's Value

32 Whoever ignores discipline despises himself,
      but the one who listens to warning gains understanding.
33 The fear of the LORD is discipline ˻leading to˼ wisdom,
      and humility comes before honor.

16TH CHAPTER

The Sevenfold Centrality Of The LORD

1 The plans of the heart belong to humans,
    but an answer on the tongue comes from the LORD.
2   A man thinks all his ways are pure,
      but the LORD weighs motives.
3   Entrust your works to the LORD,
          and your plans will succeed.
4 The LORD has made everything for His own purpose,
    and even the wicked for the Day of Trouble. *a*
5   Everyone with a conceited heart is disgusting to the LORD;
      certainly ˻such a person˼ will not go unpunished.
6   By mercy and faithfulness guilt is atoned for,
          and by the fear of the LORD evil is avoided.
7   When a man's ways are pleasing to the LORD,
              He makes even his enemies to be at peace with him. *b*

---

16 *a-* 4 Or "day of trouble."
     b- 7 Pronouns ambiguous.

Honesty And Planning

8 Better a few ˌpossessionsˌ gained honestly
   than many gained through injustice. [c]

9 A person may plan his own journey,
   but the LORD directs his steps.

Kings [d]

10 When a divine revelation is on a king's lips,
    he cannot voice [e] a wrong judgment. [f]

11 Honest balances and scales belong to the LORD;
    He made the entire set of weights. [g]

12 Wrongdoing is disgusting to kings,
    because a throne is established through righteousness.

13 Kings delight in honest words,
    and whoever speaks what is right is loved.

14 A king's anger announces death, [h]
    but a wise man can calm him down.

15 When the king is cheerful [i] there is life,
    and his favor is like a cloud bringing spring rain.

Wisdom's Highway

16 How much better it is to gain wisdom than gold,
    and the gaining of understanding should be chosen over silver.

17 The highway of the upright turns away from evil;
    whoever watches his way preserves his own life.

Pride

18 Pride precedes a disaster,
    and an arrogant attitude precedes a fall;

19 better to be humble with the lowly
    than to share plunder with the proud.

Words That Give Understanding

20 Whoever gives attention to the LORD's word [j] prospers,
    and blessed is the one who trusts the LORD.

---

c- 8 Heb: "*belo' mishpat*"; see *MISHPAT* on p. 100.

d   Verses 10-15 constitute the *first* of five verse units that deal with the subject of "kingship" within
     Proverbs. The others are: 20:2-8; 25:2-7; 30:29-31; 31:4-7. Other references to "king" within
     Proverbs are: 1:1; 8:15; 14:28,35; 19:12; 20:26,28; 21:1; 22:11,29; 24:21; 25:1; 29:4,14;
     30:22,27; 31:1,3; see "KINGSHIP," WITH SPECIAL REFERENCE TO *PROVERBS* on p. 87.

e- 10 Lit.: "his mouth cannot make."

f- 10 Heb: "*mishpat*"; "*mishpat*" is translated "honest" at v. 11; "outcome" at v. 33; "judge" at 24:23;
      see *MISHPAT* on p. 100.

g- 11 Lit.: "He made all the stones in the bag."

h- 14 Lit.: "A king's anger is messengers of death."

i- 15 Lit.: "In the light of the face of the king."

j- 20 See 13:13.

21   The person who is truly wise is called "Understanding,"[k]
        and speaking sweetly helps others learn.
22   Understanding is *a fountain of life* to the one who has it,
        but stubborn fools punish themselves with their stupidity.
23   A wise man's heart controls his speech,
        and what he says helps others learn.
24   Pleasant words are ⌊like⌋ honey from a honeycomb —
        sweet to the spirit and healthy for the body.

Negative Personality Types

25   There is a way that seems right to a man,
        but eventually it ends in death.
26   A laborer's appetite works to his advantage
        because his hunger drives him on.
27   A worthless man plots trouble,
        and *his speech is like a burning fire.*
28   A devious man spreads quarrels,
        and a gossip separates the closest of friends.
29   A violent man misleads his neighbor
        and leads him on a path that is not good.
30   Whoever winks his eye is plotting something devious;
        whoever bites his lips has finished his evil work.

General Advice And Observations[l]

31   Silver hair is a beautiful crown found in a righteous life.
32   Better to get angry slowly than to be a hero, and
        better to be even-tempered than to capture a city.
33   The dice are thrown,[m]
        but the Lord determines every outcome.

17TH CHAPTER

1   Better a bite of dry bread ⌊eaten⌋ in peace
    than a family feast filled with strife.
2   A wise slave will become master over a son who acts shamefully,
        and he will share the inheritance with the brothers.
3   *The crucible is for refining silver and the smelter[a] for gold,
    but the One who purifies hearts by fire is the Lord.*
4   An evildoer pays attention to wicked lips;
        a liar opens his ears to a slanderous tongue.

---

22 *Jn 4:14; Rev 7:17; 21:6*   **27** *Jas 3:6*   **3** *1 Pet 1:7*

---

k- 21   Lit.: "To the wise of heart he will be called 'Understanding.'"
l   Reading unit comprises 16:31–17:6.
m- 33   Lit.: "The lot is thrown into a lap."
17 a- 3   The technical terms "crucible" and "smelter" indicate different types of furnaces used for
refining various metals (also at 27:21).

5 Whoever makes fun of a poor person insults his Maker;
   whoever is happy ⌊to see someone⌋ in distress will not escape punishment.
6   Grandchildren are the crown of grandparents,^{b}
       and parents are the glory of their children.

The Consequences Of Being A Fool

7 Refined speech is not fitting for a godless fool^c —
   how much less does lying fit a noble person!
8   A bribe seems ⌊like⌋ a jewel to the one who gives it;^{d}
       wherever he turns he prospers.
9 Whoever forgives an offense seeks love, but
   whoever keeps bringing up the issue separates the closest of friends.
10   A scolding impresses a person who has understanding
       more than a hundred lashes impress a fool.

The Consequences Of Evil Living

11 A rebel looks for nothing but evil;
    therefore, a cruel messenger will be sent ⌊to punish⌋ him.
12   Better to meet a bear robbed of her young
       than a fool ⌊carried away⌋ with his stupidity.
13 Whoever pays back evil for good —
    evil will never leave his home.
14   Starting a quarrel is ⌊like⌋ opening a floodgate,
       so stop before the argument gets out of control.
15 Whoever justifies the wicked and whoever condemns the righteous —
    both are disgusting to the LORD.

The Mind Of A Fool

16 Why should a fool have money in his hand to acquire wisdom
    when he doesn't have a mind to grasp anything?
17   A friend always loves,
       and a brother is born to share trouble.
18 A person without good sense closes a deal with a handshake;
    he guarantees a loan in the presence of his friend.^{e}
19   Whoever loves sin loves a quarrel;
       whoever builds his city gate high invites destruction.
20 A twisted mind never finds happiness,
    and one with a devious tongue ⌊repeatedly⌋ gets into trouble.
21   The parent of a fool has grief,
       and the father of a godless fool has no joy.
22 A joyful heart is good medicine,
    but depression drains one's strength.

---

b- 6 Lit.: "older people."
c- 7 "Godless fool" also at v. 21; 30:22; see THE "FOOL" IN *PROVERBS* on p. 91.
d- 8 Or "who receives it."
e- 18 Indicating that a person who co-signs for another is a person without good sense. Cf. 6:1 (and
        note "a"); 20:16; 22:26 (also 11:15; 27:13).

23   A wicked person secretly accepts a bribe
         to corrupt the ways of justice.
24   Wisdom is right there in front of an understanding person,
         but the eyes of a fool ˌare looking aroundˌ all over the world.

4. Set 4: Description of a foolish son (17:25–19:12)

A Foolish Son

25   A foolish son is a heartache to his father
         and bitter grief to his mother.

Self-control

26   To punish an innocent person is not good;
         to strike down noble people is not right.
27   A person who has knowledge controls his words,
           and a man who has understanding is even-tempered.

About Fools *f*

28   Even a stubborn fool is thought to be wise if he keeps silent;
         he is considered intelligent if he keeps his lips sealed.

18TH CHAPTER

1   The loner is out to get what he wants for himself;
       he opposes all sound reasoning.
2   A fool does not delight in understanding
         but only in expressing his own opinion.

Aspects Of Wickedness

3   When wickedness comes, contempt also comes,
       and insult comes along with disgrace.
4   The words of a man's mouth are ˌlikeˌ deep waters;
         the fountain of wisdom is an overflowing stream.
5   It is not good to be partial toward the wicked,
             thereby depriving the innocent of justice.

A Fool's Mouth

6   By talking, a fool gets into an argument,
         and his mouth invites a beating.
7   A fool's mouth is his ruin,
         and his lips are a trap to his soul.

---

f   Reading unit comprises 17:28–18:2.

8 The words of a gossip are swallowed greedily,
     and they go down into a person's innermost being.

Laziness

9 Whoever is lazy in his work is a brother to a vandal.

Two Types Of Safety

10 The Name of the Lord is a strong tower;
     a righteous person runs to it
         and is safe.
11 A rich person's wealth is his strong city
     and is like a high wall in his imagination.

Human Attitudes

12 Before destruction a man's heart is proud,
     but humility comes before honor.
13 Whoever gives an answer before he listens is stupid and shameful.
14 A man's spirit can endure sickness,
     but who can bear a broken spirit?
15 The mind of a person who has understanding acquires knowledge,
     and the ears of the wise seek knowledge.
16 A gift opens doors for the giver[a]
     and brings him into the presence of great people.

Contentions

17 The first to state his case seems right —
   ⌐until⌐ his neighbor comes and cross-examines him.
18   Flipping a coin[b] ends quarrels
     and settles ⌐issues⌐ between the powerful.
19   An offended brother is more ⌐resistant⌐ than a strong city,
     and disputes are like the locked gate of a castle tower.

Talking

20 A man's speaking ability provides for his stomach;
     his talking provides him a living;
21   the tongue has the power of life and death,
   and those who love to talk will have to eat their own words.

Companions

22 He who finds a wife finds something good
     and has obtained favor from the Lord.

---

18 *a-* 16 Lit.: "The gift of a person makes broad for him."
    b- 18 Lit.: "Casting lots."

23   A poor person is timid when begging,
        but a rich person is blunt when replying.
24   A man and his friends can destroy one another,[c]
            but there is a loving friend who sticks closer than a brother.

19TH CHAPTER

Poverty And Knowledge; Poverty And Wealth

1   Better to be a poor person who lives innocently
    than to be one who talks dishonestly and is a fool.
2   A person without knowledge is no good,
        and a person in a hurry makes mistakes.
3   The stupidity of a person turns his life upside down,
            and his heart rages against the LORD.
4   Wealth adds many friends,
                but a poor person is separated from his friend.

Deception

5   *A lying witness* will not go unpunished,
    and *one who utters lies* will not escape.
6   Many try to win the kindness of a generous person,
        and everyone is a friend to a man who gives gifts.
7   All the brothers of a poor man hate him—
            how much more do his friends keep their distance from him;
            when he chases them with words,
            they are gone.
8   A person who gains sense loves himself;
        one who guards understanding finds something good.
9   *A lying witness* will not go unpunished,
    and *one who utters lies* will perish.

Being Near The Fool, The Wise Person, And The King

10 Luxury does not fit a fool,
    much less a slave ruling over princes.
11   A person with good sense is patient,
        and it is to his credit[a] that he overlooks an offense.
12   The rage of a king is like the roar of a lion,
            but his favor is like dew on the grass.

---

5 Acts 6:13   9 Acts 6:13

---

c- 24 Or "A man has friends as companions."
19 *a*- 11 Lit.: "glory."

5. Set 5: Description of a foolish son (19:13-25)

Home Life

13 A foolish son ruins his father,
     and a quarreling woman is ⌊like⌋ constantly dripping water.
14 Home and wealth are inherited from fathers,
     but a sensible wife comes from the LORD.

Laziness And Life

15 Laziness throws one into a deep sleep,
     and an idle person will go hungry.
16 He who keeps the law[b] preserves his life,
     ⌊but⌋ he who despises His [the LORD's] ways will be put to death.

Good Advice

17 *Whoever has pity on the poor lends to the LORD,*
     and He will repay him for his good deed.
18   Discipline your son while there is still hope;
            do not be the one responsible for his death.
19   A person who has a hot temper will pay for it;
            if you rescue him you will have to do it over and over.
20   Listen to advice and accept discipline
            so that you may be wise the rest of your life.
21   Many plans are in a man's heart,
            but the advice of the LORD will endure.
22 Loyalty is desirable in a person,
     and it is better to be a poor man than a liar.

Contrasting Harm And Benefit

23 The fear of the LORD leads to life,
     and such a person will rest easy without suffering harm.[c]
24   A lazy person puts his fork in his food;[d]
            he doesn't even bring it back to his mouth.
25   Strike a mocker
                 and a gullible person may learn a lesson;
            warn an understanding person
                 and he will gain more knowledge.

---

17 *Matt 25:40*

---

b- 16 Heb: "*mitzwah*" (also at note "e" at 13:13); see *TORAH* AND *MITZWAH* on p. 96.
c- 23 Heb meaning of this line uncertain.
d- 24 Lit.: "A lazy person buries his hand in a dish" (see 26:15).

6. Set 6: Description of a foolish son (19:26–22:16)

A Foolish Son

26 A son who assaults his father
ᵧandᵧ who drives away his mother
brings shame and disgrace.
27 If you stop listening to instruction, my son,
you will stray from the words of knowledge.

Mockers[e]

28 A worthless witness mocks justice,
and the mouth of the wicked swallows up trouble.
29 Punishments are set for mockers
and beatings for the backs of fools.

20TH CHAPTER

1 Wine ᵧmakes peopleᵧ mock;
liquor ᵧmakes themᵧ noisy;[a]
and everyone under its influence is unwise.

From A King's Point Of View[b]

2 The screaming rage of a king is like the roar of a lion;
whoever makes him angry forfeits his life.
3 It is honorable for a man to avoid a quarrel,
but any stubborn fool can start a fight.
4 A lazy person does not plow in the fall;[c]
he looks for something in the harvest but finds nothing.
5 A motive in a man's heart[d] is ᵧlikeᵧ deep waters,
and a person who has understanding draws it [the motive] out.
6 Many a person declares himself loyal,
but who can find a man who is ᵧreallyᵧ trustworthy?
7 A righteous person lives on the basis of his integrity —
blessed are his children after him!
8 A king who sits on his throne to judge
sifts out every evil with his eyes.

---

26 1 Tim 1:9

---

e   Reading unit comprises 19:28–20:1.
20 *a-* 1 Lit.: "Wine is a mocker;
liquor is a noisy brawler."
b   See note "d" at heading for 16:10-15.
c- 4 Fall was the start of the planting season in Palestine.
d- 5 Lit.: "Counsel in the heart of a man"; see *LEB*: "HEART" AND "MIND" on p. 95.

Inner Aspects Of Life

9 Who can say,
  "I've made my heart pure;
  I'm cleansed from my sin"?
10 A double standard of weights and measures —
both are disgusting to the LORD!
11   Even a child makes himself known by his actions,
  whether his deeds are pure or right.
12 The ear that hears;
the eye that sees:
  the LORD made them both!
13 Do not love sleep or you will end up poor;
keep your eyes open ˎandˌ you will have plenty to eat.

The Mouth In Action

14 "Bad! Bad!" says the buyer;
  then, as he goes away, he brags ˎabout his bargainˌ.
15 There is gold and plenty of jewels,*e*
  but ˎwhatˌ precious gems*f* are the lips of knowledge!
16 Hold on to the garment of one who guarantees a stranger's loan,
  and hold responsible the person
    who makes a loan in behalf of a foreigner.*g*
17 Food gained dishonestly tastes sweet to a man,
  but afterward his mouth will be filled with gravel.
18 Plans are confirmed by getting advice,
  and with guidance one wages war.
19 Whoever goes around as a gossip tells secrets;
do not associate with a person whose mouth is always open.

Good And Bad Judgment Contrasted

20 *Whoever curses his father and mother,*
  *his lamp will be snuffed out in total darkness.*h
21 An inheritance quickly obtained in the beginning
  will never be blessed in the end.
22 *Do not say, "I'll get even with you!"*i
  Wait for the LORD
    and He will save you.

---

20 *Matt 15:4; Mk 7:10*   **22** *Rom 12:17,19; 1 Thess 5:15; 1 Pet 3:9*

---

e- 15 Lit.: "plenty of coral."
f- 15 Lit.: "precious vessel."
g- 16 Lit.: "foreign woman" (cf. 27:13). This verse refers to an action that is to be taken against a
  co-signer who has guaranteed a loan for a total stranger. Cf. 6:1 (and note "a"); 17:18; 22:26;
  (also 11:15).
h- 20 Or "snuffed out as darkness approaches."
i- 22 Lit.: "I will pay back the evil."

23 A double standard of weights is disgusting to the LORD,
        and dishonest scales are no good.
24 The LORD is the One who directs a man's steps;
      how then can a man understand his own way?
25   It is a trap for a person to say impulsively:
          "This is a holy offering!"
              and later to have second thoughts about those vows.
26 A wise king scatters the wicked
      and then runs them over.*j*
27   A person's soul is the LORD's lamp;
          it searches his entire innermost being.

Kings, Good People, And Evil People

28 Mercy and truth protect a king,
      and with mercy he maintains his throne.
29   While the glory of young men is their strength,
          the splendor of older people is their silver hair.
30   Brutal beatings cleanse away wickedness;
              such beatings cleanse the innermost being.

21ST CHAPTER

The Ways Of Life

1 The king's heart is ⌊like⌋ streams of water,
      both are under the LORD's control;
          He turns them in any direction He chooses.
2 *A man thinks everything he does is right,*
      but the LORD weighs hearts.
3 Doing what is right and just
      is more acceptable to the LORD than offering a sacrifice.
4 A conceited look and a proud heart,
      which are the lamp of the wicked, are sins.
5 The plans of a hardworking person certainly lead to prosperity,
      but everyone who is ⌊always⌋ in a hurry certainly ends up in poverty.*a*
6 Those who gather wealth by lying are wasting time;*b*
      they are looking for death.
7 The violence of the wicked will drag them away
      since they refuse to do what is just.

---

2 Lk 16:15

j- 26 Lit.: "A wise king winnows the wicked
              and drives the threshing wheel over them."
          "Winnows" and "threshing wheel" are farm terms describing the preparation of wheat for the mill.
21 *a-* 5 Parallel non-Biblical proverb: "The hurrier I go;
                      the behinder I get!"
  b- 6 Lit.: "are a fleeting vapor."

8 The way of the guilty is crooked,
   but the behavior of the pure is upright. [c]

Life With The Wicked

9 Better to live on a corner of a roof
   than to share a home with a quarreling woman.
10   The mind of a wicked person desires evil
       and has no consideration for his neighbor.
11   When a mocker is punished,
           a gullible person becomes wise,
           and when a wise person is instructed,
           he gains knowledge.
12   The Righteous One wisely considers the house of the wicked;
               He throws the wicked into disaster.
13   Whoever shuts his ear to the cry of the poor;
               someday that person will call and not be answered.
14 A gift ˌgiven, in secret calms anger,
    and a secret bribe calms great fury.
15   When justice is done, the righteous are delighted,
       but troublemakers are terrified.
16   A person who wanders from the way of wise behavior
       will rest in the assembly of the dead.
17   Whoever loves pleasure will become a poor man;
       whoever loves wine and expensive food [d] will not become rich.
18   The wicked becomes a ransom for the righteous,
       and the treacherous will take the place of the upright.
19 Better to live in a desert
    than with a quarreling and angry woman.

The Wealth Of The Wise

20 There is costly treasure and wealth [e] in the home of the wise,
       but a foolish man devours it.
21 Whoever pursues righteousness and mercy
       will find life, righteousness, and honor.

The Wise Man Versus Pride

22 A wise man attacks a city of warriors
    and *pulls down the strong defenses* in which they trust.
23   Whoever guards his mouth and his tongue
       keeps himself out of trouble.
24   A proud, conceited person is called a mocker;
           he acts with extreme pride.

---

22 2 Cor 10:4

---

c- 8 Heb meaning of this verse uncertain.
d- 17 Lit.: "wine and olive oil."
e- 20 Lit.: "olive oil," a symbol of wealth because of its great value.

The Lazy Person

25 The desire of a lazy person will kill him,
     because his hands refuse to work;
26   all day long he feels greedy,
               but a righteous person gives
                 and does not hold back.

The Way Of The Wicked And The Upright

27 The sacrifice of the wicked is disgusting,
     especially if they bring it with evil intent.
28 A *lying witness* will perish,
     but a man who listens to advice will continue to speak.
29 A wicked person puts up a bold front,
     but an upright person's way of life is his own security.

The LORD Is Over Everything

30 There is no wisdom, no understanding, and no advice
     ⌊that can stand up⌋ against the LORD.
31   The horse is made ready for the day of battle,
     but the victory belongs to the LORD.

22ND CHAPTER

A Good Name

1 A good name is more desirable than great wealth;
   respect is better than silver or gold.

General Advice And Observations

2 The rich and the poor have this in common:
   the LORD is the Maker of them all.
3   A sensible person foresees trouble and hides ⌊from it⌋,
     but gullible people go ahead and suffer ⌊the consequence⌋.
4 ⌊Coming⌋ on the heels of humility (the fear of the LORD)
   are riches and honor and life.
5   A devious person has thorns and traps ahead of him;
     whoever guards himself will stay far away from them.
6 Train a child in the way he should go,
     and even when he is old he will not turn away from it.
7 The rich person rules over the poor,
     and the borrower is a slave to the lender.

---

28 Acts 6:13

8 Whoever sows injustice will reap trouble,
    and this weapon of his own fury will be destroyed.
9 Whoever is generous will be blessed,
    for he has shared his food with the poor.
10 Drive out a mocker and conflict will leave;
    quarreling and abuse will stop.
11 Whoever loves a pure heart
   ⌊and⌋ whose speech is gracious,
       has a king as his friend.
12   The LORD's eyes watch over knowledge,
    but He overturns the words of the treacherous.
13 A lazy person says,
  "There's a lion outside!
    I'll be murdered in the streets!"
14   The mouth of an adulterous woman is a deep pit;
    the one who is cursed by the LORD will fall into it.
15   Foolishness is firmly attached to a child's heart;
    spanking[a] will remove it far from him.
16 Oppressing the poor for profit
   ⌊or⌋ giving to the rich
     certainly leads to poverty.

C. The Words of the Wise (22:17–24:34)
1. Opening comments (22:17-21)[b]

17 Open your ear and hear the words of the wise,
and set your mind on the knowledge I give you,
18   for it is pleasant if you keep them in mind
   ⌊so that⌋ they will be on the tip of your tongue,
19   so that your trust may be in the LORD.
Today I have made them known to you, especially to you.
20 Didn't I write to you previously with advice and knowledge
21   in order to teach you the very words of truth,
     so that you can give an accurate report to those who send you?

2. Practical advice (22:22–24:22)

Robbing The Poor

22 Do not rob the poor,
    because he is poor
or trample on the rights of those in distress at the city gate,[c]
23   because the LORD will plead their case
    and will take[d] the lives of those who rob them.

---

22 *a-* 15 Lit.: "the rod of discipline"; see note "e" at 10:13.
    b   See PROVERBS 22:17–24:22 AND THE "THIRTY SAYINGS" on p. 115. Some have called this
        section "the *thirty* sayings," basing it upon a different translation of the word "previously" in
        v. 20.
    c- 22 The phrase "at the city gate" means "where *courts* were in session."
    d- 23 Lit.: "will rob."

Associating With Hotheads

24 Do not be a friend of one who has a bad temper
     and never keep company with a hothead,
25   or you will learn his ways
         and set a trap for yourself!

Concerning Loans

26 Do not be ˌfoundˌ among those who make deals with a handshake,
     among those who guarantee other people's loans.ᵉ
27   If you have no money to pay back ˌa loanˌ,
         why should your bed be repossessed?

Protect Your Property

28 Do not move an ancient boundary marker
         that your ancestors set in place.

The Skilled Worker

29 Do you see a man who is efficient in his work?
         He will serve kings;
         he will not serve unknown people.

23RD CHAPTER

The Food Of A Ruler

1 When you sit down to eat with a ruler,
         pay close attention to what is before you,
2   and put a knife to your throat if you have a big appetite;
3   do not crave his delicacies,
             for this is food that deceives you.

Getting Rich

4 Do not wear yourself out getting rich;
     be smart enough to stop!
5   Will you catch only a fleeting glimpse of wealth before it is gone?
         For it makes wings for itself like an eagle flying off into the sky.

Eating With Selfish People

6 Do not eat the food of one who is stingy and
     do not crave his delicacies,

---

e- 26 See 6:1 (and note "a"); 17:18; 20:16 (also 11:15; 27:13).

7   for as he calculates the cost to himself, this is what he does:
      he tells you, "Eat and drink,"
      but he doesn't really mean it.*a*

8   You will vomit up the little bit you have eaten
      and spoil your pleasant conversation.

Talking To Fools

9   Do not talk in front of a fool
      because he will despise the wisdom of your words.

Protect The Property Of Orphans

10   Do not move an ancient boundary marker
      or enter the fields of orphans,*b*

11   because their Redeemer is strong;
      He will plead their case against you.

Disciplined Living

12   Live a more disciplined life*c*
      and listen carefully to words of knowledge.

Child Discipline

13   Do not hesitate to discipline a child;
      if you spank him*d* he will not die.

14   Spank him yourself,
      and you will save his soul from hell.*e*

What Makes A Father Rejoice

15   My son, if you have a wise heart,
      my heart will rejoice as well;

16   my heart*f* rejoices when you speak what is right.

Sin Versus Hope

17   Do not envy sinners in your heart,
      but rather, continue in the fear of the LORD.

18   There is indeed a future,
      and your hope will never be cut off.

---

23 *a-* 7 Lit.: "but his heart is not with you"; see *LEB*: "HEART" AND "MIND" on p. 95.
  b- 10 Orphans were often deprived of their property because they were defenseless.
  c- 12 Lit.: "Set your heart to discipline."
  d- 13 Lit.: "if you beat him with a rod" (also at v. 14); see note "e" at 10:13.
  e- 14 Heb: "*sheol*"; see DEATH AND *SHEOL* on p. 103.
  f- 16 Lit.: "my kidneys."

Associating With Drunks And Gluttons

19 My son! Listen and be wise,
 and keep your mind going in the right direction.
20   Do not associate with those who drink too much wine,
   with those who eat too much meat,
21   because both a drunk and a glutton will become poor,
     and drowsiness will dress a person in rags.

Parental Advice

22 Listen to your father since you are his son,
 and do not despise your mother just because she is old:
23   Buy truth (and do not sell it),
   ˻that is,˼ buy wisdom, discipline, and understanding.
24   A righteous person's father will certainly rejoice;
     one who has a wise son will enjoy him.
25   May your father and your mother be glad,
     and may she who gave birth to you rejoice.

Against Prostitution

26 My son, give me your heart;
 let your eyes take delight in my ways:
27   A prostitute is a deep pit,
   and a loose woman*g* is a narrow well;
28   she is like a robber, lying in ambush;
     she spreads unfaithfulness throughout society.

The Misery Caused By Drinking

29 Who has woe? Who has misery?
 Who has quarrels? Who has a complaint?
 Who has wounds for no reason? Who has bloodshot eyes? —
30   Those who drink glass after glass of wine;
   who go and mix it with everything!
31 Do not look at wine
     just because it is red,
     just because it sparkles in the cup, and
     just because it goes down smoothly;
32   later on it bites like a snake
     and strikes like a poisonous snake.
33 Your eyes will see strange sights,
   and your mouth will say embarrassing things.*h*
34 You will be like someone lying down in the middle of the sea
 or like someone lying down on top of a ship's mast, ˻saying˼:
35   "They strike me, ˻but˼ I feel no pain;
     they beat me, ˻but˼ I'm not aware of it.
         Whenever I wake up
             I'm going to look for another drink."

---

g- 27 Lit.: "foreign woman," meaning a prostitute from another nation.
h- 33 Lit.: "your heart will speak perverse things"; see *LEB*: "HEART" AND "MIND" on p. 95.

24TH CHAPTER

Wrong Thoughts; Wrong Company

1 Do not envy evil men
    or wish you were with them,
2   because their minds plot violence,
        and their lips talk trouble.

Spiritual Building Materials

3 A house is built with wisdom;
    its foundation is understanding;
4 its rooms are filled with knowledge,
        with every kind of riches, both precious and pleasant.

Strategic Planning

5 A wise man is strong,
    and an intelligent man has strength,
6   for with the right strategy you can wage war,
        and with many advisers there is victory.

Foolish Scheming

7 Matters of wisdom are beyond the grasp of a stubborn fool;
        at the city gate*a* he does not open his mouth.
8 Anyone who plans to do evil will be known as a schemer.
9 Foolish scheming is sinful,
        and a mocker is disgusting to everyone.

Caring And Its Reward

10 If you faint in a crisis,
        you reveal that you are weak.
11 Rescue captives ⌞condemned⌟ to death,
        and spare those staggering toward their slaughter.
12 When you say, "Look, we didn't know this,"
        won't He who weighs hearts take note of it? And
        won't He who guards your soul know it? And
        won't *He pay back everyone according to what he does*?

Honey And Wisdom Compared

13 Eat honey, my son, because it is good;
        honey that flows from the honeycomb tastes sweet;

---

12 Matt 16:27; Rom 2:6; 2 Tim 4:14; Rev 2:23; 20:12; 22:12

---

24 *a-* 7 In ancient Israelite cities the city gate was the place where *court* was held, important business
        decisions were made, and leaders of the city met. Cf. 31:23.

14 the knowledge of wisdom is just like that for your soul —
  if you find it, then there is a future,
  and your hope will never be cut off.

The Resilient Righteous; The Devastated Damned

15 You wicked one, do not lie in ambush at the home of the righteous;
 do not rob his house,
16 for a righteous person may fall seven times —
  but he gets up again;
  however, in a disaster wicked people fall. *b*

How To React To Your Enemies' Misfortune

17 Do not be happy when your enemies fall
 and do not feel glad when they stumble,
18 or the L ORD will see it and not like it
  and turn His anger away from them [the enemies].

Level-headed Restraint

19 Do not get overly upset with evildoers;
 do not envy wicked people,
20 because an evil person has no future,
  and *the lamp of the wicked will be snuffed out.*

Godly Traditions Cushion Misery

21 *Fear the L ORD*, my son
 (*fear the king* as well);
 do not associate with those who always insist upon change,
22 because disaster will come on them suddenly,
  and who knows what misery both may bring?

3. Closing comments (24:23-34)

Partiality And Fairness

23 These also are ⌊the sayings⌋ of the wise:
 It is not good to show partiality as a judge.
24 Whoever says to the guilty
 "You are innocent"*c*
  will be cursed by people and condemned by nations,
25 but it will be a delight for those who convict the guilty,
  and a great blessing will come upon them.
26 Giving a straight answer is ⌊like⌋ a kiss on the lips.

---

20 Matt 25:8   *21 1 Pet 2:17*

---

b- 16 Meaning "wicked people will stumble and never get up again."
c- 24 Lit.: "righteous"; according to Israelite law a person was guilty until proved innocent
 (righteous).

Plan Ahead!

27 Prepare your work outside
      and get things ready for yourself in the field —
      then afterwards, build your house.

Don't Try To Get Even

28 Do not testify against your neighbor without a reason,
      and do not deceive ˌanyoneˌ with your lips.
29 *Do not say,*
      "I'll treat him like he treated me;
      I'll pay him back for what he's done to me."

Learn From The Laziness Of Others

30 I passed by a lazy man's field,
      the vineyard belonging to a man without sense.
31   And look, it was all overgrown with thistles;
      the ground was covered with weeds,
      and its stone fence was torn down!
32 When I observed ˌthisˌ, I took it to heart;
      I saw it ˌandˌ learned my lesson.
33   "Just a little sleep,
      just a little slumber,
      just a little nap."[d]
34   Then your poverty will come ˌupon youˌ like a drifter,
      and your need will come ˌupon youˌ like a bandit.

25TH CHAPTER

D. The Proverbs of Solomon Copied Out by the "Men of Hezekiah"[a]
(25:1–29:27)

Introduction

1 These also are Solomon's proverbs which were copied
      by the men of King Hezekiah of Judah.

In Relation To Kings[b]

2 It is the glory[c] of God to hide things,
      but the glory of kings to investigate them.

---

29 Rom 12:17; 1 Pet 3:9; 1 Thess 5:15

---

    d- 33   See 6:10.
25 *a*   Cf. 2 Chr. 29:1–32:33.
      b   See note "d" at heading for 16:10-15.
      c- 2   Or "the rightful power, prerogative."

3 ⌊Like⌋ the high heavens and the deep earth,
　　so the mind of kings is unsearchable.
4 Take dross away from silver[d]
　　and a vessel is ready for the silversmith to mold.[e]
5 Take the wicked person away from the presence of a king
　　and justice[f] will make his throne secure.
6 Do not brag about yourself before a king
　　or stand in the spot that belongs to notable people;
7　　　because it is better to be told, *"Come up here,"*
　　　　than to be put down in front of a prince
　　　　whom your eyes have seen.

Lawsuits, Libel, And Level-headedness

8 Do not be in a hurry to go to court,
　　for what will you do in the end if your neighbor disgraces you?
9 Present your argument to your neighbor,
　　but do not reveal another person's secret;
10　　otherwise, when he hears about it, he will humiliate you,
　　　and his evil report about you will never disappear.

The Word Is Like...

11 ⌊Like⌋ golden apples in silver settings,
　　⌊so⌋ is a word spoken at the right time.
12 ⌊Like⌋ a gold ring and an ornament of fine gold,
　　⌊so⌋ constructive criticism is to the ear of one who listens.
13 Like the coolness of snow on a harvest day,
　　⌊so⌋ is the trustworthy messenger to those who send him:
　　　he refreshes his masters.
14 ⌊Like⌋ a dense fog or a dust storm,
　　⌊so⌋ is the man who brags about a gift that he does not give.

Moderation In Human Relations

15 With patience you can persuade a ruler,
　　and a soft tongue can break bones.

16 When you find honey, eat only as much as you need;
　　otherwise, you will have too much and vomit.
17 Do not set foot in your neighbor's house too often;
　　otherwise, he will see too much of you and hate you.

---

7 *Lk 14:10*

---

d- 4 "Silver dross" refers to the impurities that are removed while silver is being refined. See note "d" at 26:23.
e- 4 Lit.: "and a vessel goes out for the silversmith."
f- 5 Lit.: "righteousness" (Heb: "*tzedeq*").

18 ₍Like₎ a club and a sword and a sharp arrow,
      ₍so₎ is the man who gives false testimony against his neighbor.
19 ₍Like₎ a broken tooth and a lame foot,
      ₍so₎ is confidence in an unfaithful person in a ₍time of₎ crisis.

20 ₍Like₎ taking off a coat on a cold day
          or pouring vinegar on baking soda,
              so singing songs is to one who has an evil heart.

21 *If your enemy is hungry, give him some food to eat, and*
    if he is thirsty, give him some water to drink;
22   *for ₍in this way₎ you will heap^g burning coals on his head,^h*
        and the LORD *will reward you.*

23 ₍As₎ the north wind brings rain,
          so the whispering tongue brings angry looks.
24 Better to live on a corner of a roof
          than to share a home with a quarreling woman.

25 ₍Like₎ cold water to a thirstyⁱ soul,
          so is good news from far away.
26 ₍Like₎ a muddied spring and a polluted well,
          ₍so₎ is the righteous person who gives in to the wicked.

27 Eating too much honey is not good,
          and searching for honor is not honorable.^j
28 ₍Like₎ a city broken into ₍and₎ left without a wall,
          ₍so₎ is a man who lacks self-control.

26TH CHAPTER

The Fool

1 Like snow in summertime and rain at harvest time,
        so honor is just not right for a fool.
2 Like a fluttering sparrow,
    like a darting swallow,
        so a hastily spoken curse does not come to rest.
3 A whip is for the horse,
    a bridle is for the donkey, and
        a rod^a is for the back of fools.

21, 22 Matt 6:4,6; Rom 12:20

---

g- 22 Lit.: "will snatch up."
h- 22 Meaning that it is better now to feel the *guilt* and *shame* (the *coals of fire*) than the *punishment*
        later (cf. Ps. 140:10).
i- 25 Lit.: "faint, weary."
j- 27 Heb meaning of this line uncertain.
26 a- 3 See note "e" at 10:13.

4 Do not answer a fool with his own type of stupidity,
      or you will be just like him.
5 Answer a fool with his own type of stupidity,
      or he will think he is wise.
6 Whoever uses a fool to send a message
         cuts off his own feet
            and brings violence upon himself. ᵇ
7 ⌞Like⌟ a lame person's limp legs,
      so is a proverb in the mouth of fools.
8 Like tying a stone to a sling,
      so is giving honor to a fool.
9 ⌞Like⌟ a thorn stuck in a drunk's hand,
      so is a proverb in the mouth of fools.
10 ⌞Like⌟ many people who destroy everything,
      so is one who hires fools or drifters.
11 *As a dog goes back to his vomit,*
      ⌞so⌟ a fool repeats his stupidity.
12 Have you met a man who thinks he is wise?
      There is more hope for a fool than for him.

The Lazy Person

13 A lazy person says,
      "There's a lion out on the road!
      There's a lion loose in the streets!"
14 ⌞As⌟ a door turns on its hinges,
      so the lazy person turns on his bed.
15 A lazy person puts his fork in his food; ᶜ
      he wears himself out bringing it back to his mouth.
16 A lazy person thinks he is wiser
      than seven people who give a sensible answer.

Concerning Meddling

17 ⌞Like⌟ grabbing a dog by the ears,
      ⌞so⌟ is a bystander
         who gets involved in someone else's quarrel.
18 Like a madman
      who shoots flaming arrows, arrows, and death [to capture a city],
19   so is the man who tricks his neighbor
         and says, "I was only joking!"

Avoid Gossip

20 Without wood a fire goes out, and
   without gossip a quarrel dies down.

---

11 2 Pet 2:22

---

b- 6 Lit.: "and drinks violence"; NET has reversed the two Heb lines for sake of Eng flow.
c- 15 See 19:24.

21   ⌊As⌋ charcoal fuels burning coals and wood fuels fire,
          so the quarrelsome man fuels a dispute.
22   The words of a gossip are swallowed greedily,
          and they go down into a person's innermost being.

The Evils Of Lying

23   ⌊Like⌋ a clay pot covered with silver dross,[d]
          ⌊so⌋ is smooth talk which covers up an evil heart.[e]
24   One filled with hate disguises it with his speech,
          but inside he holds on to deceit.
25   When he talks charmingly, do not trust him
          because of the seven disgusting things[f] in his heart.
26   His hatred is deceitfully hidden,
          but his wickedness will be revealed in the community.
27   Whoever digs a pit[g] will fall into it;
      whoever rolls a stone, it will roll back on him.
28   A lying tongue hates its victims, and
          a flattering mouth causes ruin.

27TH CHAPTER

General Advice And Observations

1   *Do not brag about tomorrow,*
          because you do not know what another day may bring.
2   Praise should come
          from another person and not from your own mouth,
          from a stranger and not from your own lips.

3   A stone is heavy and sand weighs a lot,
          but annoyance caused by a stubborn fool is heavier than both.
4   Anger is cruel and fury is overwhelming,
          but who can stand before jealousy?
5   Open criticism is better than unexpressed love.
6   Wounds made by a friend are intended to help,
          but an enemy's kisses are too much to bear.[a]
7   One who is full despises honey,
          but to one who is hungry, even bitter food tastes sweet.

---

1 Jas 4:13-16

---

d- 23 "Silver dross" refers to the impurities that are removed while silver is being refined. Such dross was used as "glaze" to give the appearance of real silver, thus a clay pot would look like a *cheap* silver pot.
e- 23 Lit.: "⌊so⌋ are burning lips and an evil heart."
f- 25 See 6:16-19.
g- 27 Heb: "*shahath*"; see DEATH AND *SHEOL* on p. 103.
27 a- 6 Heb meaning of "are too much to bear" uncertain.

8 Like a bird wandering from its nest,
   so is a man wandering from his home.

9 Perfume[b] and incense make the heart glad,
   but the sweetness of a friend is a fragrant forest.[c]
10 Do not abandon your friend or your father's friend;
   do not go to your brother's home when you are in trouble;
   a neighbor living nearby is better than a brother far away.

11 Be wise, my son, and make my heart glad,
   so I can answer anyone who criticizes me.
12 A sensible person foresees trouble ˎandˌ hides,
   ˎbutˌ gullible people go ahead ˎandˌ suffer.
13 Hold on to the garment of one who guarantees a stranger's loan, and
   hold responsible the person who makes a loan in behalf of a foreigner.[d]
14   Whoever blesses his friend early in the morning with a loud voice —
   his blessing is considered a curse.
15 Constantly dripping water on a rainy day is like a quarreling woman.
16 Anyone who can control her can control the wind;
   ˎhe canˌ even pick up olive oil with his right hand.[e]
17 ˎAsˌ iron sharpens iron,
   so one man sharpens the wits[f] of another.
18 Whoever takes care of a fig tree can eat its fruit, and
   whoever protects his master is honored.
19   As a face is reflected in water,
   so a person is reflected by his heart.
20 *Sheol* and *Abaddon*[g] are never satisfied,
   and a person's eyes are never satisfied.
21 The crucible is for refining silver and the smelter[h] for gold,
   but a man ˎis testedˌ by the praise given to him.
22 If you crush a stubborn fool in a mortar with a pestle,
   along with grain,[i]
   ˎeven thenˌ his stupidity will not leave him.

Rural Routines

23 Be fully aware of the condition of your flock,
   and pay close attention to your herds,
24   for wealth is not forever,
   nor does a crown always last.

---

20 Rev 9:11

---

b- 9 Lit.: "oil" (see Ex. 30:23-25).
c- 9 Or "is sincere advice"; Heb meaning of "fragrant forest" uncertain.
d- 13 Lit.: "foreign woman" (cf. 20:16). Also, this verse is not speaking about repossessing
    something, but responsibly securing a loan for someone unfamiliar to you.
e- 16 Heb meaning of this line uncertain.
f- 17 Lit.: "face."
g- 20 See note at 15:11.
h- 21 See note at 17:3.
i- 22 Heb meaning of "grain" uncertain.

25 ⌊When⌋ grass is removed, the tender growth appears
      and vegetables are gathered on the hills;
26   lambs ⌊will provide⌋ you with clothing,
            and the money from the male goats will buy a field.
27   There will be enough goats' milk to feed you,
                  to feed your family,
                        and to keep your servant girls alive.

28TH CHAPTER

General Advice and Observations

1 A wicked person flees when no one is chasing him,
      but the righteous are as bold as a lion.
2 When a country is in revolt it has many rulers,
      but only with a person who has understanding and knowledge
        will it last a long time.
3 A poor man who oppresses poorer people
      is ⌊like⌋ a driving rain that leaves no food.
4 Those who abandon ⌊God's⌋ teaching praise the wicked,
      but those who keep ⌊God's⌋ teaching oppose them.
5 Evil men do not understand justice,
      but those who seek the LORD understand everything.
6 Better to be a poor person who has integrity
      than to be rich and double-dealing.
7 Whoever keeps ⌊God's⌋ teaching is a wise son,
  whoever associates with gluttons disgraces his father.
8   Whoever becomes wealthy through ⌊unfair⌋ loans and interest[a]
      collects them only to lose it [the wealth]
      to the one who is kind to the poor.
9 Whoever refuses to listen to ⌊God's⌋ teaching,
  even his prayer is disgusting.
10   Whoever misleads the upright into evil will fall into his own pit,
      but the innocent will inherit good things.
11 A rich man is wise in his own eyes,
      but a poor man with understanding sees right through him.
12 When the righteous triumph, there is great glory,
      but when the wicked rise, people hide themselves.
13 Whoever covers over his sins does not prosper, but
   whoever confesses and abandons them receives compassion.
14   Blessed is the one who is always fearful ⌊of sin⌋,
      but *whoever is hard-hearted falls into disaster*.
15 ⌊Like⌋ a roaring lion and
   ⌊like⌋ a prowling bear,
        ⌊so⌋ is the wicked person who rules over poor people.

---

14 Rom 2:5

---

28 *a-* 8 Cf. Ex. 22:25; Lev. 25:36; Deut. 23:19,20.

16 A leader without understanding taxes ˏhisˏ peopleˏ heavily,
       but those who hate unjust gain will live longer.
17 A person burdened with the guilt of murder
       will be a fugitive down to his grave[b] —
           no one should help him.
18 Whoever lives honestly will be safe, but
   whoever lives dishonestly will fall all at once.
19   Whoever works his land will have plenty to eat; but
       whoever chases rainbows[c] will have plenty of nothing.
20 A trustworthy man has many blessings,
       but anyone in a hurry to get rich will not escape punishment.
21 It is not good to play favorites
       because some men will turn on you even for a piece of bread.
22 A stingy man is in a hurry to get rich,
       not realizing that poverty is about to overtake him.
23 Eventually, whoever criticizes someone will be more highly regarded
       than the one who flatters with his tongue.
24 The one who robs his father or his mother
       and says, "It isn't wrong!" is a companion to a vandal.
25 A greedy person stirs up a fight,
       but whoever trusts the LORD prospers.
26 Whoever trusts his own heart is a fool, but
   whoever walks in wisdom will survive.
27   Whoever gives to the poor lacks nothing, but
       whoever ignores the poor ˏreceivesˏ many curses. [d]
28 When the wicked rise, people hide, but
   when they perish, the righteous increase.

29TH CHAPTER

Observing Some Patterns Of Life

1 A man who will not bend after many warnings
       will suddenly be broken beyond cure.
2 When the righteous increase, the people ˏof Godˏ rejoice,
       but when a wicked person rules, everybody groans.
3 A man who loves wisdom makes his father happy,
       but one who pays prostitutes wastes his wealth.
4 By means of justice a king builds up a country,
       but a man who confiscates religious contributions[a] tears it down.
5 A man who flatters his neighbor
       is spreading a net for him to step into.

---

b- 17 Heb: "*bor*"; see DEATH AND *SHEOL* on p. 103.
c- 19 See 12:11.
d- 27 Lit.: "but those who hide their eyes ˏreceiveˏ many curses."
29 a- 4 The Heb word translated "religious contributions" is always employed in the OT concerning
        items given to be used by the priests in the Temple. Kings often thought of these items as
        being their own personal property.

6 To an evil man sin is bait in a trap,
     but a righteous person runs away from it[b]
        and is glad.
7 A righteous person knows the just cause of the poor;
     but a wicked person does not understand this.
8 Men who mock create an uproar in a city,
     but the wise turn away anger.
9 When a wise man goes to court with a stubborn fool,
     he may rage or laugh,
        but there is no peace and quiet.
10 Bloodthirsty men hate an innocent person,
     but upright people seek ˌto protectˌ his life.
11 A fool expresses all his emotions,
     but a wise person controls them.
12 If a ruler pays attention to lies,
     all his servants become wicked.
13 A poor man and an oppressor have this in common:
     the LORD gives both of them sight.
14 When a king judges the poor with honesty,
     his throne will always be secure.

General Truths

15 A spanking[c] and a warning produce wisdom,
     but an undisciplined child disgraces his mother.
16 When the wicked increase, crime increases,
     but the righteous will witness their downfall.
17 Correct your son and he will give you peace of mind,
     and he will bring delight to your soul.
18 Without prophetic vision people run wild,
     but blessed are those who keep ˌGod'sˌ teaching.
19 A slave cannot be disciplined with words;
     he will not respond though he may understand.
20 Have you met a man who is quick to answer?
     There is more hope for a fool than for him.
21 Pamper a slave from childhood
     and later on he will be ungrateful.[d]
22 An angry man stirs up a fight,
     and a hothead does much wrong.
23 *A person's pride will humiliate him,*
     but a humble spirit gains honor.
24 Anyone who is a thief's partner hates his own life;
     he will not testify under oath.[e]

---

23 Matt 23:12; Lk 18:14

---

b- 6 Heb meaning of "runs away from it" uncertain.
c- 15 See note "e" at 10:13.
d- 21 Heb meaning of "ungrateful" uncertain.
e- 24 See Lev. 5:1.

25 A person's fear sets a trap ˌfor himˌ,
  but one who trusts the LORD is safe.
26 Many seek an audience with a ruler,
  but justice for mankind comes from the LORD.
27 An unjust man is disgusting to righteous people,
  and a person who is upright is disgusting to the wicked.

30TH CHAPTER

E. The Words of Agur (30:1-33)

Introduction

1 The words of Agur the son of Jakeh, his prophetic revelation!

God Is A Mystery!

[To God:]
  This man's declaration:
    "I'm weary, O God;
    I'm weary, O God, and
    I'm worn out,*a* for
2   I'm more ˌlikeˌ a dumb animal than a man, and
        I don't ˌevenˌ have human understanding, and
3   I haven't learned wisdom, and
        I don't have knowledge of the Holy One!"*b*

[To the audience:]
 4 *"Who has gone up to heaven and come down?*
  Who has gathered the wind in the palm of His hand?
  Who has wrapped up water in a garment?
  Who has set up the earth from one end to the other?
  What is His Name or the Name of His *Son*?*c*
    Certainly you must know!"

The Strength Of God's Word

 5 "Every word of God*d* has proven to be true.
  He is a Shield to those who come to Him for protection.
 6 *Do not add to His words*
    or He will scold you,
      and you will be found to be a liar."

---

4 *Jn 3:13; Rom 10:6*   *6* *Rev 22:18*

---

30 *a-* 1 Or "The words of Agur the son of Jakeh, his prophetic revelation, this man's declaration to
      Ithiel, to Ithiel and Ucal."
  b- 3 Or "holy ones" ("angels").
  c- 4 Notice how the NT solves the question and the overall problem of Agur and other OT believers:
      Matt. 13:11; Col. 1:26,27; 1 Tim. 3:16.
  d- 5 Heb: "*Elohim*" (also at vv. 1,9; 25:2); see GOD: HIS DESIGNATIONS AND NAMES on
      p. 80.

A Prayer

[To God:]
7 "I've asked You for two things;
　　don't keep them from me before I die:
8　　　Keep vanity and lies far away from me;
　　　don't give me either poverty or riches;
　　　　feed me ⌊only⌋ the food I need
9　　　or I may feel satisfied and deny ⌊You⌋
　　　　and say, 'Who is the LORD?' —
　　　or I may become poor and steal
　　　　and give the Name of my God a bad reputation."

Against Slander

[To the audience:]
10 "Do not slander a slave to his master
　　or he will curse you
　　　and you will be found guilty."

Four Kinds Of People

11 There is a certain kind of person who curses his father
　　and does not bless his mother.
12 There is a certain kind of person who thinks he is pure
　　but is not washed from his own feces [human waste]. *e*
13 There is a certain kind of person — how arrogantly he looks about
　　and how conceited he is.
14 There is a certain kind of person
　　whose teeth are ⌊like⌋ swords and
　　whose jaws are ⌊like⌋ knives,
　　　　devouring the oppressed from the earth
　　　　and the needy from among mankind.

Human Bloodsuckers

15 The bloodsucking leech has two daughters — "Give!" ⌊and⌋ "Give!"

Four Things That Are Never Satisfied

　　There are three things that are never satisfied,
　　four that never say, "Enough!":
16　　the grave *f*
　　　and a barren womb;
　　　a land that never gets enough water
　　　and a fire that does not say, "Enough!"

---

8 Matt 6:11

---

e- 12 Blunt Heb term but not considered vulgar.
f- 16 Heb: "*sheol*"; see DEATH AND *SHEOL* on p. 103.

Disrespectful Children: Their Punishment

17 The eye that makes fun of a father and hates to obey a mother
      will be plucked out by ravens in the valley
        and eaten by young vultures.

Four Things Of Intrigue

18 Three things are too wonderful for me,
      even four which I cannot understand:
19   an eagle ˌmakingˌ its way through the sky;
        a snake ˌmakingˌ its way over a rock;
        a ship ˌmakingˌ its way through high seas;ᵍ
        a man ˌmakingˌ his way with a virgin. ʰ

About The Adulteress

20 This is the way of an adulterous woman:
      She eats and wipes her mouth
      and says, "I haven't done anything wrong!"

Four Things That Are Intolerable

21 Three things cause the earth to tremble,
      even four it cannot bear up under:
22   a slave when he becomes king and
        a godless fool when he is filled with food;
23   a woman who is unloved when she gets marriedⁱ and
        a maid when she replaces her mistress.

Four Things Small—Yet Smart And Strong

24 Four things on earth are small,
      yet they are very wise:
25   ants are not a strong species,
          yet they store their food in summer;
26   rock-badgers are not a mighty species,
          yet they make their home in the rocks;
27   locusts have no king,
          yet all of them divide into swarms by instinct;
28   a lizard you can hold in your hands,
          and yet it can even be found in royal palaces.

Four Things That Move Like A Kingʲ

29 There are three things that walk ˌlikeˌ a king,
      even four that march ˌlikeˌ a king:

---

g- 19 Lit.: "the way of a ship in the heart of the sea."
h- 19 Lit.: "maiden," that is, a young girl of marriageable age (12 or older) who is presumed to be a
        virgin.
i- 23 Meaning "a woman from her wedding day until the day she dies."
j   See note "d" at heading for 16:10-15.

30   a lion, mightiest among animals, which turns away from nothing,
31   a strutting rooster[k] or
      a male goat, and
      a king at the head of his army.[l]

Keep Calm And Quiet

32 If you are such a godless fool as to honor yourself, or
    if you scheme evil,
        you had better put your hand over your mouth,
33   for just as churning milk[m] produces butter
            and squeezing a nose produces blood,
                so stirring up anger[n] produces a fight.

31ST CHAPTER

F. The Counsel of Lemuel's Mother (31:1-9)

Introduction

1   The sayings of King Lemuel, a prophetic revelation,
    used by his mother to discipline him.

Don't Make Yourself Vulnerable!

2 "What, my son? And
   what, son of my womb? And
   what, son of my prayers?[a]
3   Don't give your strength to women
       or your power[b] to those who ruin kings."

       ·

The Use Of Liquor[c]

4 "It is not for kings, Lemuel;
   it is not for kings to drink wine,
   that is, for rulers to crave liquor;
5   otherwise, they drink and forget what ⌊they have⌋ decreed
       and change the standard of justice for all the oppressed.
6 Give liquor to the person who is perishing
   and wine to one who feels bitter.

---

k- 31 Heb meaning of this line uncertain.
l- 31 Heb meaning for "at the head of his army" uncertain.
m- 33 Lit.: "squeezing milk."
n- 33 Lit.: "as squeezing milk...and squeezing a nose [nostril]...so squeezing noses [two nostrils]." A non-Biblical proverb:
        "Hit me once I may bleed;
        hit me twice I'll fight back."
31 a- 2 Lit.: "my vows"; see 1 Sam. 1:11.
    b- 3 Lit.: "your ways."
    c   See note "d" at heading for 16:10-15.

7   Such a person drinks
         and forgets his poverty
         and does not remember his trouble anymore."

Defending The Poor And The Needy

8 "Speak out for the one who cannot speak,
         for the rights of those who are doomed.
9 Speak out,
         judge fairly,
         and defend the rights of the oppressed and needy."

G. A Wife with Strength of Character (31:10-31)

An Alphabetic Poem^d

א
| א | 'Aleph | 10 | "Who can find a wife with strength of character? |

א   'Aleph   10 "Who can find a wife with strength of character?
                    She is worth far more than jewels. *e*
ב   Beth   11   Her husband trusts her with ₌all₌ his heart,
                    and he does not lack any good thing;
ג   Gimel   12   she helps him
                    and never harms him all the days of her life.

ד   Daleth   13   "She seeks out wool and linen ₌with care₌
                    and works with willing hands.
ה   He   14   She is like merchant ships;
                    she brings her food from far away.
ו   Waw   15   She wakes up while it is still dark
                    and gives food to her family
                    and a share of food to her servant girls.

ז   Zayin   16   "She picks out a field and buys it;
                    she plants a vineyard from the profits she has earned.
ח   Heth   17   She *puts on strength like a belt*
                    and goes to work with energy;*f*
ט   Teth   18   she sees that she is making a good profit;
                    her lamp burns late at night.

---

17 *1 Pet 1:13*

---

d   See POETIC STRUCTURES THAT CONVEY TEXTUAL MEANINGS on p. 105.
e- 10 Lit.: "pieces of coral."
f- 17 Lit.: "She ties strength around her waist
              and makes her arms strong."

י	*Yod*	19	"She puts her hands on the distaff,[g] and her fingers hold a spindle.
כ	*Kaph*	20	She opens her hands to the oppressed and stretches them out to the needy.
ל	*Lamed*	21	She does not fear for her family when it snows because her whole family has a double layer of clothing.[h]
מ	*Mem*	22	She makes quilts for herself; her clothes are ˌmade ofˌ linen and purple.[i]
נ	*Nun*	23	"Her husband is known at the city gates[j] when he sits with the elders of the land.
ס	*Samek*	24	"She makes linen garments and sells them and delivers belts to the merchants;
ע	*'Ayin*	25	she dresses with strength and nobility, and she smiles at the future.
פ	*Pe*	26	"She speaks with wisdom, and on her tongue there is tender instruction.
צ	*Tzade*	27	She keeps a close eye on the conduct of her family, and she does not eat the bread of idleness.
ק	*Qoph*	28	Her children stand up and bless her; her husband ˌtooˌ; in addition, he sings her praises, ˌsayingˌ,
ר	*Resh*	29	'Many women have done noble work, but you have surpassed them all!'
ש	*Shin*	30	"Charm is deceptive, and beauty evaporates, ˌbutˌ a woman who has the fear of the LORD — she is to be praised!
ת	*Taw*	31	"Reward her for what she has done, and let her achievements praise her at the city gates!"

g- 19 This is a difficult Heb word. "Distaff" means a staff for holding the yarn or wool in spinning.

h- 21 Some render the word for "double layer of clothing" as "scarlet clothing." This color would indicate high quality.

i- 22 Purple dye was very expensive; only those of high rank and nobility could afford it.

j- 23 In ancient Israelite cities the "city gates" were the place where *court* was held, important business decisions were made, and leaders of the city met. This verse implies that the husband of the poem's ideal wife is one of the leaders of the city (see also 31:31). Cf. 24:7.

STUDIES IN *PROVERBS*

STUDIES IN *PROVERBS*

Parallel to the APPENDIXES of the NET NT are these "Studies in *Proverbs*." They are designed to lead the reader to a fuller understanding of the Biblical text. In so doing, they aim to glorify God and educate His people.

While these studies are geared to *Proverbs* in particular, they more or less have ramifications for other OT literature as well. Some topics are so broad that they will reappear each time another NET OT text goes to press. For example, Study 4, which deals with terms and names for *God*, is crucial for overall OT comprehension. It will be expanded for books such as *Genesis* and *Exodus*, and even divided into *two* articles when numerous names of the Messiah appear in books like the *Psalms*, *Isaiah*, and *Zechariah*. Eventually the more comprehensive information from these articles will accompany the combined publication of the NET OT and NT.

Study 1
"WISDOM" IN *PROVERBS*

Many people divide the books of the OT into five categories: the Five Books of Moses (Gk: *Pentateuch* = "five volumes"—*Genesis* to *Deuteronomy*), the Historical Books (*Joshua* to *Esther*), the Poetic Books (*Job* to *Song of Solomon*), the Major Prophets (*Isaiah* to *Daniel*), and the Minor Prophets (*Hosea* to *Malachi*).

This type of division can be misleading to new readers of the Bible since these categories are too limiting. True, they do describe major distinctions and emphases, but they exclude information pertaining to significant *overlappings*. For example, both *Genesis* and the Minor Prophets are very *historical*, while at the same time they contain important *poetic* sections, the latter grouping being predominately *poetic*.

In addition, both *Psalms* and *Proverbs* are classified as Poetic Books. However, they have as many dissimilarities as similarities. The psalms, as one case in point, were certainly meant to be sung; the proverbs were most likely meant to be read and spoken, but *not* sung. More importantly, both *Proverbs* and many of the psalms (e.g., Ps. 1; 32; 33; 37; 49; 50; 73; 90; 94) belong to a type of Biblical literature called "wisdom literature." They could both be classified as *practical* and *reflective* in terms of "wisdom literature." Yet the remainder of the psalms are quite diverse from *Proverbs* in their *main* emphasis. The majority of these psalms are *initially practical* as *to worship in congregational settings*; in contrast, the proverbs are *initially practical as to advice for everyday life situations.* Obviously, both aspects touch *all* phases of faith and life. The practical aspect of *Proverbs* is expanded and repeatedly reinforced below since it is so key to its character.

A. Biblical "wisdom literature"—its approach and scope

Readers of the Bible who have been educated in western culture may expect Biblical "wisdom literature" to read like ancient Greek philosophy or modern philosophy. For instance, they may expect to find a very orderly and systematized thought pattern. They may also expect the writers of this literature to try to convince the reader of certain opinions by means of western standards of logic and argumentation, and—with such argumentation and logic—to try to prove that the Biblical writers are indeed wise, intelligent, smart, and clever. This, however, is not the goal of Biblical "wisdom literature." It does not run along lines of western thought patterns of philosophy in terms of systematic expression, but it does contain magnificent *content*. Rather than philosophizing or impressing the reader with western standards of logic, Scripture's "wisdom literature" is more concerned with explaining how to handle the challenges of life and how to get along in life. As stated above, this literature, especially *Proverbs*, gives the reader all sorts of *practical advice for everyday living.* As such, *Proverbs* presents "sanctified common sense" that helps its readers get through life.

In fact, Biblical "wisdom literature" deals with the crucial questions of philosophy, science, and culture. *Job* takes up the question, "Why do the righteous suffer?" *Ecclesiastes* faces the question that most people have asked at one time or another, "Is life worth living at all?" Some of the wisdom psalms also deal with such topics.

Proverbs also seems to start with in-depth concepts. Its stated purpose in 1:1-6 could give this sole impression if not read thoughtfully:

> The proverbs of Solomon son of David, king of Israel,
> given in order
>> to grasp wisdom and discipline,
>> to understand deep thoughts,
>> to acquire the discipline of wise behavior
>>> —righteousness and justice and fairness—
>> to give insight to gullible people,
>> to give knowledge and foresight to the young—
>>> a wise person will listen and continue to learn,
>>> and an understanding person will gain direction
>> to understand a proverb and a clever saying,
>> to understand the words of the wise and their riddles.

The formality of this *statement of purpose* fits perfectly with the profound doctrinal presentation found in chapter 8. However, when contrasted with a section like 10:8-14, one of many examples, the reader receives a totally different impression:

The one who is truly wise accepts commands, but
the one who talks foolishly will be thrown down headfirst.
    Whoever lives honestly will live securely, but
    whoever lives dishonestly will be found out.
    Whoever winks with his eye causes heartache, and
the one who talks foolishly will be thrown down headfirst.
    The mouth of the righteous is a fountain of life, but
    the mouth of the wicked conceals violence.
    Hate starts quarrels, but
    love covers every wrong.
Wisdom is found on the lips of a person who has understanding,
    but a rod is for the back of one without sense.
Those who are wise store up knowledge,
    but by the mouth of a stubborn fool ruin comes near.

All of a sudden the individual words and concepts of 1:1-6 come to life on a different, more practical level. Proverb after proverb is presented in terms of the ordinary, everyday routine of life—with all its ups and downs, its temptations and frustrations.

Or, consider 23:1 and 15:1, respectively, where advice is given in regard to the unforgettable events of life as well as to the ones that are mundane:

When you sit down to eat with a ruler,
    pay close attention to what is before you,
        and put a knife to your throat if you have a big appetite;....

A gentle answer turns away rage,
    but a harsh word stirs up anger.

And so it goes on throughout the book. No wonder *Proverbs* has been likened to a string of pearls on a necklace—one "pearl of wisdom" after another, and most of them are a "guide for everyday living"!

As we might expect, *Proverbs* is replete with *moral* and *spiritual* advice. Honesty, righteousness, and other virtues are common themes on its pages:

Dishonest scales are disgusting to the LORD,
    but accurate weights are pleasing to Him. (11:1)

Riches are of no help on the Day of Fury,
    but righteousness saves from death;.... (11:4)

It is this spiritual *flavor* which the reader can *taste* throughout the book of *Proverbs* and which sets Biblical "wisdom literature" apart from the rest of the world's "wise" literature. The book of *Proverbs* is written with specific readers in mind, namely, the children of God "who are in the world but are not of the world." They are living in a spiritual relationship with God and their neighbor under God's grace [undeserved love].

On the other hand, *Proverbs* is also quite applicable to non-Christians for two reasons: (1) the power of its word, given by inspiration of the Holy Spirit, can convert their hearts to wisdom (cf. 1:8,9 with Ps. 19:7-14; Jer. 23:29); and (2) following its practical, everyday advice can benefit even unbelievers, for they can avoid certain *worldly* difficulties of foolish people by applying God's directives (19:25).

B. "Wisdom literature" in the Ancient Near Eastern context

Israel's Biblical "wisdom literature" has often been compared and contrasted to the *wisdom literature* of other Near Eastern cultures, primarily Egyptian and Mesopotamian.

In neighboring Egypt *wisdom literature* was written by officials in order to teach young men who attended the scribal schools and who wanted to become government employees. In Egypt such literature was written as if a father were talking to his son. This was the way teachers would speak to their students in the scribal schools. The purpose of these schools was not only to teach reading and writing, but also to teach public speaking skills, ethics, and proper court etiquette.

In spite of the proximity of Egypt and whatever cultural exchanges may have taken place in the area of *wisdom literature*, the concept of *wisdom in Egypt* was totally different from *wisdom in the Bible*. In Egypt *wisdom (ma'at)* was usually thought of as one of the many *gods*, but it lacked moral value and had an air of fatalism. (If one is interested in pursuing knowledge in this area, see *The Intellectual Adventure of Ancient Man*, trans. John A. Wilson. Chicago: University of Chicago Press, 1946, especially p. 103.)

Israel's other cultural contact was Mesopotamia (modern Iraq), with its two great nations of Assyria in the north and Babylonia in the south. Scholars have pointed out that Mesopotamia had virtually no comprehensive collection of *wisdom literature* such as we find in the Bible. Nevertheless there are some parallels. The *Dialogue of Pessimism* and *Ludlul bel nemeqi* are the two documents most often cited as containing parallels with the Bible's "wisdom literature." The first document touches on the ups and downs of everyday life. The second document reminds us of the book of *Job* in that it raises the similar question, "Why do the righteous suffer?"

For the most part, however, Mesopotamian *wisdom* was more concerned with practical occupational skills, from the magician's dexterity in performing his tricks to the administrative expertise of a city official. There was little concern with the *moral* aspects of Biblical "wisdom literature."

To date, there are no documents from Canaan (later Phoenicia) that could really be equated to *wisdom literature*.

Biblical *wisdom* is really only a part of what God has revealed. In fact, Biblical *wisdom* points away from itself to the only true God, for it is based upon one simple, overarching concept: "The fear of the L<small>ORD</small> is the beginning of wisdom,..." (Prov. 9:10). Also in contrast to other ancient *wisdom literature*, *wisdom* in the Bible always reflects the highest ethical standard, and there is a complete absence of fatalism. Readers of Biblical *wisdom literature* know that their God cares about them in all aspects of life and loves them dearly.

Study 2
HEBREW TERMS FOR "WISDOM"

The basic Hebrew word for "wisdom" is *hokmah*. It occurs over 150 times in the Hebrew OT, and 32 of those occurrences are in the book of *Proverbs*. It is a noun whose grammatical gender is *feminine*, both because it is an abstract noun in its meaning and because it is a noun that ends with the stressed (accented) Hebrew suffix *-ah* (see GENDER AND HEBREW GENDER on p. 109).

In Hebrew, as with all other Semitic languages, the basic meaning of a noun or verb is indicated by its root, usually made up of three consonants, as is the case with the root of *hokmah—hkm*. More importantly, its meaning is ultimately determined by *context*, that is, how the word is used in a phrase, line of poetry, sentence, paragraph, chapter, or even in an entire book of the Bible.

A. *Hokmah*: its meanings

Standard Hebrew lexicons list five or six different meanings for *hokmah*, with groupings of Bible references following each one of those meanings. The English reader of Scripture may be surprised to learn that all lexicons list the first, and perhaps the original, meaning of *hokmah* as "technical skill, aptitude." According to Ex. 31:1-6 Bezalel, Oholiab, and other workers were filled with the "skill" (*hokmah*) to make everything that the Lord needed for the Tabernacle in the wilderness. A second, closely related meaning is "experience, good sense, shrewdness" (2 Sam. 20:22). Other meanings include "*wisdom*, [as] in administration" (*BDB*) or "worldly wisdom" (Holladay). This latter concept can be found in 1 Kgs. 4:30-32. *Hokmah* is also associated with righteous people. In *Proverbs* it is intimately tied to the ethical and religious *wisdom* which comes from God and shows up in the lives of His people (9:10-12).

Whatever shade of meaning *hokmah* carries in specific contexts, it is never merely an abstract, philosophical idea. Rather, it is always *practical* since it supplies a spiritual "know-how" that springs from a reverent "fear of the Lord" (1:7—see THE "FEAR" OF THE LORD on p. 77). This *hokmah*/ "wisdom" is especially helpful to God's people as they struggle against their sinful flesh throughout life (Ps. 90:12; Prov. 1:2-4).

Yet there is still more to *hokmah*. *Hokmah* also occurs in Scripture as one of God's *attributes* (Prov. 2:10-19; 3:13-18). In Prov. 8 the description of *Hokmah*/"Wisdom" goes beyond simply being one of God's attributes—it is God Himself! Here *Wisdom*, namely, the Son of God, identifies *Itself* as the "Master Craftsman" who was at the Father's side during Creation (v. 30; the reader should realize that God's Son is the *pre-incarnate* "It" or "Being" in Lk. 1:35 where the text and note in the NET NT indicate that Gabriel uses a *neuter* gender to describe Jesus, the Son of God—see CHRIST, THE "WISDOM" OF GOD on p. 83). Of interest also is Prov. 9, where *wisdom* is personified. The imagery of *wisdom* in this context may be that of a woman, since it is contrasted to "the woman, Stupidity"—see GENDER AND HEBREW GENDER on p. 109.

B. Synonyms and words associated with *hokmah*

Most of the Hebrew synonyms for *hokmah* are mentioned right at the beginning of *Proverbs* and are then repeated several times throughout the book. In the order of their occurrence in 1:2-4, the synonyms for *hokmah* (v. 2b - "wisdom") are: *musar* (v. 2b - "discipline"); *binah* (v. 2c - "deep thoughts" and the related word *tebunah* in 2:2a - "understanding"); *haskel* (v. 3a - "wise behavior" and the related words *maskil* in 10:5a - "wise" and *sekel* in 12:8a - "insight," meaning "wise behavior"); *'ormah* (v. 4a - "insight," meaning "good sense"); *da'ath* (v. 4b - "knowledge"); and *mezimmah* (v. 4b - "foresight"). At times the words *'ormah* and *mezimmah* carry the *negative* idea of "scheming." The observant reader will note that there are *seven* (7) "*wisdom* words" in this 1:2-4 section, the *perfect* number of words for *perfect wisdom*—see THE SYMBOLICAL NUMBERS OF REVELATION in the NET NT (1990) on p. 567.

Of all the synonyms, *musar* occurs most frequently, some fifty times in the Hebrew OT and thirty times in *Proverbs*. Eighty per cent of the time the NET has translated *musar* as "discipline" and most of the remaining times as "instruction." This meaning of "discipline" seems to be the closest, comprehensive meaning for *musar* in English. At first glance we might think of this word as being associated with athletes in training. This is close to the mark, since *musar* implies "oral instruction as received from a coach"— which can come in the form of positive reinforcement or negative warning. *Musar* also involves the regular exercise and practice of self-discipline.

The next most frequently occurring synonyms for *hokmah* in *Proverbs* are *tebunah* (nineteen times) and *binah* (fourteen times); the NET has rather consistently translated both words as "understanding." Both *binah* and *tebunah* are derived from the Hebrew verb *bin* ("to perceive"). The concept behind both of these words is an internal "eyesight" that views things through "the mind's eye." This is why at times the NET has also translated *binah* as "insight."

The other synonyms referred to in 1:2-4 occur less frequently. Each carries its own shade of meaning as it approaches the subject of *wisdom*.

One synonym not mentioned in 1:2-4 is *tushiyyah*. It occurs only four times in *Proverbs*, and the NET chose to translate it as "priceless *wisdom*."

The many words that God uses for *wisdom* sparkle like the facets of a priceless gem. They capture the Divine light from slightly different angles and together radiate it with a brilliance that none could give by itself. Indeed, according to 8:10,11, God's *wisdom* surpasses in value any earthly treasure:

> Take my discipline (*musar*), not silver,
> and my knowledge (*da'ath*) rather than fine gold,
>> because wisdom (*hokmah*) is better than jewels,
>> and nothing you desire can equal it.

Study 3
THE "FEAR" OF THE LORD

The phrase "fear of the LORD" is one of the major themes of the book of *Proverbs*. The importance of comprehending its meaning cannot be emphasized enough. That meaning is the key to understanding the purpose of *Proverbs* and receiving the greatest of benefits. (The phrase "fear of the LORD" occurs fifteen times in the book, while "fear the LORD" appears two times.)

Two types of "fear." The word "fear" occurs frequently in English Bibles. However, it is a mistake to assume that the English word "fear" is a translation of the same Hebrew word each time it appears. In the OT there are at least seventeen Hebrew words from different roots which are rendered by the term "fear"! Both in Hebrew and in English the term "fear" has a twofold meaning: (1) "to be apprehensive, afraid of, or terrified of"; (2) "to regard with awe or reverence, to venerate." The *fear of the LORD* is either of a *"servile"* (master/slave) nature, meaning to be afraid or terrified of God's punishment; or, it is of a *"filial"* (parent/child) nature, meaning reverence, awe, and the respect toward our heavenly Father which grows out of a confident faith in the salvation He has given to us.

Servile fear is the dread of the LORD which Adam and Eve experienced when they violated His holy Word and then fled in fear before the presence of God (Gen. 3:10). Theirs was a *fear* of God which comes to all people because of sin. It is a fright or terror arising from the threats of the Law. The ungodly person is terrified before God as a slave who is about to be punished by his master. But this is *not* the God-pleasing *fear* of which Moses speaks, "And now, Israel, what does the LORD your God ask of you? He asks that you *fear* the LORD your God, walk in all His ways, love Him, and serve the LORD your God with your whole heart and with your whole self" (Deut. 10:12).

Filial fear is the *proper* fear which the LORD desires. It is an attitude which only "a child of God" can have. Paul makes a distinction between these two kinds of fear when he writes in Rom. 8:15: "For you did not receive the spirit of slaves to make you feel afraid again, but you received the spirit of God's adopted children by which we call out, 'Abba, Father!'" In slave-like manner the unregenerate try to conform their lives to the demands of God's Law out of fear of punishment. This is "the spirit of slaves" to which Paul refers.

On the other hand, a Christian—in faith—reveres the LORD, just as a dear child would revere a dear father. Filial fear is a joyous, loving, willing reverence of the LORD which grows out of the Gospel of salvation. It is a fruit of saving faith in Christ's redemptive sacrifice, which is worked alone by the Holy Spirit through the Gospel (Rom. 1:16; 1 Cor. 12:3). It is found only in those who are truly converted and who, as regenerated children of God, serve Him in sincere faith and love.

Filial fear is a spontaneous attitude of the heart which has experienced the full and complete forgiveness of Christ (Ps. 130:4). The proper *fear of the* LORD is a respect and reverence of the LORD that results from faith in the Savior. When the filial *fear of the* LORD is ascribed to a person in the Hebrew language, it is usually expressed with some form of the verb *yr'*. Expressions like the "fear of the LORD" and the "fear of God" in most cases refer to the *proper* "fear of the LORD" that grows out of faith in His salvation.

This section has been summarized nicely by the following piece of wisdom:

> Slavelike fear is afraid God will come;
> childlike fear is afraid He will go away.

"Fear," its positive side. The *fear* of God makes itself known through the desire both to do what is pleasing to God and to avoid what is displeasing to Him. It does not function out of a terror of the punishment that will follow. Rather, it operates out of a thankfulness for all that our heavenly Father has already done and will continue to do for us. It is faithful service to and worship of the LORD (Deut. 6:13). Luther, the great Bible translator, once wrote: "The *fear* of God is nothing else than to serve God with the heart inwardly and with the conduct outwardly which consists in this, that one holds Him in honor, reveres Him, and does and omits nothing but what he knows pleases Him." Such a *fear* of God leads to a fleeing from sin as is seen in the life of Joseph (Gen. 39). Because Joseph did not want to offend the loving, heavenly Father, he did not commit adultery with Potiphar's wife. "The fear of the LORD is to hate evil" (Prov. 8:13).

"Fear" compared to "knowledge and wisdom." The *filial* "fear of the LORD is the beginning of knowledge" and ultimate "wisdom" (Prov. 1:7; 9:10; Ps. 111:10). There is a fundamental relationship between "the fear of the LORD" and "knowledge and wisdom." The latter finds its origin in such *fear*. People cannot be expert in the complexities of life unless they begin with the *knowledge* and *wisdom* of God. Those who revere the Name of the LORD know that their relationship with the LORD is the most important thing in their life. They can lose all other things, but if they lose their LORD they have lost everything.

"Fear" and the Word of God. The proper "fear of the LORD," which is the source of true "knowledge and wisdom," is intimately connected to the Word of the LORD. In fact, the phrase "fear the LORD" is parallel to "delight in His commandments" (Ps. 112:1) and "keep His precepts" (Ps. 119:63). This even reveals that "fear of the LORD" is at times *virtually synonymous* with phrases which express a knowledge of God's Word. The "fear of the LORD" is an instruction for that *wisdom* which is taught only through the Word (Ps. 119:79). The one who *fears the* LORD makes the Word a daily part of his life. He meditates continually on the life-giving Word, that Word through which the LORD comes to him, dwells in him, strengthens and nourishes him, and gives true wisdom to him from above (cf. Ps. 119:99; Prov. 14:26,27).

"Fear," its benefits. The "fear of the LORD," or childlike reverence of God, is ever so *practical*. People who properly *fear* the LORD will not be afraid of what others can do to them (Prov. 19:23). Godly fear drives out all fear of other human beings. Those who "fear the LORD" live in His peace and serenity because He protects them. The Angel of the LORD camps around those who *fear* Him, and He rescues them (Ps. 34:7). This is seen in the lives of the three men in the fiery furnace (Dan. 3) as well as Daniel in the lions' den (Dan. 6): The "fear of the LORD" made them fearless.

Those who "fear the LORD" are blessed already in this lifetime (Ps. 112:1; Prov. 22:4). The LORD has compassion on the one standing in awe of Him, just as a father has compassion on his child. Those who "fear the LORD" have everything they truly need (Ps. 34:9). Their homes will be filled with everything good (Ps. 112:3), for in the God-fearing household there will be joy and contentment since the LORD will be the *center* of that home. The children of its household will grow in the "fear of the LORD," as they are protected by their God.

The "fear of the LORD" also contains the promise of salvation, for His salvation is near to those who fear Him (Ps. 85:9; Prov. 14:26,27). The LORD *forgives* those who fear Him (Ps. 130:4). Already in this present life, they are His holy ones, forgiven by the Savior's redemptive work. Therefore they are blessed in this life and have the confident hope of that wonderful home above where they will live with the LORD forever (Ps. 23:6; Prov. 1:33).

Study 4
GOD: HIS DESIGNATIONS AND NAMES

Many are the designations for deity on the pages of Scripture. Some of these designations are *generic* indicators, translated with terms such as "God" or "god(s)" (Heb: *elohim/eloah*; Gk: *theos*) as well as "Lord" or "lord" (Heb: *adonai/adon*; Gk: *kurios*); others serve as proper names or epithets for the true God. In fact, Jesus Himself has over one hundred (100) such titles ascribed to Him in the Bible. Such names describe *characteristics* or *goals* as well as *accomplishments* of given personalities. For this reason the *importance* of "designations and names" cannot be overemphasized.

With the exception of the Name "Holy One" (*Qdshm*) in 9:10, *Proverbs* limits itself to one generic designation for "God" (*Elohim*) and to the proper Name "Lord" (*YHWH*).

A. *Elohim*

The term *Elohim*, first used in Scripture at Gen. 1:1 in the sentence "In the beginning *God* created the heavens and the earth," occurs fifteen times in *Proverbs*. Identical to its use in Gen. 1:1 the term is *plural* but is translated as *singular* when referring to the true God ("God" not "gods"). Some call this a "plural of majesty," implying that the *greatness* of God is expressed in plurality since He is all in all and above anything or anyone else (cf. Ps. 95:3). Others view the plural as an indicator for the Father, Son, and Holy Spirit— the one true God.

This general term for God comes from a root that indicates "strength" or "power." Thus God is "the strong or powerful One," who deserves to be held in fear, awe, and honor.

People of today are very familiar with the ongoing conflicts in the Middle East. They will be interested to know that *allah*, the Arab designator for deity, is related to the Hebrew *elohim* (note the consonants "l" and "h" in both terms).

The use of *Elohim* as a *compound* name in Hebrew terms such as *El Elyon* (God Most High) or *El Shaddai* (God Almighty) will be discussed in connection with books such as *Genesis*.

B. *YHWH*

The second term that refers to God in *Proverbs* is the Hebrew *YHWH*, the Tetragrammaton (*tetra* - "four" + *gramma* - "letter"). The term is generally vocalized as *Yahweh*, a popular designation being written at times in English as "Jehovah" (see below).

NET translation. There are many theories concerning the origin and meaning of this term, and general conjectures exist pertaining to the ancient pronunciation of *YHWH*.

Our translators debated long and hard as to how *YHWH* should be represented in the NET text. It has been suggested that the NET follow the New Jerusalem Bible (JB) and use *Yahweh*, as in "Yahweh is my Shepherd" (Ps. 23:1). Three primary factors caused hesitation to do this: (1) Some readers might view the textual presence of *Yahweh* as an endorsement of the opinion that this term validates the rediscovery of the "God" of the OT, the God whom they then identify as someone other than the "God" of the NT. Scripture, however, knows no such separation. (2) There is too much uncertainty as to the original vocalization (vowels used in pronunciation) of *YHWH*. Therefore, the NET would leave itself open to linguistic criticism if it used *Yahweh* in the text. (3) The NET is a modern language, down-to-earth translation that aims to reach people on an easy-to-read, easy-to-understand, easy-to-listen-to level. The unnecessary retention of a Hebraism like *Yahweh* would seem out of place in the NET translation model.

Therefore, the NET has chosen to render *YHWH* as "Lord" (with large and small caps), as does the KJV and most other translations, including the Jewish Publication Society's version that is recommended as a standard version on many college campuses. Such capitalization solves a problem for the eye, though, to be sure, *not* for the ear. The problem is this. The sound "lord" indicates a *generic* Name for God, certainly not a *proper* Name. Other so-called gods are called "lord," and at times the true God is referred to as "Lord" (with upper and lower case letters). This confusing problem is at least overcome *on the printed page* when the NET utilizes the *marked term* "Lord." An article like this present one should help one overcome such a barrier.

Historical usage. As implied above, the ancient pronunciation of *YHWH* is anyone's guess. Such knowledge was lost during the Middle Ages, if not earlier. By the time of the Second Temple (Ezra, Nehemiah, Malachi) this holy term had been eliminated from *public* reading; later it was not even spoken by Jews *in private*. In time the Jews simply substituted the Hebrew word *adonai* ("Lord") whenever they came to *YHWH*. This is still a Jewish custom in our day.

In this way the Jewish community attempted to reemphasize *YHWH* as the "wonderful and awesome Name" of God (Deut. 28:58). Passages like Lev. 24:11,16 had avoided *YHWH*; there God was just called "the NAME." (Cf. 2 Chr. 7:14 and Is. 43:7 where the people of God are connected to His "Name.") Obviously the sixty-eight hundred (6,800) occurrences of *YHWH* on the pages of the OT show that God did not ban its usage. Of interest, however, is the fact that Matthew speaks of "the Kingdom of *heaven*," not "the Kingdom of *God*," in his Gospel. In line with Jewish custom this may be a possible avoidance of the use of God's Name.

The Gentiles also adopted their own unique approach. They took the *vowels* of *adonai* and erroneously placed them with the *consonants* of *YHWH*. This formed the hybrid *Jehovah*, as mentioned above. (The initial "e" of *Jehovah* comes from the *shewa* of the compound *hateph-patah*, *patah* being a short "a." Note also that the Hebrew "y" and "w" come over into English as "j" and "v," respectively.)

The technical aspect. There is general consensus that *YHWH* is a *proper name*, designating the true God. In Is. 42:8 *YHWH* Himself makes clear that this is His most important Name, while Deut. 5:9 uses *YHWH* as the supreme term to qualify the generic *Elohim*, namely, "I, the Lord (*YHWH*) your God (*Elohim*), am a jealous God (*El*)."

Conversely, there is little consensus as to the precise Hebraic verb form (and intended meaning) behind the term *YHWH*. General agreement exists that *YHWH* is connected with the verb *hyh* and its earlier root form *hwh* ("to be"). So it is in the case of *YHWH*: "to be" or *to be more*—that is the question!

Key passages in the overall discussion must include Ex. 3:14 and 6:3. These will be dealt with in an expansion of this article in connection with the NET publication of *Exodus*. For the present, however, it will suffice to say that some see *YHWH* as a stative ("to be") or indicative ("to exist") verb form. This twofold view is a hairline distinction, and in practical analysis both sides would grant obvious overlapping. This overlapping view would see the "I AM that I AM" (first person; cf. "He is" - third person) as revealing that the Name *YHWH* means "I am alive, present, active," that is, "I reveal My existence when and where I will."

A second viewpoint sees *YHWH* as a *hiphil* verb form, indicating *causative* action. Thus, "I bring into being" means "I cause to happen what I desire to cause to happen."

Those interested in reading at length on all these technicalities should consult the *Theological Dictionary of the Old Testament*, "*YHWH*," by D. N. Freedman and M. P. O'Connor, vol. 5, pp. 500-521.

The differences of these two viewpoints are being played out in an "either/or" arena, whereas sound exegetical application and practical theology could argue for a "both/and" solution. A "both/and" conclusion could dictate that *YHWH*, the Lord of Creation and Salvation, is the One who "exists" by the very fact that He "is." At the same time inherent in His very existence is His power to *cause* anything He wills to come into existence—and to be sustained in that existence according to His will. Thus is the totality of *YHWH*: being, existing, causing to exist, continuing to exist, and continuing to cause to exist.

Most pertinent, and having deep significance to *Proverbs*, is the fact that totally new faith relationships between humans and God as well as godly relationships between humans themselves come into being when true "knowledge" of the NAME (*YHWH*) enters a person's life (Ex. 33:12,18,19; Jn. 17:6; cf. Prov. 1:7; 18:10).

Study 5
CHRIST, THE "WISDOM" OF GOD

To the careful reader of *Proverbs*, it becomes readily apparent that Prov. 8 serves as a focal point to much of the material in Prov. 1-9, both in content and especially in the way that *Wisdom* (*Hokmah*) is portrayed. The content of *Proverbs*, as it leads up to chapter 8, is basically in the form of advice from King Solomon to his son. Within that content *wisdom* is referred to primarily as an *abstract* idea: (1) as the *main topic* of the entire book (1:2; 9:10); (2) as the *best teaching* Solomon has to offer to his son (2:1-19); and (3) as the *highest good*, a *treasure* more valuable than gold, silver, or jewels (4:6-9; 3:14,15).

In addition to the abstract concept, *wisdom* is also described by various figures of speech, that is, Solomon describes the abstract idea of *wisdom* as if it were an imaginary person (personification) or he gives certain human characteristics to wisdom (anthropomorphism) or he describes wisdom as some other thing (metaphor): (1) *wisdom* may be portrayed as a female who calls out (1:20,21, personification); (2) *wisdom* is "a tree of life" whose fruit is "long life...riches and honor" (3:16-18, metaphor); (3) as the highest good, *wisdom* can be embraced and will crown the child of God with "a graceful garland" or "a beautiful crown" (4:6-9, anthropomorphism); (4) *wisdom* is to be an intimate part of one's life, like a sister or some other relative (7:4, anthropomorphism); and (5) *wisdom* gives a banquet that is especially prepared for the gullible fools of the city (9:1-12, personification).

Besides these references, there is one place at which *wisdom* reaches its highest point—at 8:22-31. Here *wisdom* is described in a way far different from all the other places in the book. Chapter 8:1-3 seems to begin with a personification of *wisdom* similar to 1:20-33. Then, at verse 4 and continuing all the way to the end of the chapter (v. 36), "wisdom/Wisdom" delivers a discourse in the first person singular, a discourse longer than any other speech in *Proverbs* (cf. 1:22-33). Without going into a word-by-word, verse-by-verse exegesis of the passage, "wisdom/Wisdom" here describes itself as the *highest good* (v. 6), *holy* (vv. 7,8), *more valuable than anything else* (vv. 10,11), *indispensable* for kings and rulers (vv. 15-21), the *"Master Craftsman"* who worked side by side with the LORD at the very creation of the world (vv. 22-31). And then, in verses 32-36 the reader is encouraged to find and hold onto *Wisdom* throughout life. Thus, the *special way* in which *Wisdom* is presented in this chapter motivates the reader to become thoroughly wise and to walk in *Wisdom*'s ways (v. 33), because in so doing the reader will find true "life" and "favor" from the LORD (v. 35).

Others have also noticed the greater distinction between *Wisdom* in Prov. 8 and *wisdom* throughout the rest of *Proverbs*. In the fourth century A.D. a lively and sometimes violent debate raged throughout the whole Christian church because of two differing interpretations of Prov. 8, especially verse 22:

> The LORD already possessed Me
>> long ago, when His way began,
>> before any of His works.

Both parties in the Christological controversy agreed that verse 22 referred to the *Logos* ("the Word"), the pre-incarnate Christ of Jn. 1:1-18. However, the one party—led by a priest named Arius—argued that the *Proverbs* passage clearly made the *Logos* a "Creature" of God, meaning that the *Logos* had been created and had not existed from all eternity. Arius argued that *Wisdom* was a Creature set apart from all the rest of creation and was especially created by the Father to assist in the rest of the whole creation. The arguments of Arius were based in total on the LXX translation of verse 22:

> The LORD *created* Me
>> as the first of His ways, *for* His works.
>> Before the age He established Me
>> in the beginning,
>> before He made the earth
>> and before He made the oceans.

The words "*created* Me...*for* His works" tell the whole story. For Arius "Wisdom/the *Logos*/Christ" was *not* "eternal." The English reader should also be reminded that the LXX of *Proverbs* is, in particular, very inferior to the MT.

The exegesis of 8:22-31, especially verse 22 in the context of the whole, became both the initial reason for the Arian controversy as well as its very focal point. We shall not repeat how Arius and his supervising bishop, Alexander of Alexandria in Egypt, disputed over Prov. 8; nor will we enlarge upon the other details of the ensuing controversy, including the role of the faithful Athanasius. Instead, we address the main question of the controversy: Is Christ who came to earth to reunite God and mankind the same divine Being who rules heaven and earth as the supreme *Wisdom* of God, or is He just the Word (*Logos*) reduced to a semi-divine being or demigod?

In other words, was Jesus Christ really God, the Jesus who was born in Bethlehem and who died outside Jerusalem and rose three days later? Was He God Almighty, the Creator of heaven and earth? Or, was He more than a man, more than an angel, perhaps a god, but *not quite* God Almighty? Finally, was there a time when Jesus, as the *Wisdom* of God, did not exist? In short, was Christ eternal, without beginning—or not?

The conclusion of the Arian controversy resulted in the condemnation of the Arians and the adoption of the Niceno-Constantinopolitan Creed of A.D. 381, commonly referred to as the Nicene Creed, in which those Christians who recite creeds confess that they believe "...in one Lord Jesus Christ, the only-begotten Son of God, begotten of His Father before all worlds, God of God, Light of Light, very God of very God, begotten, not made, being of one substance with the Father, by whom all things were made."

As a result of such church history, the description of *Wisdom* in Prov. 8 has caught the attention of Christians down through the ages. What or who is this *Wisdom*? Most scholars today would agree that *hokmah*/"wisdom" is *personified* in 8:22-31. But is there more?

The conclusion to the question seems to hinge specifically on how the Hebrew verb *qnh* is to be taken in 8:22. The basic meaning of *qnh* is "to acquire" (see 4:5,7 where *qnh* is used in each verse, and both times the NET has translated with the term "acquire"). Recall from above that the LXX (and the Arians) translated *qnh* as "created" in verse 22. Following the MT and in agreement with the basic meaning "to acquire," the NET has translated *qnh* as "possessed" in this context:

> The LORD already possessed [acquired] Me....

Recent scholarship has found that Ugaritic literature (from a fourteenth-century B.C. Semitic culture which preceded the Canaanites in Northern Canaan and which had roots related to the Hebrew language) calls the goddess Asherah the "Creatress of the gods" (*qnyt 'ilm*). On this basis those making the connection between *qnyt* and *qnh* would assume that the same was true of 8:22, namely, that the LORD was "the Creator of the gods," the Creator of "wisdom." Thus, "Wisdom/the Son of God/Christ/Jesus" was "created." With this, Scripture would not agree.

This Ugaritic translation has been challenged by others, and there is good reason to keep the basic meaning of "acquire" for our key Hebrew verb. In fact, the concept behind the Hebrew verb *qnh* in the Prov. 8 context seems to imply the simple *relationship of a family*, where all members refer to one another—at least this is our custom in English—with the simple verb "have" (e.g., I *have* a father, a mother, a son, a daughter, a brother, a sister). So even though the NET has translated this verb *qnh* as "possessed," it does not mean to imply that the LORD possessed *Wisdom* as a *thing*, but rather as a *relative*, in a Father-Son relationship. For a fuller discussion of *qnh*, see Derek Kidner, *Proverbs* (Downers Grove, Illinois: InterVarsity Press, 1964), pp. 79,80.

Coupled with the discussion of the Hebrew verb *qnh* is the other question asked by modern scholars concerning 8:22-31: Is this passage simply a *personification* of *Wisdom* or is it a *hypostasis* of *Wisdom*? The answer to both of these questions should help identify "what" or "who" *Wisdom* really is. And so, at this point it would be wise to pause and again define *personification*, especially in conjunction with *hypostasis* or *hypostatic Wisdom*.

When we say that *wisdom* is *personified* outside of Prov. 8, we mean that *wisdom* is being described for the reader in *picture language*, as if it were a person—but an imaginary person. However, when we say that *Wisdom* is a Hypostasis ("Person") here in Prov. 8, we are asserting that *Wisdom* is no longer being described as an abstract idea in picture language, as if it were an imaginary person. Rather, hypostatic *Wisdom* is now being regarded as a real

Person. In fact, many Christians would argue that—although *wisdom* is one of the attributes of God—here in Prov. 8 *Wisdom* is really God Himself.

We conclude that Solomon, writing under the inspiration of the Holy Spirit, is here describing the pre-incarnate Christ, the Son of God, who is both transcendent and immanent—that is, He is a God who is a very "down-to-earth" God, literally! He is the God with whom we can walk each day and in whom we find true "life" (8:32-36). Although the Apostle Paul did not specifically quote Prov. 8, he certainly identified the *Wisdom* of Prov. 8 when he wrote in 1 Cor. 1:24: "He is Christ, God's power and God's *wisdom*,...." In Col. 2:2,3 Paul adds, "I say this so that your hearts may be encouraged..., so that you recognize the mystery of God, namely, Christ, in whom are hidden all the treasures of *wisdom* and knowledge."

Study 6
"KINGSHIP,"
WITH SPECIAL REFERENCE TO *PROVERBS*

The word *melech*, translated as "king," occurs more than twenty-five hundred (2,500) times in the OT. It appears thirty-one times in the book of *Proverbs*, of which three are in superscriptions as a title accompanying proper names: "Solomon son of David, king of Israel" (1:1), "King Hezekiah of Judah" (25:1), and "King Lemuel" (31:1). The other twenty-eight occurrences in *Proverbs* are general references; they are listed in chapter 16, note "d."

Contrary to the modern division of authority into distinct branches, kingship in the ancient Near East ordinarily embraced all governmental functions—legislative, executive, and judicial:

> First, although the king took advice from counselors who were more learned and usually older than himself, he had full authority to establish and declare law and to assign penalties for its violation. A famous extra-Biblical example of this is the Code of Hammurabi.

> Second, the king was responsible for enforcing the law of his nation and also, as he saw fit, international law. He generally did this through officers who served at his pleasure. In this connection he was the commander in chief of the armed forces and often took personal command of his troops in battle.

> Third, the king was the final judge in both civil and criminal cases, whether brought to him directly or by appeal from lower courts. In countries where concepts of tempering justice with mercy existed, kings had some latitude to pardon even those whom they had found guilty of crime.

In all these functions, however, the authority of the king had limitations. Such limitations varied, depending on the people and the era concerned. Several factors curtailed his powers: (1) previous statutes and royal precedents, (2) the common law of the nation (established custom), and (3) external authority (divine mandates mediated by priests and prophets; imperial law, if the king was a vassal in a more extensive empire; and accords of various sorts between states). An outstanding example of the first variety of limitation is furnished by the "law of the Medes and Persians" which prevented Darius, the Medo-Persian king of Babylon, from setting aside the decree which condemned Daniel to the lions' den (Dan. 6:15,16).

We might say that the concept of kingship in the ancient Near East corresponds to modern government in general. In a democracy the people themselves are the government, electing representatives (directly or indirectly) to fulfill various legislative, executive, and judicial duties. In some democracies, however, there remains a monarch whose position, together with certain prerogatives, does not derive from or through the people. The British sovereign, for one, reigns "by the grace of God." Although the sovereign does have symbolic significance, to describe the monarch as "merely symbolic" is a misunderstanding of British law. In such cases, therefore, there is an added dimension to the picture which must be considered.

In Israel royal privileges were in theory, if not always in practice, restricted considerably more than anywhere else in the ancient Near East. Elsewhere, for example, the kingship was understood as embracing "priesthood" as well, and on one or more occasions during the year the king would perform priestly functions in important public ceremonies. However, this was not the case in Israel. No one, not even her king, could intrude upon the sacred, priestly office which the LORD Himself had instituted through Moses and restricted to the Levites. Violations of this rule brought removal for Saul and leprosy to King Uzziah, even though the latter otherwise receives commendation from the sacred historians.

Actually, there was no human kingship in the original political structure of the Israelite nation. This unusual phenomenon arose from Israel's essential definition as a "theocracy" (Gk: *theokratia* = *theos* - "God" + *kratia* - "rule"). The people were to regard the LORD Himself as the King of Israel, a major consideration which we shall explain as other OT books of the NET demand explanation in relation to God and His Messiah as King.

God had foreseen that sinful Israel would not be satisfied merely with having a divine King, and so at Moses' time He had already made provision—by way of concession to the hardness of Hebrew hearts—for a human monarchy (Deut. 17:14-20; 28:36). Later, He inspired Samuel to explain, orally to contemporaries and in writing to posterity, such regulations as would make the monarchy as tolerable as possible to Him (1 Sam. 10:25). At the same time He exhorted Israel to remain faithful in the future according to these stated guidelines.

So the Israelites traveled forward in their history. But regardless of whether a particular king was faithful or faithless, once the LORD had subjoined the monarchy to the constitution of theocracy, all Israelites were bound to obey their God-given king, except when the king's command ran contrary to the command of God. Specifically, such obedience was owed to every king chosen by God until such time as God, speaking through a prophet, should absolve His people from this obligation—either transferring the crown to someone else or finally bringing the kingship to an end.

What the book of *Proverbs* says of kingship is clearly meant to apply to all kings in general, not only to Solomon and his successors in Israel. The Solomonic chapters customarily use "king" without qualification, often in the plural, sometimes in a general, all-embracing way. Here are three unit examples:

It is the glory of God to hide things,
> but the glory of kings to investigate them.

Like the high heavens and the deep earth,
> so the mind of kings is unsearchable.

Take dross away from silver
> and a vessel is ready for the silversmith to mold.

Take the wicked person away from the presence of a king
> and justice will make his throne secure.

Do not brag about yourself before a king
> or stand in the spot that belongs to notable people;
>> because it is better to be told, "Come up here,"
>>> than to be put down in front of a prince
>>> whom your eyes have seen. (25:2-7)

Locusts have no king,
> yet all of them divide into swarms by instinct;

a lizard you can hold in your hands,
> and yet it can even be found in royal palaces. (30:27,28)

There are three things that walk like a king
even four that march like a king:
> a lion, mightiest among animals, which turns away from nothing,
> a strutting rooster or
> a male goat, and
> a king at the head of his army. (30:29-31)

Significantly, the word "king" occurs several times in the advice given to and through the monarch Lemuel:

The sayings of King Lemuel, a prophetic revelation,
> used by his mother to discipline him.

"What, my son? And
what, son of my womb? And
what, son of my prayers?
> Don't give your strength to women
> or your power to those who ruin kings.

"It is not for kings, Lemuel;
it is not for kings to drink wine,
that is, for rulers to crave liquor;
> otherwise, they drink and forget what they have decreed
> and change the standard of justice for all the oppressed."

(31:1-5)

King Lemuel's mother superbly sums up the basic duty of a king, namely, the administration of justice. Such a duty required compassionate impartiality as well as legal expertise (31:8,9). Solomon makes the same point in the earlier chapters of the book (8:15; 16:10b,12; 20:8,26; 25:5; 29:4,14; cf. also 28:16).

The Biblical conception concerning governmental authority in general, above all else, pertains to *kingship*. Such application is made in the book of *Proverbs*. The Bible teaches that whatever government exists at any time in a given state possesses the authority of God Himself. It also teaches that subjects are bound by divine authority to obey their government in all its mandates except those conflicting with the commands of God. Statements of such a view are found on the lips of Jesus (Matt. 22:21) and in the epistles of Paul and Peter (Rom. 13:1-7; 1 Pet. 2:13-20; cf. Acts 5:29). In Israel's law-code the magistrates are regarded so definitely as representatives of God who exercised His authority that one who appears before a magistrate and is judged by him is said to appear "before God" and to be judged by God (Ex. 22:8,9—MT: vv. 7,8). In Ps. 82:1,6 God goes so far as to entitle those whom He has invested with divine majesty on earth as *elohim*, even if they have abused their authority. As such, He not only calls these magistrates "sons of the Most High," but also declares: "I have said, 'You are gods.'" The God who speaks is specifically the Messiah (cf. Prov. 8:12-36), thereby justifying the argument of Jesus in Jn. 10 where He proves His deity from the power of the Word of God to delegate divine authority.

Such an understanding lies behind those statements in the book of *Proverbs* which closely relate the king to God (e.g., 16:10; 24:21; 25:2,3) and those which, therefore, call subjects to reverence and obedience, fearing the king's wrath and desiring his pleasure (e.g., 14:35; 16:13-15; 19:12; 20:2; 22:29; 25:6; 30:31). The most explicit passage, however, is 8:15,16, in which the Supreme *Wisdom*, God the Son, lays claim to being the specific source of all governmental authority—including, above all, exercise of kingship:

> By Me kings reign,
>   and rulers decree just laws.
> By Me princes rule,
>   so do nobles and all just judges.

Study 7
THE "FOOL" IN *PROVERBS*

Proverbs is a book of *wisdom*, God's *wisdom*. Specifically, it is classified as "wisdom literature." On its pages—through His inspired writers—God the Holy Spirit often uses *contrast* to communicate this *wisdom*, its truth and application to the Christian life. As a skilled artist who sets his subject matter against a contrasting background, the Spirit sets the bright gem of *wisdom* against the dismal backdrop of *foolishness*.

When the Bible in general—and *Proverbs* in particular—speaks of foolishness, it is important to remember that Scripture is describing a *moral* and *spiritual* condition. This ties in with the fact that *Proverbs* denotes fools as ones who do *not* have a proper "fear of the LORD." Consequently, such people are apt to be led astray from what God's Word says; or else, they simply ignore it.

In terms of these moral and spiritual indicators, then, we should not equate the condition of foolishness with lack of academic prowess or a low IQ. Quite the contrary! Some people who are brilliant in the eyes of the world may still be fools according to God's standards. For example, many so-called scholars deny God's existence on the basis of reason, considering believers to be "fools." But God dismisses such reason and concludes that anyone who says "there is no God" is the real "fool" (Ps. 14:1).

A. Four types of "fools"

Solomon uses several different Hebrew words to describe foolish people. One is *peti*. This person is the least hardened of the various types of fools. Those who fall into this category are "gullible people" as the NET translates the word. They might also be described as "naive" and "inexperienced." These gullible people drift along aimlessly, until they fall easy prey to temptation. Prov. 14:15 sets the gullible person *in contrast* to the one who is sensible:

A gullible person believes anything,
    but a sensible person watches his step.

A gullible person who doesn't "wise up" in time may well move to another level of foolishness and become a *kesil*. This Hebrew word, occuring in its singular and plural forms and used some fifty times in *Proverbs*, is the book's most common term for describing foolish people. The NET editorial committee for *Proverbs* identifies such people as "fools," having referred to them in meetings as "generic, plain brown wrapper" fools. These fools actually come to enjoy their folly. The enjoyment of folly as well as some other negative qualities of the "fool" are described in 18:2:

A fool does not delight in understanding
    but only in expressing his own opinion.

Verses 6 and 7 of this same chapter, as well as 29:11,20, indicate that fools of this type love to hear themselves talk. But most of all, their top quality is expressed in one word—"stupidity" (13:16; 14:8,24; 15:2,14; 17:12). In accordance and addition to this, 26:1-12 has much to say about these "fools," including the tendency to repeat past foolishness. Verse 11 points out:

> As a dog goes back to his vomit,
>   so a fool repeats his stupidity.

"Stubborn fool" is the NET rendering for the next Hebrew term, *'ewil*. This Hebrew word occurs about twenty times in *Proverbs*. As the NET translation implies, individuals at this level of foolishness are more hardened and persistent (15:5). True, most of the things said of the "fool" (*kesil*) are also stated about "stubborn fools" (*'ewilim*). Yet, the latter goes a step farther by actually ridiculing what God says about sin and its guilt. As 14:9 indicates:

> Stubborn fools make fun of guilt,
>   but there is forgiveness among the upright.

"Stubborn fools" are prime candidates for the final level of foolishness. This is *nabal* territory, the home of the worst of fools. The NET translates the Hebrew *nabal* as "godless fool," since this type of fool declares, "There is no God" (Ps. 14:1, as cited above). The term *nabal* appears only three times in *Proverbs*. People who fall under this designation have closed their minds to God; they have decidedly rejected the LORD. According to 30:21-23 they belong to one of the four worst groups of people on earth:

> Three things cause the earth to tremble,
> even four it cannot bear up under:
>   a slave when he becomes king and
>   a godless fool when he is filled with food;
>   a woman who is unloved when she gets married and
>   a maid when she replaces her mistress.

Who knows what havoc such godless fools will bring to others once their physical needs are satisfied!

While these four Hebrew terms for the various types of fools have different shades of meaning, they all point to people who believe and live contrary to what God's Word teaches.

B. The "mocker" and the "lazy person"

In addition to the four types of *fools* described above, we encounter other undesirable characters on the pages of *Proverbs*. Like those fools, they stand in bold contrast to *believers in God*. Two of them deserve mention in reference to *Proverbs*.

One is the "mocker" (Heb: *letz*). This person would much rather make fun of others than be at the receiving end of constructive criticism. Prov. 9:8 says:

> Do not warn a mocker or he will hate you;
> warn a wise person and he will love you.

Such individuals are "proud, conceited" (21:24). And if they persist in their sinful ways, ultimately God Himself will mock them, as 3:34 states:

> When He mocks the mockers,
>   He is gracious to the humble.

The mocker is not to be taken lightly. He is a parallel both to the "stubborn fool" as well as to the "godless fool"; however, the "mocker" is not naive like the "gullible person" (19:25; 21:11). Rather, selfish pride is the trademark of mockers (21:24). Such people are vocal, active, and public in their denial and mockery of God (cf. Ps. 1:1,2).

The last in our gallery of the foolish are those people who are "lazy" (Heb: *atzel*). They are so tragic that observers want to cry for them at the same time as they laugh at their folly. These elements of humor and pity appear at 26:15:

> A lazy person puts his fork in his food;
>   he wears himself out bringing it back to his mouth.

Rather than expend any effort by using personal God-given talents, such a person fiddles away time in idleness. In 6:6, one of eighteen references to lazy people in *Proverbs*, Solomon observantly says:

> Consider the ant, you lazy bum;
>   watch its ways and become wise:....

When lazy people refuse to learn, they eventually come to ruin. This story is told in 24:30-32:

> I passed by a lazy man's field,
> the vineyard belonging to a man without sense.
>   And look, it was all overgrown with thistles;
>   the ground was covered with weeds,
>   and its stone fence was torn down!
> When I observed this, I took it to heart;
> I saw it and learned my lesson.
>   "Just a little sleep,
>   just a little slumber,
>   just a little nap."
>   Then your poverty will come upon you like a drifter,
>   and your need will come upon you like a bandit.

C. In summary

Whether observing fools, mockers, or people who are lazy, a Christian realizes, "Except for the grace of God, there go I!" King Saul of Israel began his reign wisely. Later he fell into sin and had to admit, "I have acted like a fool" (1 Sam. 26:21). Even the author of *Proverbs*, the great and wise King Solomon himself, became such a fool that he fell into idolatry for a time (1 Kgs. 11:4-11)!

Things have not changed over the centuries. Foolishness still permeates all nations. For that reason human beings need true *wisdom* to combat foolishness. As much as ever, today's people still need the *Wisdom* of God, namely, Jesus Christ (cf. 8:1-36 with 1 Cor. 1:24,25). It is crucial for one to have the "knowledge, wisdom, and understanding" of Him who is "Knowledge, Wisdom, and Understanding" (cf. 9:10 with 3:19,20). Our God has loved us, sacrificed Himself for us, and through faith has saved us for service on earth and glory in heaven.

Wisdom's forgiveness in Christ destroys *sin's foolishness*. Such salvation comes only by God's grace [undeserved love] through His Word, and through that Word we humans initially become wise, and afterwards, as Christians, continue to grow in true *wisdom*.

God has given His words to Christians as their daily companion (8:34). But His teachings must be taken to heart if they are to serve as an effective remedy against foolishness, mockery, and laziness. Besides, *wisdom* in Christ compels Bible-believers to reach out to sinful and foolish human beings (2 Cor. 5:14-21). Like *wisdom* in 1:22 believers need to cry out to unbelievers:

"How long will you gullible people love being so gullible, and
how long will you mockers delight in your mocking, and
how long will you fools hate knowledge?"

But Christians also need to speak the following assurance of 2:10-14 to the lost, saying to them, "Through faith in Christ

wisdom will come into your heart and
knowledge will be pleasant to your soul;
    foresight will protect you;
    understanding will guard you.

Wisdom will save you
    from the way of evil,
    from the man who speaks devious things,
    from those who abandon the paths of righteousness
        to walk the ways of darkness,
    from those who enjoy doing evil,
    from those who rejoice in the deviousness of evil;...."

Study 8
LEB: "HEART" AND "MIND"

The English language has no individual word which directly corresponds to the Hebrew word *leb* (or *lebab*) or captures the full meaning of its semantic field. This creates translation difficulties and often forces *context* to become the strong controlling factor. As a result *leb* is often translated as "heart"; at other times as "mind" or "sense."

Not all Bible readers understand this distinction. To many people in our day "heart" and "mind" seem mutually exclusive or contradictory. The word "heart" generally implies *emotions* or *feelings*, while "mind" implies *reason* or *sense*. However, the Hebrew word *leb* is more comprehensive and actually includes *both* ideas. Its root meaning seems to refer to the inner or central part of a thing, most especially, to the central part of a person's being or personality.

This human *leb* certainly includes *feelings*, *affections*, and *desires*. It is the center of *emotions*, *moods*, and *passions*. In *Proverbs, joy* (15:13; 17:22) *grief* (14:13), *ill-temper* (19:3), *hate* (5:12), and *love* (22:11) are all experienced in the "heart." Therefore, "heart" serves as a fine translation for *leb* in certain Bible passages.

At the same time the human *leb* functions as the source of *thought* and *reflection* (15:14); it *understands* (2:2), *acquires wisdom* (18:15; 22:17), and *represents the idea of choice and conscience* (6:35; 29:17). A word like "mind" is an excellent translation for *leb* in those Biblical contexts. As stated above, this seems strange when "mind" is compared to the "heart" side of *leb*. But contrary to our way of thinking, the Hebrew Scriptures never really regarded "the head" as being the center of "thought process" or of "intelligence." That was the function of the *leb*, the operations center for *decision-making* (16:9), the center for influencing and controlling *obedience* (23:19) and *intentions* (16:9; 24:2). Notes accompanying the *Proverbs* text also indicate where *leb* at times is translated with terms such as "sense" (10:13, note "f"); "attitude" (15:7); "heartache" (15:13); etc.

In summary, then, the *leb* actually represents the total inner life of human beings—all their *feelings* and *emotions*, all their *thoughts* and *intellect*. In Hebrew thought it is often used as the equivalent of "heart" and "mind," generally being translated in the NET with these two words, depending on context. As possibly surmised from the preceding discussion, neither "heart" alone nor "mind" alone can communicate the whole meaning of the Hebrew *leb* in passages where qualities of both need to be communicated. This leaves a translation difficulty but one which the reader can overcome through awareness of language limitations.

Study 9
TORAH AND *MITZWAH*
"Teaching" and "Commands"

This article explains why the NET has translated the Hebrew *torah* and *mitzwah* as "teaching" and "commands," rather than with the usual terms "law" and "commandments," respectively.

Stating the problem. *Torah* is one of the most important and frequently used words in the Hebrew Bible. Numerous English Bibles translate it almost exclusively with the term "law." Unfortunately, this translation is misleading in most instances. Its lack of precision as to nuance often causes part of the misconception that the OT is *primarily* "Law," while the NT is *primarily* "Gospel." As a consequence some give little attention to the OT. Why not, if they incorrectly perceive that a *new* way of salvation in the NT, the "Gospel" (grace and freedom in Christ), has displaced an OT religion of "Law" (God's wrath and human self-righteousness)? But such a distinction between the two Testaments is inaccurate. *Both* Testaments reveal God's requirements for obedience *and* show His way of salvation through faith in Christ.

A. *Torah*

The various meanings of *torah*. The word *torah* has a *wide range* of semantic meaning. It does not refer to the same thing every time. In a narrow sense it can refer to specific *instructions* or *laws*. At other times it is used in a much wider sense to refer to *larger units of the OT*, such as the first five books of the Bible or the entire OT—see THE OLD TESTAMENT CANON in the NET NT (1990) on p. 551.

In *Leviticus* and *Numbers* the term *torah* refers to collections of *priestly instructions* regarding sacrifices (Lev. 6:14; 7:1; 11:46; Num. 19:2; 31:21). One of the ongoing tasks of the priests was to teach the *Torah* (Jer. 18:18; Hos. 4:6; Hag. 2:11; Mal. 2:6-8). As is evident from Mal. 2:6-8, such *instruction* carried divine authority since the priests were to be God's messengers. Their role as teachers underscores the meaning of *torah* as "instruction."

Because God taught His will through Moses (Deut. 4:1,2), both the specific collections of "laws" as well as the entire Pentateuch, the Five Books of Moses, are referred to as the *Torah*. The book of *Deuteronomy* is called the *Torah* of Moses (Deut. 17:18; 28:61; 31:24-26). The revelation through Moses is comprehensively referred to as *Torah* (Josh. 1:8; 23:6; 2 Kgs. 22:8; 23:25; 2 Chr. 23:18; Ezra 7:6; Neh. 8:1; Dan. 9:11). Certainly the book of *Deuteronomy* and the rest of the Pentateuch teach much more than *laws* which demand obedience. In the Pentateuch, as throughout Scripture, the demands for obedience to specific "commandments" (*mitzwah*) are based upon God's revealed plan of redemption. This "Gospel" accent of *torah*, referring to Israel's election and deliverance (redemption) from Egypt, is especially evident in its first use in *Exodus* where the whole story of the exodus and its reenactment are highlighted by the *redemption-filled* observation of the Passover festival (cf. Ex. 13:9).

The wider sense of *torah*. In another related way *torah* is used as a synonym for the "word of God." As such it is the object of proclamation (Is. 2:3) and meditation (Ps. 1:2). It is to be in the believer's mouth and in his heart (Ps. 40:8). In Ps. 119 *torah* is equated with God's "word," which needs to be learned through "teaching" and "instruction" (Ps. 119:105-108). It is a synonym for "commandment," "decree," "precept," "statute," "discipline," and "wisdom." Ps. 19 well summarizes the Bible's great appreciation and positive understanding of *torah*, as well as its companion term, *mitzwah* (see below). According to Ps. 19:7-11, God's *revelation* has the power to restore to life, to instill wisdom, and to give joy and illumination. It is clear that *torah* understood merely in a narrow sense as God's "law" or demand for perfect obedience cannot and does not bring about such wonderful results.

The wider sense of *torah* in *Proverbs*. The meaning of *torah* as "instruction" or "teaching" is obvious in the book of *Proverbs*. For example, Prov. 4:1-6 illustrates the understanding that *torah*—throughout the book—is equivalent to "wisdom," "insight," "precepts," "discipline," "words," "commands," and "exhortation," all of which must be learned through *revelation* and *instruction*. The verb *yrh* ("to instruct," the root of the noun *torah*) is used in v. 4 to emphasize that *torah*, wisdom, and other precious concepts must be taught; it is not possible to discern, discover, or deduce the content of *torah* by one's own doing. The result of learning *torah* is *God's* doing, namely, His giving the gift of life. Humans respond to *torah* through faith and through lives of obedience based on the "teaching" of God's word (*torah*).

The NET translation of *torah*. On the pages of the OT, then, *torah* serves as a comprehensive term which refers to both accents of Scripture—*Law and Gospel*, the sum and total of God's revelation. *Torah* is often equivalent to the "word of God," the authoritative "revelation" of God's will, the divine "teaching" and "instruction" for both faith and obedience. As a consequence, the NET translation of *torah* as "teaching" in *Proverbs* proves to be a faithful and communicative rendering. It conveys the concept of *authoritative revelation* without carrying all the negative baggage and legalistic nuances which are often associated with the term "law."

B. *Mitzwah*

***Mitzwah* as compared to *torah*.** We now turn our attention to the Hebrew term *mitzwah*, comparing it to *torah*. As is frequently the case in the OT, *Proverbs* often uses *torah* and *mitzwah* as *parallel* ideas (cf. 3:1; 4:1-6; 6:20,23; 7:1,2; 13:13,14).

Most English Bibles translate *mitzwah* as "commandment" or "commandments." Once again, this causes a problem of imprecision; much of what has been said above concerning *torah* also applies to *mitzwah*. In a sense, *all* that God *says* and *does* is *mitzwah*, translated in the NET as "commands." These "commands" are the authoritative "revelation" of His will for faith and obedience (Deut. 4:1,2). Therefore, to "keep" God's *commands* means to "guard" His words in faith as well as to "live" in accord with His specific *commandments*. We need to take a close look at the connotation of the terms "commands" and "commandments" since both terms have so much overlapping in English, as does *mitzwah* in Hebrew.

The wider sense of *mitzwah*. Jesus taught that *belief* in Him was the total fulfilling of the will, words, and works of God (Jn. 5:38,45,46; 6:28,29). Christians believe that His *death* on the cross in their place wiped out all sins against God's "commandments." But of equal importance was Jesus' *life of obedience*. That obedience fulfilled God's "Law" in our place so that we, as believers, can no longer be accused of breaking God's "commandments."

In the previous paragraph, how does one perceive the term "commandments"? Most would take it as a reference to the "Ten Commandments," that is, God's "Law" in the *narrow* sense. But God's "commandments" or "commands" can refer to something broader than the "Ten Commandments." What about God's "commands" concerning *ceremonial laws* in the OT or His "commands" to "obey" or "believe" the Gospel in the NT. This is "Law" in the *broader* sense. As such, God's "commands" include all of His *instructions* concerning belief in Him, as well as *instructions* to do what is pleasing to Him. Two exceptions to this more general truth is the fact that *mitzwah* can be seen in the narrower sense of "law" (cf. 13:13; 19:16).

On the other side of the coin, the word "Gospel" also can be used in a *narrow* and *wider* sense. When speaking of faith in Jesus alone, it is used in a narrow sense. However, when the Scriptures tell us to "obey" the Gospel by both believing and living a Christian life of obedience, they are applying the "Gospel" in a wider sense.

Confusing? Not really, if one will take time to study and analyze. But it does take dedication when one tackles the five or more uses of the term "law" in the NT book of *Romans* or the content of *torah* and *mitzwah* in the books of *Psalms* and *Proverbs*. For a discussion of the Greek term for "law" in the NT, see *NOMOS* in the NET NT (1990), APPENDIX 2.C.7 on p. 544.

In perspective. When the two terms "law" and "commandments" occur in English, we generally think of the "Ten Commandments." But more often than not, the OT, including *Proverbs*, uses the terms *torah* and *mitzwah* in their *wider sense*. They include God's whole instruction concerning faith as well as His demands for obedience. For this reason the term *mitzwah*, as parallel to *torah*, is to be understood more positively and broadly as "commands," thus avoiding the narrower, negative, or legalistic connotations of the word "commandments." In this way, then, "teaching" (*torah*) and "commands" (*mitzwah*) are inclusive of God's total Word of Gospel and Law, faith and obedience. Consequently, statements such as 3:1 (NET) take on more comprehensive meaning:

> My son, do not forget my *teaching*,
> and keep my *commands* in mind,....

The words "teaching" and "commands" communicate much more broadly than translations which use words of limited meaning. For example:

> My son, do not forget my *law*,
> and keep my *commandments* in mind,....

The former communicates God's fullest truth; the latter is limiting, misleading, and imprecise.

Three additional thoughts will help in appreciating the subject matter at hand:

1. Though complex, the relationship between Law and Gospel is one of the most crucial concepts of Scripture.

2. Your understanding of this study article will open the whole of Scripture in a fresh way. For example, a passage like Ps. 119:97 will become so much more comprehensive when it is translated as

> Oh, how I love Your *teaching*;
> it is in my thoughts all day long.

and not as

> O how love I thy *law*!
> It is my mediation all the day.

The former includes a love for and a reflection of the *entire message* of Scripture, the latter again is limiting.

3. Bible readers need to comprehend the full import of words like "love" in the above verse. With the broader term "teaching," it will now be easier to see "love" in terms of the "Gospel." However, one dare not go overboard and now make the mistake of *not* also seeing God's "Law" as part of the wider *torah* or *mitzwah*. God's Law, like His Gospel, is to be "loved" because it also is pure, good, and very beneficial (1 Jn. 5:3). Jesus ties the Gospel and Law together so beautifully when He says: "If you *love* Me, you will keep My commandments" (Jn. 14:15).

Study 10
MISHPAT
"Judgment" or "Justice"

The Hebrew *mishpat* is one of the more difficult words to translate accurately into English. It has often been rendered as "judge" or "judgment," either of which is accurate in several Biblical contexts. However, these English terms tend to flatten out the multi-dimensional meaning of *mishpat* onto a single plane. For many English readers "judge" or "judgment" merely conjure up a courtroom scene where a judge sits to render a verdict and pronounce an appropriate sentence. This is the correct understanding at Deut. 1:15-17 where Moses reminds the people, "So I took the leaders of your tribes...and put them over you...and I gave orders to your judges at that time, saying: '...Do not show partiality as a judge (*mishpat*);....'" It also holds at Prov. 24:23,24:

> These also are the sayings of the wise:
>> It is not good to show partiality as a judge.
> Whoever says to the guilty
>> "You are innocent"
>>> will be cursed by people and condemned by nations,....

However, the translation "judge" or "judgment" as well as the much more preferable translation "justice" or "just" cannot completely capture the deeper dimensions of the Hebrew *mishpat*. These English terms can even be misleading at times.

A. Two deeper dimensions of *mishpat*

To begin with, *mishpat* is not merely some general or abstract principle of right and wrong. The Bible considers *mishpat* to be one of God's chief *attributes*. In Deut. 32:4 Moses defines the Name of the Lord by writing,

> The Rock!
>> His work is perfect;
>> certainly all His ways are just (*mishpat*).

Cf. also Gen. 18:25; Jer. 9:24. According to Prov. 29:26 all genuine *mishpat* originates with God alone:

> ...justice (*mishpat*) for mankind comes from the Lord.

Furthermore *mishpat* shows itself in specific acts of mercy, in caring for the helpless and needy. Deut. 10:18 says that God "...carries out justice for the orphan and the widow" (lit.: "does *mishpat* for the fatherless and the widow") "and loves the resident alien *and gives him food and clothing*." At times

God's *mishpat* also requires the punishment of those who proudly resist Him and oppress His people (cf. Deut. 32:41-43).

Perhaps *mishpat* finds its closest counterpart in the familiar NT Greek word *agape* ("love") which is also one of God's chief *attributes* (cf. 1 Jn. 4:8). God's love is also not abstract but reveals itself in self-sacrificing acts of mercy and salvation for the helpless and the sinner. For example, see Rom. 5:8 where Paul writes, "...God shows His love (*agape*) for us by this: While we were still sinners, Christ died for us."

God wants *mishpat* to characterize His people. The prophet Micah (6:8) puts it bluntly, "And what does the LORD seek from you—but to carry out justice" (lit.: "to do *mishpat*"—cf. Deut. 10:12-20) "and to love loyalty, and to walk humbly with your God?"

B. "To do *mishpat*"

Since true *mishpat* is found in God, people cannot even begin "to do *mishpat*" until they are united with the Source of *mishpat*, namely, God Himself. Such a relationship, the Bible says, is based solely on the grace [undeserved love] and free favor of God. As Moses made clear to God's OT people, it was God's *mishpat* which acted on their behalf to bring them out of captivity and to make them His own special people. And as He loved and defended His people, both while and after they were foreigners, strangers, aliens, and captives in Egypt (Deut. 10:19) and continued to do so with an everlasting love (Jer. 31:3; Lk. 1:68-75), so He takes care of His people, the Christian church, to this very day and beyond (1 Pet. 2:4-10). Through faith in Christ all Christians are one with the God of love who is their "Shield" (Prov. 2:7,8). Besides, they are thereby enabled through faith to produce acts of love and mercy (cf. Jn. 15), and, like their God, they also are able to show love and "do *mishpat*."

But there is more. Since *mishpat* is not abstract or theoretical, God's people cannot be living *mishpat* ("justly") if they are ignoring or neglecting the needs of people around them. Living *mishpat*, that is practicing "justice," will show itself in concrete acts of kindness and mercy, including, at times, the active denouncing of ungodliness. In Is. 1:17 God reminded His people "to seek justice" (*mishpat*) and all that this entailed concerning orphans and widows and those in need. In the same way Jas. 2:14-17 reflects the OT concept of *mishpat* when asking, "What good does it do, my fellow Christians, if you say you have faith but do not have any works? Can such a faith save you? If a Christian man or woman is going without clothes or daily food and one of you tells them, 'Go in peace, keep warm, and eat heartily,' but does not give them what the body needs, what good does it do? So faith, if it is not accompanied by works, is dead for that very reason."

In summary, then, *mishpat* is not mere talk. Rather, it is *action*. It involves specific acts of kindness toward those in need and the giving of help and assistance when necessary. It means drawing strength and power from God Himself, He who remains the Source of all true *mishpat*. This is the "justice" God shows us in forgiving us all our sins for Jesus' sake (1 Jn. 1:9); this is the "justice" He, in turn, expects us to show daily to those around us, as He says, "Love one another as I have loved you" (Jn. 13:34). Or, to paraphrase this command, "Do *mishpat* to one another as I have done *mishpat* to you."

C. Understanding *mishpat* in *Proverbs*

Now an exercise to understand the above a bit better—the concept of *mishpat* as **attribute** and **action** as well as **aquittal** or **accusation**! Note four examples from *Proverbs* and apply the above principles of understanding as you consider them:

> The thoughts of the righteous are just;
> the advice of the wicked is treacherous;.... (12:5)

> A wicked person secretly accepts a bribe
> to corrupt the ways of justice. (17:23)

> Doing what is right and just
> is more acceptable to the LORD than offering a sacrifice. (21:3)

> Evil men do not understand justice,
> but those who seek the LORD understand everything. (28:5)

Example 1: "just," an *attribute* of the Christian.
Example 2: "justice," the unbeliever in *action*, seeking to keep *judgment* from being "just" or fair.
Example 3: "just," the Christian in *action*, living out his religion in daily life.
Example 4: "justice," the unbeliever does not possess the *attribute*, nor perform the *action*, nor comprehend the coming *accusation* or "judgment" of *mishpat*.

May the LORD bless you as you "do *mishpat*" in this life until—in heaven above—you meet Him who is the ultimate *MISHPAT* face to face!

Study 11
DEATH AND *SHEOL*

The Hebrew word *sheol* appears either sixty-five or sixty-six times in the OT, depending on the Hebrew text being used. Nine of those appearances are in *Proverbs*. Here the NET translates *sheol* as "hell" five times (5:5; 7:27; 9:18; 15:24; 23:14), as "the grave" twice (1:12; 30:16), and twice leaves it as "*Sheol*" (15:11, 27:20).

The etymology of *sheol* is uncertain. One conjecture is that it comes from a Hebrew verb meaning "to ask" (*sh'l*). The connecting idea is that *sheol* "asks" everyone alike to enter its gates. A second guess is that *sheol* derives from a verb root which means "to be hollow" (*sh'l*). The linking thought here would relate to the "hollow cavity" of the grave.

In its translation work to date, the NET OT editorial committee has chosen one or the other of *two* basic meanings for *sheol*: (1) "grave," representing the state of physical death that both the wicked and the righteous alike enter (the translation "grave" suffices if its sense reaches beyond the mere *place of burial* and is also understood to include the more abstract *concept of death*); and (2) "hell," the eternal place of suffering for the damned.

Apart from the OT, the term *sheol* appears only once, that is, in some ancient writings from a small island in the Nile—the Elephantine Papyri (495-399 B.C.). In these Aramaic papyri the meaning of *sheol* is "grave." The significant lack of outside sources to sharpen the meaning of *sheol* emphasizes that it is the Bible—above all—that must dictate the translation of *sheol* in any given verse. Other considerations within Scripture, such as general context, descriptions within a passage, synonymous expressions in parallel parts of poetry, and the light shed on *the afterlife* by the NT aid the translator when dealing with this Hebrew term.

A common idea is that *sheol* is merely a Hebrew name for the dark and miserable underworld inhabited by the souls of *all* the dead as described in Mesopotamian writings. However, the NT clearly reveals that the souls of believers do *not* enter such a dismal netherworld at death. Therefore in those OT passages that speak of "the righteous" in relation to *sheol*, the principle of *the unity of Scripture* leads us to say that *sheol* cannot be a place where righteous souls live in agony. In other words "hell" is a possible translation in a given verse only when the focus is on the judgment of the wicked. The word *sheol* does not appear in Babylonian and Assyrian writings, and to assume that we must always equate *sheol* with an underworld place of suffering like that in Mesopotamian mythology is neither good scholarship nor sound theology. Possibly the earliest uses of *sheol* only referred to the "grave." "Hell" may be a later and more specialized meaning.

The Septuagint (LXX), the third-century B.C. Greek translation of the Hebrew OT, generally uses the Greek term *hades* for *sheol*. It does so eight times in the book of *Proverbs*. In one instance (23:14), it chooses the word *thanatos* ("death"); this may be the result of a reading other than *sheol* in the particular Hebrew text used by the Septuagint translators.

For a study of the NT terms related to *sheol*, see *HADES/GEHENNA* in the NET NT (1990), APPENDIX 2.C.4 on p. 540.

Parallel terms for *sheol* are *bor* ("pit" - 1:12) and *abaddon* ("decay" - 15:11; 27:20). The term *shahath* ("pit") does *not* serve as a parallel to *sheol* in 26:27. These three terms will be treated in more detail, along with *sheol* once again, as other NET OT texts are published.

Study 12
POETIC STRUCTURES THAT CONVEY
TEXTUAL MEANINGS

This study article speaks of the structure and importance of OT poetry. On the basis of several Scriptural passages from the book of *Proverbs*, specific examples will be given that illustrate *how* OT meaning is beautifully conveyed and aided by a knowledge of its poetic structure.

A. Poetry in the OT

Much of the OT consists of poetry. This not only includes books normally thought of as the Poetical Books (i.e., *Job, Psalms, Proverbs, Ecclesiastes, Song of Solomon, Lamentations*) but also large portions of the Prophetic Books as well as sections of the Pentateuch and the Historical Books (e.g., Ex. 15:1-18). Like other cultures of the Ancient Near East, the Israelites did not rely primarily on rhyme or meter to produce their poetry. Scholars still debate the place of meter in Hebrew poetry, and rhyme is very rare.

Instead, poetry was characterized by a device called *parallelism*. Parallelism consists of two or more lines of poetry whose meanings are related to one another in some fashion. This makes it possible to translate the poetry of the OT so that much of the poetic "feeling" survives. Faithful translation into other languages, such as English, would not be possible if it were important to retain the meter or rhyme of the original Hebrew.

Scholars have identified several types of parallelism in the OT. A few of the more common are:

SYNONYMOUS	ANTITHETICAL	CONSTRUCTIVE		STAIRLIKE
A	A	A	A	A
A	B	B	B	B
			C	C
				D

"Synonymous parallelism" (A-A) means that a second line repeats the thought of the first but in different words. "Antithetical parallelism" (A-B) indicates that a second line says the opposite of the first. "Two-line constructive parallelism" (A-B) and "three-line constructive parallelism" (A-B-C) are used to build ideas as a second and even third line add to the preceding line(s). "Stairlike parallelism" (A-B-C-D) moves downward on the page but upward in content as each line adds a thought to the former. ("Stairlike parallelism" is merely "constructive parallelism" extended over a longer series of lines.)

A positioning of the various lines in a *vertical* or *slanted* lineup helps to indicate meanings. Examples will be cited below.

The reader of *Proverbs* will notice that, unlike most Bibles, the NET has chosen to set type *across the entire page* rather than divide the page into two columns. This feature is *crucial* if one is going to keep each individual line of poetry from wrapping onto a second line. Nonwrapping is vital so that certain lines can be seen as being parallel in meaning to companion lines. In fact, since spacing is so valuable if wrapping is to be avoided, the NET has chosen to go with a wide page format; it also has set its *poetry* sections in a smaller type than its prose. This has obviously permitted more words per poetic line. An added benefit is that it also has made for an attractive page format which assists the reader's understanding.

The commitment to superb communication on the part of NET Publishing dictates that Scripture's poetry be presented in the best possible way, so that Scripture's valuable structures may continue to convey full, rich textual meanings.

B. Examples of Parallelism in *Proverbs*

1. Synonymous parallelism (A-A)
(Slanted or vertical lineup for readability)

16:18　**A** Pride precedes a disaster,
　　　　A　　and an arrogant attitude precedes a fall;....

31:31　**A** Reward her for what she has done,
　　　　A and let her achievements praise her at the city gates!

2. Antithetical parallelism (A-B)
(Slanted or vertical lineup for readability)

"Antithetical parallelism" is perhaps the most widely used type of parallelism in *Proverbs*. It is particularly suited to *comparisons*. Individual proverbs often compare the wicked to the righteous, one situation to another, the industrious to the lazy, or the wise to the foolish.

10:32　**A** The lips of the righteous announce good will,
　　　　B　　but the mouth of the wicked is devious.

11:14　**A** A nation will fall when there is no direction,
　　　　B but with many advisers there is victory.

13:4　**A** A lazy person craves food and there is none,
　　　　B　　but the appetite of hardworking people is satisfied.

15:20　**A** A wise son makes his father happy,
　　　　B　　but a foolish child despises its mother.

3. Constructive parallelism (A-B-C)
(Slanted or vertical lineup for readability)

"Constructive parallelism" is used in a variety of ways in *Proverbs*. Below are examples of its more common usages:

a. Conclusion

Often the first line makes a statement from which the following lines *draw a conclusion*.

14:7   **A** Stay away from a fool,
       B   because you will not receive knowledge from his lips.

16:3   **A** Entrust your works to the LORD,
       B and your plans will succeed.

26:3   **A** A whip is for the horse,
       B a bridle is for the donkey, and
       C   a rod is for the back of fools.

b. Comparison

At times the first lines state a situation, while the following line(s) *by way of comparison* offer insight into living.

10:26 **A** Like vinegar to the teeth and
       B like smoke to the eyes,
       C   so the lazy person is to those who send him on a mission.

26:2   **A** Like a fluttering sparrow, and
       B like a darting swallow,
       C   so a hastily spoken curse does not come to rest.

c. Stairlike

"Stairlike parallelism" is merely "constructive parallelism" extended over several lines. It is used in sections of *Proverbs* where an ongoing discussion of one subject occurs.

1:1-6   The proverbs of Solomon son of David, king of Israel,
             given in order
         A   to grasp wisdom and discipline,
         B   to understand deep thoughts,
         C   to acquire the discipline of wise behavior...
         D   to give insight to gullible people,
         E   to give knowledge and foresight to the young...
         F   to understand a proverb and a clever saying,
         G   to understand the words of the wise and their riddles.

4. Various types of parallelism in combination

At times various types of parallelisms are united in order to communicate meaning by way of comparison or contrast. This ties certain proverbs together.

19:25 **AA** Strike a mocker
    AB   and a gullible person may learn a lesson;
    BC warn an understanding person
    BD   and he will gain more knowledge.

In this verse the first two lines are "constructive parallelism" (A-B). The next two lines are also "constructive parallelism" (C-D). At the same time the first two lines stand in "antithetical parallelism" to the last two lines (vertically, AA-BB).

C. Acrostic (alphabetic) poetry

Another poetic device used in the OT is the "acrostic poem." In a *singlefold* acrostic the first word of each new verse begins with a different letter of the Hebrew alphabet. This is done in alphabetical order until the entire alphabet is represented. There is one such acrostic in 31:10-31, a poem about the ideal wife. Such an acrostic serves to bind a given set of proverbs into a single unit. This acrostic feature is pointed out to the reader of the NET by including each of the twenty-two (22) letters of the Hebrew alphabet with its appropriate textual verse. (The *threefold* acrostic of Lam. 3 and the *eightfold* acrostic of Ps. 119 will be dealt with in later NET articles on OT poetry.)

Study 13
GENDER AND HEBREW GENDER

The topic at hand deals with *gender*—gender in language; gender in society; gender in translation, interpretation, and communication. Some would not touch this topic with a ten-foot pole since it can be so *controversial*; others because it is so *difficult*. Yet, it is so *important* to OT translation work that one cannot produce a proper translation without addressing gender in some way, especially in relation to the book of *Proverbs*. The purpose of this study is to show that the "gender" of a language does matter and must be understood and handled intelligently (minus the baggage of emotional presuppositions) if correct translation and communication are to take place.

Such grammatical gender distinctions become important in our day when English usages are being altered by certain elements in society. We need only to think of the "pagan" New Age Movement, which refers to "Mother Earth" as a "goddess"; or of those persons who discard the Biblical terms for deity— "Father" and "Son"—and then speak of God as "Mother"; or, finally, who altogether avoid the gender indicators in the baptismal formula of Matt. 28:19 by substituting "Creator" and "Redeemer" for "Father" and "Son." In short, this new approach to gender has caused tension in Christian circles and necessitates a study article such as this one, especially since certain voices would like to identify "wisdom" (Heb: *hokmah*; Gk: *sophia*) as a "goddess" in Prov. 8, not as the "Son of God"—see CHRIST, THE "WISDOM" OF GOD on p. 83. What is also being done with God the Father should be evident from modern book titles, such as, *Created in Her Image* and *When God Was a Woman*. This alone should encourage Bible readers to learn more about Hebrew gender for sake of accurate understanding.

Many readers do not realize that certain gender designators (the form of the noun) show a *communication purpose* or *function* in Scripture. God as "Father" and "Son" (masculines) or people as "sons of God" express the concept of having "responsibility" for various things, such as preserving creation, redeeming the world, forgiving sins, or spreading the Gospel (Ps. 2:7-9; Lk. 23:34,46; Gal. 4:4-7). On the other hand, when *female* imagery like "daughter of Zion" is employed, Scripture stresses "endearment"—how much God's people ought to love others, or how much God loves His people and cares for them (Ps. 9:14; Is. 66:13). By way of application one could say that *wisdom* in Prov. 9 functions according to this female imagery since *she* shows "endearment" to gullible people by inviting these sinners to come to faith (vv. 1-6). However, in Prov. 8 the context calls for masculine or neuter reference, not feminine, since the "Son of God" is here portrayed as "Wisdom," who had the "responsibility" of being the "Master Craftsman" of Creation at the Lord's side (v. 30).

The *translation problem* in a nutshell is that the Hebrew language has only *two* grammatical genders, masculine and feminine, while the English has *three*, masculine, feminine, and neuter. What are translators to do with this dilemma between the two languages as they move from Hebrew to English?

A. The problem of gender in the book of *Proverbs*

The point of concern regarding gender in *Proverbs* involves words such as "ant." Traditionally, English Bibles have translated pronouns referring to "ant" as "she" and "her," because this noun is *feminine* in Hebrew. However, the NET Bible has translated pronouns referring to "ant" as "it" and "its" (6:6-8). English-speaking people will not be surprised, since they themselves generally regard *ants* as things that are neuter, not feminine.

But when it comes to a *concept* like "wisdom" (Heb: *hokmah*), translation becomes particularly challenging. The question is whether "wisdom" should be forced to remain the feminine Hebrew gender "she" and "her" when spoken of by means of pronouns, or should "wisdom" agree with its neuter English gender "it" and "its," especially in light of the surrounding subject matter. Take for example the imagery of Prov. 8. In this chapter the concept "wisdom," ultimately revealed as an obvious reference to the male designation "Son of God," was referred to as an "it" in verses 1-3. This was done because chapter 8 makes an extensive reference to the *pre-incarnate* Christ who is also spoken of with a *neuter* in Lk. 1:35 ("Being"—see CHRIST, THE "WISDOM" OF GOD on p. 83). Elsewhere in *Proverbs*, wherever the usual form for the word "wisdom" (*hokmah*) appears, the NET consistently translated the pronoun as "it" (2:4; 3:13-18; 4:5-9).

However, in addition to "it" and "its," the pronouns "she" and "her" were also used for "wisdom" in the NET. The distinction between the use of the *neuter* and the *feminine* was made solely on the basis of the Hebrew. "She" and "her" were used exclusively when the pronouns in 1:20,21 and 9:1-4 referred to a special form of the word "wisdom" (Heb pl.: *hokmoth*). The Hebrew *plural* in these passages where imagery is used indicates *personification* (see below). This special plural form of the word occurs only *two* other times in the whole Old Testament (Prov. 24:7; Ps. 49:3).

Those interested in more in-depth information on the topic of grammatical gender in Hebrew and English will want to continue with the rest of this article.

B. In general

In the Hebrew language all nouns are classified according to their gender as being either *masculine* or *feminine*. For the English reader who is unfamiliar with this very common linguistic phenomenon, it must be emphasized that when we say nouns in Hebrew are either masculine or feminine, we are *not* saying that all nouns in Hebrew are *male* or *female* or that they refer to something male or female. The *grammatical gender* of a noun in many languages like English (masculine, feminine, or neuter) is not really the same thing as the *natural sex* of a noun (male or female; more rarely, neuter). In fact, in most languages where there is grammatical gender, there is only a *partial* correspondence between the *natural* gender of a noun and the *grammatical* gender of the noun. For example, if a noun represents an animate object (a person or an animal of the male or female *sex*), usually the grammatical gender of the noun corresponds: it is either masculine or feminine. For this reason the Hebrew noun "father" (*'ab*) is a noun of the *masculine* gender because that noun refers to a person of the male gender (sex), and similarly the Hebrew word for "mother" (*'em*) is a noun of the *feminine* gender because that noun refers to a person of the female gender (sex). However, if a noun represents an inanimate object (e.g., door, goodness, evil, song, city), that noun is obviously not associated with any sex, and so the gender assignment (to our way of thinking) is purely *arbitrary*. Since Hebrew, contrary to many other languages, has no *neuter* gender, all of its nouns are referred to either as a "he" or a "she."

By way of contrast, English speakers usually refer only to people as "he" or "she." All other nouns in English are usually referred to as "it." The only exception to this "rule," which is also pertinent to our understanding of *Proverbs*, is due to what is called *personification*. *Personification* is that literary device where the writer treats an inanimate or abstract noun as if it were a person. In fact, in those languages which have grammatical gender for nouns and at the same time personify a noun, that noun is personified *according to the grammatical gender of that noun*, not according to some vague association of that noun with a certain male or female stereotype. For example, when inanimate nouns are personified in English, the noun is frequently referred to as a "she" ("God bless our native land, firm may *she* ever stand..."); however, when expanding on phrases such as "the man in the moon" and "Old Man River," one would use *masculine* pronouns.

C. The specifics of Hebrew gender

1. Masculine nouns

In Hebrew most masculine nouns are *unmarked*, that is, there is no special ending on the noun which marks it as masculine. When the noun is animate and portrays natural "male" sex (e.g., "father"), that noun is easily recognizable as *masculine*. However, outside the category of animate nouns, the gender of all other *masculine* nouns must be memorized since, as we said earlier, gender is arbitrarily assigned to nouns.

2. Feminine nouns

a. Marked—by form

This section deals with *feminine* nouns that are *gender-marked* in Hebrew. Some feminine nouns are also *unmarked* in Hebrew (e.g., "mother"). Yet there are many feminine nouns which are *marked*, that is, there are special endings on some nouns, which "mark" them as *feminine*. In Hebrew the *marked* nouns may be classified feminine if they *visually*:

1. end in stressed (accented) -ah (like hokmah, "wisdom").

2. end in -ath (an alternate form of -ah, as in hokmath elohim, "the wisdom of God").

3. end in -th (Heb: berith, "covenant").

4. end in -eth (Heb: kapporeth, traditionally translated "mercy seat"; also "propitiation, atonement cover").

b. Marked—by semantic range

Not only are the *marked* feminine nouns classified by their "markers" (their endings), but they may also be categorized by their *meaning* (their semantic range). Several major types or categories of nouns are found among the *marked* feminine nouns:

1. Abstract nouns (e.g., "strength, goodness, evil"). Many of these Hebrew nouns are derived from adjectives and end in stressed (accented) -ah. For example the noun tobah, "goodness," is derived from the adjective tob, "good"; likewise the noun ra'ah, "evil," is derived from the adjective ra', "evil." Our famous hokmah/"wisdom" is in this same category, i.e., an abstract noun also marked by its stressed ending -ah.

   Under this same category Hebrew also uses for nouns or adjectives the feminine plural ending -oth to indicate *abstract* concepts (see Prov. 2:12 where "devious things" in that verse is an adjective ending in the Hebrew feminine plural, indicating an abstract concept). Technically speaking, these feminine plurals expressing abstract concepts are not restricted to the feminine gender alone. This way of expressing *abstract* ideas is more a feature of *plural* forms of nouns in general, masculine and feminine alike, rather than just a characteristic of the gender feminine plural alone (see Prov. 1:3 where "fairness" translates an adjective ending in the masculine plural in Hebrew, also indicating an *abstract* concept). In this connection the Hebrew word hokmah occurs not only with the marked feminine suffix -ah, but also with the feminine *plural* ending -oth as in hokmoth, also indicating an *abstract* concept. A suggested differentiation between these two abstract suffixes will be discussed in the "Conclusion" of this study.

2. Collective nouns (e.g., "caravan, poor people"). These nouns end in the marked endings listed above (-ah, -ath, -th, or -eth).

3. The single unit from a collective noun (e.g., a "vessel" from a fleet; a "hair" from the head). Primarily these nouns make use of the first two marked endings that were listed above (-ah or -ath).

4. Some figurative nouns (e.g., the word for a "suckling child" with a feminine ending produces the noun "a sucker" or "a shoot" from a plant). These nouns have the marked endings that are listed above (*-ah*, *-ath*, *-th*, or *-eth*).

c. Unmarked

While the majority of *unmarked* Hebrew nouns are masculine, there are two important categories of *unmarked* nouns which are *feminine* in Hebrew:

1. Parts of the body, especially those parts which occur in symmetrical pairs, are usually *feminine* (ear, eye, hand, foot, but also tongue and stomach).

2. Many names of cities or countries are *feminine* because the nouns for "city" and "country/land" are feminine in Hebrew. This is true even though the terms "city" or "country/land" may not be present in the Hebrew text (e.g., city of Jerusalem or land of Canaan). Traditionally these geographical words were explained as being *feminine* because they were viewed as the "mother" of the people. But it may be better to understand these words as feminine because other nouns are understood to be connected with the name of a given city or country/land. For example, the noun "Judah" is *masculine* in Is. 3:8 probably because the Hebrew masculine noun "house of" is understood to go with it. Yet in Is. 7:6 "Judah" is *feminine* probably because the Hebrew feminine noun "land of" is understood to go with it.

D. Conclusion

In keeping with modern English usage, the translators of the NET OT have used "it" to refer to *inanimate* nouns that are masculine and feminine in Hebrew. However, when an *inanimate* noun is *personified*, the NET has followed the general English style of using the pronouns "she" or "her" to refer to that noun, which the Hebrew does already in 1:20,21; 9:1-4.

The committee of translators of the NET OT discussed the grammatically feminine Hebrew noun, *hokmah*/"wisdom," principally in Prov. 1-9. What complicated the discussion were the different contexts in which the term "wisdom" appears. What helped in reaching a conclusion was that in Prov. 2:1-19; 3:13-18; 4:5-9, and Prov. 8 *hokmah* is used for "wisdom/Wisdom," but in Prov. 1:20; 9:1 the form *hokmoth* is used. The general conclusion was that the use of the feminine *plural hokmoth always* indicates *personification*. But in those passages where *hokmah* occurs, only the context ultimately decides whether "wisdom" refers to a mere *abstract* idea, whether it is *personified*, or whether it is a *hypostasis*—see CHRIST, THE "WISDOM" OF GOD on p. 83 for a fuller explanation of *hypostasis*.

The NET committee has concluded that the feminine *singular hokmah/* "wisdom" is *never* personified; it only occurs as the abstract idea (2:1-19; 3:13-18; 4:5-9). All the other occurrences in *Proverbs* (whether the singular *hokmah* or the plural *hokmoth*) serve as pointers to the ultimate "Wisdom" of Prov. 8:22-31 and its subsection at 3:19, where the singular *Hokmah/* "Wisdom" is used in a very special way as a reference to Christ—see CHRIST, THE "WISDOM" OF GOD on p. 83.

In both cases where "wisdom"/*hokmoth* is personified due to the plural (1:20,21; 9:1-6), the NET editorial committee kept the pronouns as feminine singulars, as they are in Hebrew. To repeat, in all other cases (2:1-19; 3:13-18; 4:5-9) the committee kept the English pronouns "it" and "its" because *hokmah/*"wisdom" is an *abstract* idea.

Finally, in highlighting "Wisdom" in Prov. 8 in relation to all other contexts, the committee of translators concluded that *Wisdom* in Prov. 8 is a Hypostasis, that is, *Wisdom* is not portrayed as an imaginary woman, but it is, in fact, making reference to a Person of the Godhead, the pre-incarnate Christ. Here Wisdom is God Himself!

Much of the material in this article is drawn from the following reference works:

Brugmann, Karl. *The Nature and Origin of the Noun Genders in the Indo-European Languages*. New York: Scribner, 1897; cited by Muhammad Hasan Ibrahim. *Grammatical Gender: Its Origin and Development*. The Hague: Mouton, 1973.
Waltke, Bruce K., and M. O'Connor. *An Introduction to Biblical Hebrew Syntax*. Winona Lake, Indiana: Eisenbrauns, 1990.

Study 14
PROVERBS 22:17–24:22 AND THE "THIRTY SAYINGS"

Prov. 22:17–24:22 contains a very interesting textual consideration. It pertains to the translation of the Hebrew word *shilshom* in 22:20. The question: Should this term be translated, "Did I not write to you *previously?*" or "Did I not write to you *thirty sayings?*"

The Hebrew term literally means "*three* days ago," that is, "formerly/previously." Some—by changing one consonant—say it means *thirty*. In any event the word is used twenty-five times in the OT. In twenty-four of these instances it is coupled with the Hebrew word meaning "yesterday." The phrase is a *time expression* equivalent in meaning to "yesterday and the day before"—thus the sense of "previously." Only in 22:20 does it appear *without* its companion word—"yesterday," and there is no manuscript evidence for its inclusion. In this instance it may thus be used in that *sense* of "previously."

Furthermore, there exists an Egyptian composition written by a man named Amenemope. His document, containing *thirty* chapters, is variously dated from as early as 1570 B.C. to as late as the Persian Period, possibly around 500 B.C. Because the composition has *thirty chapters dealing with grooming for success in the political arena* and Prov. 22:17–24:22 *possibly* could be divided into *thirty sayings dealing with godly living*, and because there seem to be a number of verbal similarities between these two writings, some have felt that an *interdependence* exists. This has led to varying conclusions, namely, (1) that Solomon borrowed from Amenemope; (2) that Amenemope borrowed from Solomon; (3) that both borrowed from another source that was Semitic in nature; or (4) that there is no adequate basis for assuming a specific relationship either way.

While no definitive answer has been reached, a few observations are in place: (1) The text of 22:20 may very well employ a *solitary use* of a temporal adverb. In this case the Hebrew term would simply be translated as "previously/formerly." As such, no *numerical* significance would be attached. (2) There is a measure of disagreement on the number of proverbs actually contained in 22:17–24:22. Some feel there are more than *thirty*, others less than *thirty*. Any number other than *thirty* tends to end the discussion. Those who feel that there are *thirty* do not necessarily agree on their division or numbering. (3) If interdependence does exist, there is some indication that Amenemope may have borrowed from *Proverbs*. This is deduced from translation problems evident in the Egyptian text, alleged translation problems that stem from a misunderstanding of the Hebrew text. However, some feel that the exact opposite of this is the more likely. (4) If anyone borrowed, it is more likely that Amenemope—of little or no fame and whose work is dated by some as being subsequent to Solomon's—took his ideas from Solomon, rather than assuming that the wise Solomon derived his ideas from Amenemope.

Regardless of comparative studies and conclusions concerning the above, the text of Prov. 22:17–24:22 is unaffected in meaning and intent.

AN ABRIDGED CONCORDANCE

This concordance is provided as a useful tool for studying *Proverbs*. Often the key words in the entries were chosen on the basis of those verses that are more commonly and frequently quoted.

All key word entries are capitalized and in alphabetical order. Each is followed by selected references and the corresponding context phrases containing the key word. The key word within the phrase is abbreviated to the first letter of the word which appears in boldface type, for example, "blessed" would appear as "**b.**"

WORDS

ABADDON
15:11 If Sheol and A lie open before the LORD—
27:20 Sheol and A are never satisfied, and a
ABUSE
9:7 a mocker receives a, and whoever warns a
22:10 quarreling and a will stop.
ACHE
14:13 a heart can a, and joy can end in grief.
ACHIEVEMENTS
31:31 done, and let her a praise her at the
ACTIONS
5:21 He surveys all his a; the wicked person
20:11 known by his a, whether his deeds are pure
ADD
9:11 and years will be a to your life.
10:22 rich, and hard work a nothing to it.
19:4 Wealth a many friends, but a poor person is
30:6 Do not a to His words or He will scold you,
ADULTEROUS
2:16 save you from the a woman, from the
5:3 the lips of an a woman drip with honey,
5:20 with an a woman and fondle a loose
6:33 The a man will find disease and
7:5 yourself from the a woman, from the
22:14 The mouth of an a woman is a deep pit;
30:20 is the way of an a woman: She eats and
ADVICE
1:25 you ignored all my a and you did not want
1:30 They refused my a; they despised my every
3:32 LORD; His intimate a is with the upright.
12:15 who listens to a is wise.
13:10 but those who take a gain wisdom.
15:22 Without a plans go wrong, but with many
19:20 Listen to a and accept discipline so that
19:21 heart, but the a of the LORD will endure.
21:28 man who listens to a will continue to speak.
ADVISERS
11:14 but with many a there is victory.
15:22 but with many a they succeed.
24:6 war, and with many a there is victory.
ALLOW
10:3 The LORD will not a the righteous person to
ALONE
5:17 should be yours a so do not share them with
9:12 if you mock, you a will be held responsible.
ANCESTORS
22:28 marker that your a set in place.
ANCIENT
22:28 Do not move an a boundary marker that your
23:10 Do not move an a boundary marker or enter
ANGER, ANGRY
14:29 is slow to become a, but a short temper is
15:1 away rage, but a harsh word stirs up a.
16:32 Better to get a slowly than to be a hero,
20:2 whoever makes him a forfeits his life.
21:14 in secret calms a, and a secret bribe calms
21:19 a quarreling and a woman.
24:18 it and turn His a away from them
25:23 tongue brings a looks.

27:4 A is cruel and fury is overwhelming, but who
29:8 uproar in a city, but the wise turn away a.
29:22 An a man stirs up a fight, and a hothead
30:33 so stirring up a produces a fight.
ANSWER
15:1 A gentle a turns away rage, but a harsh
15:28 considers how to a, but the mouth of the
21:13 that person will call and not be a.
24:26 Giving a straight a is like a kiss on the
26:4 Do not a a fool with his own type of
26:5 A a fool with his own type of stupidity, or
26:16 than seven people who give a sensible a.
ANT
6:6 Consider the a, you lazy bum; watch its ways
30:25 they are very wise: a are not a strong
APPETITE
6:30 to satisfy his a; but when he is caught,
13:2 ability, but the a of the treacherous
13:4 is none, but the a of hardworking people
13:25 to satisfy his a, but the belly of the
16:26 A laborer's a works to his advantage
23:2 if you have a big a do not crave his
APPLES
25:11 Like golden a in silver settings, so is
ARGUMENT
17:14 so stop before the a gets out of control.
18:6 fool gets into an a, and his mouth
25:9 Present your a to your neighbor, but do
ASSOCIATE
13:20 wise, but whoever a with fools will
20:19 secrets; do not a with a person whose
23:20 Do not a with those who drink too much
24:21 as well); do not a with those who
28:7 wise son, whoever a with gluttons
ATONED
16:6 guilt is a for, and by the fear of the LORD
ATTENTION
4:1 and pay a in order to gain understanding,
4:20 My son, pay a to my words; open your
5:1 My son, pay a to my wisdom; open your
7:24 to me, and pay a to the words of my
13:18 but whoever pays a to constructive
16:20 Whoever gives a to the LORD's word
17:4 An evildoer pays a to wicked lips; a
29:12 If a ruler pays a to lies, all his
ATTITUDE
15:7 but a foolish a does not.
16:18 and an arrogant a precedes a fall; better

BALANCES
16:11 Honest b and scales belong to the LORD;
BEAR
17:12 Better to meet a b robbed of her young than a
28:15 like a prowling b, so is the wicked
BEATING
18:6 an argument, and his mouth invites a b.
19:29 for mockers and b for the backs of fools.
20:30 Brutal b cleanse away wickedness; such

20:30 wickedness; such b cleanse the innermost
BEAUTIFUL, BEAUTY
4:9 will hand you a b crown.
6:25 Do not desire her b in your heart; do not
11:22 snout, so is a b woman who lacks good
16:31 Silver hair is a b crown found in a
31:30 is deceptive, and b evaporates, but a
BED
7:16 I've made my b, with colored sheets of
7:17 I've sprinkled my b with myrrh, aloes, and
22:27 why should your b be repossessed?
26:14 hinges, so the lazy person turns on his b.
BEGINNING
1:7 the LORD is the b of knowledge; wisdom
4:7 The b is wisdom: Acquire wisdom!
9:10 the LORD is the b of wisdom, and the
BEHAVIOR
1:3 discipline of wise b—righteousness and
8:13 arrogance, evil b, and twisted speech.
21:8 crooked, but the b of the pure is upright.
21:16 the way of wise b will rest in the
BETTER
3:14 silver; its yield is b than fine gold.
8:11 because wisdom is b than jewels, and
8:19 What I produce is b than gold, pure gold;
8:19 what I yield is b than fine silver.
12:9 B to be unimportant and have a slave than
15:16 B to have a little with the fear of
15:17 B to have a dish of vegetables where there
16:8 B a few possessions gained honestly than
16:16 How much b it is to gain wisdom than gold,
16:19 precedes a fall; b to be humble with the
16:32 B to get angry slowly than to be a hero,
16:32 to be a hero, and b to be even-tempered
17:1 B a bite of dry bread eaten in peace than
17:12 B to meet a bear robbed of her young than a
19:1 B to be a poor person who lives innocently
19:22 a person, and it is b to be a poor man than
21:9 B to live on a corner of a roof than to
21:19 B to live in a desert than with a
22:1 wealth; respect is b than silver or gold.
25:7 because it is b to be told, Come up here,
25:24 B to live on a corner of a roof than to
27:5 Open criticism is b than unexpressed love.
27:10 living nearby is b than a brother far away.
28:6 B to be a poor person who has integrity
30:32 evil, you had b put your hand over your
BIRD
1:17 to spread a net within the sight of any b.
6:5 hunter and like a b from the hand of the
7:23 his heart), like a b darting into a trap, he
27:8 Like a b wandering from its nest, so is a man
BITTER
5:4 the end she is as b as wormwood, as sharp
17:25 to his father and b grief to his mother.
27:7 who is hungry, even b food tastes sweet.
31:6 is perishing and wine to one, who feels b.
BLESS, BLESSED, BLESSING
3:13 B is the one who finds wisdom and the one

3:18 and those who cling to it are **b**.
3:33 the wicked, but He **b** the home of the
5:18 own fountain be **b** and enjoy the girl you
8:32 sons, listen to Me: **b** are those who keep
8:34 **B** is the person who listens to Me,
10:6 **B** cover on the head of the righteous,
10:7 the righteous is **b**, but the name of the
10:22 It is the LORD's **b** that makes a person
11:11 With the **b** of the upright a city is
11:26 grain, but a **b** will be upon the head of
14:21 neighbor sins, but **b** is the one who is
16:20 word prospers, and **b** is the one who trusts
20:7 his integrity—**b** are his children after
20:21 will never be **b** in the end.
22:9 generous will be **b**, for he has shared his
24:25 guilty and a great **b** will come upon them.
27:14 loud voice—his **b** is considered a curse.
28:14 **B** is the one who is always fearful
28:20 man has many **b**, but the anyone in a
29:18 run wild, but **b** are those who keep God's
30:11 father and does not **b** his mother.
31:28 stand up and **b** her; her husband too; in

BLOOD
1:16 and hurry to shed **b**, for it does no good to
30:33 a nose produces **b**, so stirring up anger

BLOODTHIRSTY
29:10 **B** men hate an innocent person, but

BODY
3:8 Then your **b** will have healing and your
4:22 who find them, and they heal the whole **b**.
5:11 end comes, when your **b** and flesh are consumed,
14:30 makes for a healthy **b**, but jealousy is like
15:30 the heart; good news refreshes the **b**.
16:24 sweet to the spirit and healthy for the **b**.

BONE
3:8 healing and your **b** will have nourishment.
12:4 him is like **b** cancer.
14:30 jealousy is like a **b** cancer.
25:15 a ruler, and a soft tongue can break **b**.

BOUNDARY
22:28 move an ancient **b** marker that your
23:10 move an ancient **b** marker or enter the

BRAG
20:14 as he goes away, he **b** about his bargain
25:6 Do not **b** about yourself before a king or
25:14 so is the man who **b** about a gift that he
27:1 Do not **b** about tomorrow, because you do

BREAD
6:26 is only a loaf of **b**, but a married woman
9:5 says: Come, eat my **b** and drink the wine I
17:1 a bite of dry **b** eaten in peace than a
28:21 men will turn on you even for a piece of **b**.
31:27 does not eat the **b** of idleness.

BREAK
15:4 a deceitful tongue **b** the spirit.
25:15 a soft tongue can **b** bones.

BRIBE
6:35 and the largest **b** will not satisfy him.
15:27 but whoever hates **b** will live.
17:8 A **b** seems like a jewel to the one who
17:23 secretly accepts a **b** to corrupt the ways of
21:14 anger, and a secret **b** calms great fury.

BROKEN
18:14 but who can bear a **b** spirit?
25:19 Like a **b** tooth and a lame foot, so is

BROTHER
17:2 will share the inheritance with the **b**.
17:17 loves, and a **b** is born to share trouble.
18:19 An offended **b** is more resistant than a
18:24 loving friend who sticks closer than a **b**.
19:7 All the **b** of a poor man hate him—how
27:10 do not go to your **b** home when you are in
27:10 is better than a **b** far away.

BUILD
9:1 Wisdom has **b** her house; she has carved out
14:1 The wisest of women **b** up her home, but a
17:19 a quarrel; whoever **b** his city gate high
24:3 A house is **b** with wisdom; its foundation is
24:27 then afterwards, **b** your house.
29:4 of justice a king **b** up a country, but a man

BUM
6:6 the ant, you lazy **b**; watch its ways and become
6:9 How long will you lie there, you lazy **b**?

BUY, BUYER
20:14 says the **b**; then, as he goes away, he brags
23:23 **B** truth (and do not sell it), that is, **b**
31:16 out a field and **b** it; she plants a vineyard

BYSTANDER
26:17 ears, so is a **b** who gets involved in

CALAMITY
1:26 laugh at your **c**; I will make fun of you
1:27 storm, and when **c** strikes you like a

CALM
15:18 holds his temper **c** disputes.
16:14 but a wise man can **c** him down.
21:14 given in secret **c** anger, and a secret
21:14 and a secret bribe **c** great fury.

CARELESS
12:18 **C** words stab like a sword, but the words
14:16 evil, but a fool is **c** and overconfident.

CASE
18:17 first to state his **c** seems right—until
22:23 will plead their **c** and will take the lives of
23:11 He will plead their **c** against you.

CAUGHT
3:26 and He will keep your foot from getting **c**.
5:22 and he will be **c** in the ropes of his own
6:2 your own mouth, **c** by your own promise.
6:31 but when he is **c**, he has to repay it seven

CHAIN
1:9 head and a golden **c** around your neck.

CHANGE
24:21 always insist upon **c**, because disaster will

CHARACTER
12:4 with strength of **c** is the crown of her
31:10 Who can find a wife with strength of **c**?

CHARM
7:21 all her seductive **c** she persuades him; with
31:30 **c** is deceptive, and beauty evaporates, but

CHEERFUL
15:13 heart makes a **c** face, but with a
15:15 person, but a **c** heart has a continual
16:15 When the king is **c** there is life, and his

CHILD, CHILDREN
4:3 a tender and only **c** of my mother.
14:26 confidence, and His **c** will have a place
15:20 happy, but a foolish **c** despises its mother.
17:6 and parents are the glory of their **c**.
20:7 blessed are his **c** after him!
20:11 a **c** makes himself known by his actions,
22:6 Train a **c** in the way he should go, and even
22:15 attached to a **c** heart; spanking will
23:13 to discipline a **c**; if you spank him he will
29:15 an undisciplined **c** disgraces his mother.
31:28 Her **c** stand up and bless her; her husband

CHOOSE
1:29 and did not **c** the fear of the LORD.
3:31 man, and do not **c** any of his ways, for the

CITY
10:15 is his strong **c**; poverty ruins the poor.
11:10 righteous prosper, a **c** is glad; when the
11:11 of the upright a **c** is exalted, but by the
16:32 to be even-tempered than to capture a **c**.
18:11 wealth is his strong **c** and is like a high
18:19 than a strong **c**, and disputes are like the
21:22 A wise man attacks a **c** of warriors and pulls
25:28 Like a **c** broken into and left without a
29:8 an uproar in a **c**, but the wise turn away

CLEANSE
20:30 Brutal beatings **c** away wickedness; such
20:30 such beatings **c** the innermost being.

CLEVER
1:6 a proverb and a **c** saying, to understand the

CLING
3:18 and those who **c** to it are blessed.
4:4 me: Let your heart **c** to my words; keep my
4:13 **C** to discipline; do not relax your grip on

CLOTHES, CLOTHING
6:27 fire in his lap without burning his **c**?
27:26 you with **c**, and the money from the male
31:21 whole family has a double layer of **c**.
31:22 for herself; her **c** are made of linen and

COALS
6:28 walk on red-hot **c** without burning his feet?
25:22 will heap burning **c** on his head, and the
26:21 fuels burning **c** and wood fuels fire, so the

COMMANDS
2:1 and treasure my **c** within you, paying
3:1 and keep my **c** in mind, because they will
4:4 my words; keep my **c** so that you may live:
7:1 and treasure my **c** that are within you.
7:2 Keep my **c** so that you may live, and keep
10:8 wise accepts **c**, but the one who talks

COMPANY
22:24 and never keep **c** with a hothead, or you

COMPASSION
12:10 animals, but the **c** of the wicked person
28:13 and abandons them receives **c**.

CONCEITED
16:5 Everyone with a **c** heart is disgusting to
21:4 A **c** look and a proud heart, which are
21:24 A proud, **c** person is called a mocker; he
30:13 about and how **c** he is.

CONDEMNED
12:2 but the LORD **c** everyone who schemes.
17:15 wicked and whoever **c** the righteous—
24:24 by people and **c** by nations, but it will

CONFESSES
28:13 but whoever **c** and abandons them receives

CONFIDENCE
3:26 LORD will be your **c** and He will keep
11:7 moreover his **c** in strength vanishes.
14:26 there is strong **c**, and His children
25:19 foot, so is **c** in an unfaithful person

CONFLICT
6:14 evil all the time; he spreads **c**.
6:19 person who spreads **c** among brothers.
22:10 out a mocker, and **c** will leave;

CONSIDER, CONSIDERATION
3:7 Do not **c** yourself wise; fear the LORD and
6:6 **C** the ant, you lazy bum; watch its ways
12:15 A stubborn fool **c** his own way the right
15:28 carefully **c** how to answer, but the mouth
17:28 silent; he is **c** intelligent if he keeps
21:10 evil and has no **c** for his neighbor.
21:12 One wisely **c** the house of the wicked; He
27:14 his blessing is **c** a curse.

CONSTRUCTIVE CRITICISM
13:18 attention to **c** criticism will be
25:12 fine gold, so **c** criticism is to the

CONTEMPT
18:3 wickedness comes, **c** also comes, and

CONTROL
12:24 hands gain **c**, but lazy hands do slave
17:14 stop before the argument gets out of **c**.
21:1 under the LORD's **c**; He turns them in any
27:16 Anyone who can **c** her can control the wind;

CONVICT
24:25 for those who **c** the guilty and a great

CORRECT, CORRECTION
5:12 heart despised **c**; I didn't listen to
9:7 Whoever a **c** mocker receives abuse, and
12:1 but whoever hates **c** is a dumb animal.
29:17 **C** your son and he will give you peace of

CORRUPT
17:23 accepts a bribe to **c** the ways of justice.

COST
7:23 realize that it will **c** him his life.
23:7 as he calculates the **c** to himself, this is

COUNTRY
28:2 When a **c** is in revolt it has many rulers,
29:4 a king builds up a **c**, but a man who

COURT
25:8 in a hurry to go to **c**, for what will you do
29:9 a wise man goes to **c** with a stubborn fool,

COVENANT
2:17 who forgets the **c** with her God.

COVERS
10:12 quarrels, but love **c** every wrong.
28:13 Whoever **c** over his sins does not prosper,

CRAVE
13:4 A lazy person **c** food and there is none, but
23:3 appetite; do not **c** his delicacies, for this
23:6 stingy and do not **c** his delicacies, for as

CRIME
29:16 wicked increase, **c** increases, but the

CRISIS
24:10 If you faint in a **c**, you reveal that you
25:19 in an unfaithful person in a time of **c**.

CRITICISM
13:18 to constructive **c** will be honored.
25:12 so constructive **c** is to the ear of one
27:5 Open **c** is better than unexpressed love.

CROOKED
2:15 their paths are **c**, and their ways are
8:8 nothing twisted or **c** in it; all of it is
21:8 of the guilty is **c**, but the behavior of

CROWN
4:9 your head; it will hand you a beautiful **c**.
12:4 of character is the **c** of her husband, but
14:24 The **c** of the wise is their wealth; the
16:31 hair is a beautiful **c** found in a righteous
17:6 are the **c** of grandparents, and parents are

CRUEL
5:9 your years to some **c** person; or strangers
11:17 himself, but a **c** man hurts himself.
27:4 Anger is **c** and fury is overwhelming, but
CURSE
11:26 People will **c** the one who hoards grain, but
20:20 Whoever **c** his father and mother, his lamp
24:24 innocent" will be **c** by people and condemned
26:2 so a hastily spoken **c** does not come to rest.
27:14 voice—his blessing is considered a **c**.
28:27 ignores the poor receives many **c**.
30:10 master or he will **c** you and you will be
30:11 kind of person who **c** his father and does

DARK, DARKEST, DARKNESS
2:13 walk the ways of **d**, from those who enjoy
4:19 is like deep **d**; they do not know what
7:9 the evening, in the **d** hours of the night.
7:27 down to the **d** vaults of death.
20:20 his lamp will be snuffed out in total **d**.
31:15 up while it is still **d** and gives food to her
DAUGHTERS
30:15 leech has two **d**—Give! and Give!
DAVID
1:1 of Solomon son of **D**, king of Israel, given
DEAL
11:15 the closing of a **d** remains secure.
17:18 good sense closes a **d** with a handshake; he
22:26 those who make a **d** with a handshake, among
DEATH
10:2 no one, but righteousness rescues from **d**.
11:4 saves from **d**; the righteousness of the
11:7 At the **d** of the wicked person, hope vanishes;
11:19 so whoever pursues evil finds his own **d**.
12:28 and along its path there is no eternal **d**.
13:14 to turn one away from the grasp of **d**.
14:12 to a man, but eventually it ends in **d**.
14:27 to turn one away from the grasp of **d**.
14:32 but even in his **d** a righteous person has a
16:14 anger announces **d**, but a wise man can calm
16:25 to a man, but eventually it ends in **d**.
18:21 power of life and **d**, and those who love to
19:18 do not be the one responsible for his **d**.
21:6 are wasting time; they are looking for **d**.
24:11 condemned to **d**, and spare those staggering
DECEIT, DECEITFUL,
  DECEIVE, DECEPTIVE
4:24 mouth and put **d** speech far away from
12:20 **D** is in the heart of those who plan evil,
15:4 of life, but a **d** tongue breaks the
24:28 reason, and do not **d** anyone with your
26:24 his speech, but inside he holds on to **d**.
31:30 Charm is **d**, and beauty evaporates, but
DEEP
1:2 to understand **d** thoughts, to acquire the
3:20 By His Knowledge the **d** waters were divided
4:19 the wicked is like **d** darkness; they do not
4:21 things; keep them **d** within your heart,
18:4 mouth are like **d** waters; the fountain of
19:15 throws one into a **d** sleep, and an idle person
20:5 heart is like **d** waters, but a person who
22:14 woman is a **d** pit; the one who is cursed by
23:27 A prostitute is a **d** pit, and a loose woman is
25:3 high heavens and the **d** earth, so the mind of
DEFEND
31:9 judge fairly, and **d** the rights of the
DEPRESSION
15:13 face, but with a heartache comes **d**.
17:22 medicine, but **d** drains one's strength.
DESCEND
5:5 Her feet **d** to death; her steps lead
DESCENDANTS
11:21 but the **d** of the righteous will escape.
DESIRE
6:25 Do not **d** her beauty in your heart; do not
10:3 rejects the **d** of the wicked.
10:24 grants the **d** of the righteous.
11:23 The **d** of the righteous ends only in good,
21:10 of a wicked person **d** evil and has no
21:25 The **d** of a lazy person will kill him,
DESPISE
1:7 and discipline are **d** by stubborn fools.
1:30 my advice; they **d** my every warning.
5:12 and how my heart **d** correction; I didn't
6:30 Nobody **d** a thief who is hungry when
11:12 A person who **d** a neighbor has no sense,
13:13 Whoever **d** God's word will pay the
15:5 A stubborn fool **d** his father's discipline,

15:32 ignores discipline **d** himself, but the one
23:9 because he will **d** the wisdom of your words.
23:22 son, and do not **d** your mother just because
DESTROY, DESTRUCTION
1:32 indifference, fools **d** themselves; but
3:25 nor of the **d** of the wicked when it
14:11 wicked will be **d**, but the tent of the
18:12 Before a man's heart is proud, but
22:8 this weapon of his own fury will be **d**.
26:10 many people who **d** everything, so is one
DETERMINE
8:28 above, when He **d** the currents in the
16:33 but the LORD **d** every outcome.
DICE
16:33 The **d** are thrown, but the LORD determines
DIE
5:23 his own sin; he will **d** for his lack of
10:21 but stubborn fools **d** because they have no
15:10 path; anyone who hates a warning will **d**.
23:13 a child; if you spank him he will not **d**.
30:7 from me before I **d**: Keep vanity and lies far
DIRECTION, DIRECTS
1:5 person will gain **d** to understand a
11:14 when there is no **d**, but with many
16:9 but the LORD **d** his steps.
20:24 is the One who **d** a man's steps; how then
21:1 turns them in any **d** He chooses.
23:19 keep your mind going in the right **d**.
DISASTER
1:33 and will be free from the dread of **d**.
6:15 That is why **d** will come on him suddenly;
13:21 **D** hunts down sinners, but the righteous
16:18 Pride precedes a **d**, and an arrogant
24:16 however, in a **d**, wicked people fall.
24:22 change, because **d** will come on them
28:14 whoever is hard-hearted falls into **d**.
DISCIPLINE
1:2 grasp wisdom and **d**, to understand deep
1:7 wisdom and **d** are despised by stubborn
1:8 to your father's **d** and do not neglect
3:11 Do not reject the **d** of the LORD, my son,
4:13 Cling to **d**; do not relax your grip on it;
5:12 Oh, how I hated **d** and how my heart
8:33 Listen to **d** and become wise.
10:17 Whoever practices **d** is on the way to
12:1 Whoever loves **d** loves to learn, but
13:24 loves his son **d** him from early on.
15:32 Whoever ignores **d** despises himself, but
15:33 of the LORD is **d** leading to wisdom,
19:18 **D** your son while there is still hope;
19:20 advice and accept **d** so that you may be
23:13 not hesitate to **d** a child; if you spank
DISGRACE
3:35 inherit honor, but fools will bear **d**.
6:33 dishonor, and his **d** will not be blotted
13:5 wicked person behaves with shame and **d**.
14:34 but sin is a **d** in any society.
18:3 comes, and insult comes along with **d**.
19:26 away his mother brings shame and **d**.
DISGUSTING
3:32 devious person is **d** to the LORD; His
8:7 and wickedness is **d** to my lips;
11:1 scales are **d** to the LORD, but accurate
11:20 in heart are **d** to the LORD, but He is
12:22 Lips that lie are **d** to the LORD, but
15:26 evil people are **d** to the LORD, but
16:5 heart is **d** to the LORD; certainly
16:12 Wrongdoing is **d** to kings, because a
20:23 of weights is **d** to the LORD, and
24:9 and a mocker is **d** to everyone.
26:25 of the seven **d** things in his heart.
28:9 teaching, even his prayer is **d**.
29:27 An unjust man is **d** to righteous people,
29:27 who is upright is **d** to the wicked.
DISHONEST
6:19 to do wrong, a **d** witness spitting out
11:1 **D** scales are disgusting to the LORD, but
11:18 person earns **d** wages, but whoever
14:5 not lie, but a **d** witness breathes lies.
20:23 to the LORD, and **d** scales are no good.
DISPUTE
15:18 but one who holds his temper calms **d**.
18:19 a strong city, and **d** are like the locked
26:21 fire, so the quarrelsome man fuels a **d**.
DOE
5:19 were young, a loving **d** and a graceful deer.
DOG
26:11 As a **d** goes back to his vomit, so a fool
26:17 Like grabbing a **d** by the ears, so is a

DONKEY
26:3 bridle is for the **d**, and a rod is for the
DOUBLE, DOUBLE-DEALING
20:10 from my sin" A **d** standard of weights and
20:23 A **d** standard of weights is disgusting to
28:6 integrity than to be rich and **d**.
DOWNFALL
29:16 but the righteous will witness their **d**.
DREAD
1:33 be free from the **d** of disaster.
10:24 which the wicked **d** happens to him, but
DRIFTER
6:11 upon you like a **d**, and your need will
24:34 upon you like a **d**, and your need will
26:10 so is one who hires fools or **d**.
DRINK
5:15 **D** water out of your own cistern and running
7:18 Come, let's **d** our fill of love till morning;
9:5 eat my bread and **d** the wine I have mixed;
23:7 tells you, Eat and **d**, but he doesn't really
23:20 with those who **d** too much wine, with those
23:30 Those who **d** glass after glass of wine;
23:35 I wake up I'm going to look for another **d**.
25:21 him some water to **d**; for in this way you
31:4 is not for kings to **d** wine, that is, for
31:5 otherwise, they **d** and forget what
31:7 Such a person **d** and forgets his poverty and
DRIPPING
19:13 like constantly **d** water.
27:15 Constantly **d** water on a rainy day is like
DRUNK
23:21 meat, because both a **d** and a glutton will
26:9 a thorn stuck in a **d** hand, so is a proverb
DUMB
12:1 correction is a **d** animal.
30:2 I'm more like a **d** animal than a man, and I

EAGLE
23:5 for itself like an **e** flying off into the sky.
30:19 understand: how an **e** making its way
EARNS
11:18 A wicked person **e** dishonest wages, but
11:18 righteousness **e** honest pay.
EAT
1:31 They will **e** the fruit of their lifestyle and
4:17 stumble, for they **e** food obtained through
12:9 than to act important and have nothing to **e**.
13:2 A man **e** well as a result of his speaking
13:25 The righteous person **e** to satisfy his
18:21 to talk will have to **e** their own words.
20:13 eyes open and you will have plenty to **e**.
23:1 When you sit down to **e** with a ruler, pay
23:6 Do not **e** the food of one who is stingy and do
23:20 with those who **e** too much meat, because
24:13 **E** honey, my son, because it is good; honey
25:16 When you find honey, **e** only as much as you
25:21 him some food to **e**, and if he is thirsty, give
27:18 of a fig tree can **e** its fruit, and whoever
28:19 will have plenty to **e**; but whoever chases
30:20 woman: She **e** and wipes her mouth and says, I
31:27 and she does not **e** the bread of idleness.
ELDERS
31:23 he sits with the **e** of the land.
EMBRACE
4:8 you honor when you **e** it; it will give you
EMOTIONS
29:11 expresses all his **e**, but a wise person
EMPTY
13:25 but the belly of the wicked is always **e**.
ENCOURAGING
12:25 him down, but an **e** word makes him
END
5:4 than oil, but in the **e** she is as bitter as
5:11 groan when your **e** comes, when your body
11:23 of the righteous **e** only in good, but the hope
11:23 hope of the wicked **e** only in fury.
14:12 but eventually it **e** in death.
14:13 ache, and joy can **e** in grief.
16:25 but eventually it **e** in death.
18:18 Flipping a coin **e** quarrels and settles
20:13 sleep or you will **e** up poor; keep your eyes
20:21 the beginning will never be blessed in the **e**.
21:5 in a hurry certainly **e** up in poverty.
25:8 will you do in the **e** if your neighbor
ENDURE
18:14 A man's spirit can **e** sickness, but who can
19:21 heart, but the advice of the LORD will **e**.

ENEMY
16:7 He makes even his e to be at peace with
24:17 be happy when your e fall and do not feel
25:21 If your e is hungry, give him some food to
27:6 to help, but an e kisses are too much to

ENTRANCE
1:21 calls out; at the e to the city she
8:3 the city; at the e wisdom sings its

ENTRUST
16:3 E your works to the LORD, and your plans

ENVY
3:31 Do not e a violent man, and do not choose
23:17 Do not e sinners in your heart, but rather,
24:1 Do not e evil men or wish you were with them,
24:19 evildoers; do not e wicked people, because

ESCAPE
6:29 who touch her will e punishment.
11:21 the descendants of the righteous will e.
12:13 a righteous person e from trouble.
17:5 distress will not e punishment.
19:5 and one who utters lies will not e.
28:20 get rich will not e punishment.

EVEN-TEMPERED
16:32 better to be than to capture a
17:27 a man who has understanding is e.

EVIL
1:16 they rush to do e and hurry to shed blood,
4:27 the right or to the left; walk away from e!
8:13 the LORD is to hate e; I hate pride,
11:21 Certainly an e person will not go unpunished,
11:27 whoever looks for e finds it.
15:3 watching the e and the good.
17:13 Whoever pays back e for good—e will
28:10 the upright into e will fall into his own pit,
29:6 To an e man sin is bait in a trap, but a

FACE
15:13 makes a cheerful f, but with a heartache
27:19 As a f is reflected in water, so a person is

FAITHFUL, FAITHFULNESS
14:22 are merciful and f plan good?
16:6 By mercy and f guilt is atoned for,

FALL
11:5 but the wicked f by his own wickedness.
11:14 A nation will f when there is no direction,
16:18 attitude precedes a f; better to be humble
24:16 righteous person may f seven times—but he
24:17 when your enemies f and do not feel glad
26:27 digs a pit with f into it; whoever rolls a

FALSE
25:18 the man who gives f testimony against his

FAMILY
11:29 trouble upon his f inherits only wind,
12:7 no more, but the f of the righteous
15:27 trouble upon his f, but whoever hates
17:1 in peace than a f feast filled with strife.
27:27 you, to feed your f, and to keep your
31:15 gives food to her f and a share of food to

FAVOR
3:4 Then you will find f and much success in the
12:2 good person obtains f from the LORD, but
13:15 Good sense brings f, but the way of the
16:15 is life, and his f is like a cloud bringing
18:22 and has obtained f from the LORD.

FEAR, FEARFUL
1:7 The f of the LORD is the beginning of
8:13 The f of the LORD is to hate evil; I hate
9:10 The f of the LORD is the beginning of wisdom,
10:27 The f of the LORD lengthens the number
13:13 but the one who f His law will be rewarded.
14:2 Whoever lives right f the LORD, but the
14:27 The f of the LORD is a fountain of life to
16:6 and by the f of the LORD evil is avoided.
19:23 The f of the LORD leads to life, and such a
24:21 The LORD, my son (f the king as well);
28:14 one who is always f of sin but whoever
31:21 She does not f for her family when it snows
31:30 a woman who has the f of the LORD—she is

FEED
10:21 of the righteous f many, but stubborn fools
15:14 the mouth of fools f stupidity.
30:8 poverty or riches; f me only the food I

FEEL
21:26 all day long he f greedy, but a righteous
23:35 strike me, but I f no pain; they beat me,
24:17 fall and do not f glad when they stumble,
30:9 food I need or I may f satisfied and deny
31:6 and wine to one who f bitter.

FIGHT
15:18 hothead stirs up a f, but one who holds his
20:3 but any stubborn fool can start a f.
28:25 person stirs up a f, but whoever trusts the
29:22 man stirs up a f, and a hothead does much
30:33 blood, so stirring up anger produces a f.

FIRE
6:27 Can a man carry f in his lap without burning
16:27 trouble, and his speech is like a burning f.
17:3 purifies hearts by f is the LORD.
26:20 Without wood a f goes out, and without gossip
26:21 and wood fuels f, so the quarrelsome man
30:16 enough water and a f that does not say,

FIRST
3:9 wealth and with the f and best part of all
8:23 appointed, from the f, before the earth
8:26 or fields or the f dust of the world.
18:17 The f to state his case seems right—

FLATTERS
28:23 than the one who f with his tongue.
29:5 A man who f his neighbor is spreading a

FLEES
28:1 wicked person f when no one is chasing him,

FLOCK
27:23 condition of your f, and pay close attention

FOG
25:14 Like a dense f or a dust storm, so is the

FOLLOW
1:15 My son, do not f them in their way; do not
7:22 Immediately he f her, like a steer on its

FOOD
6:8 it stores its f supply, at harvest time it
13:4 A lazy person craves f and there is none, but
19:24 his fork in his f; he doesn't even bring it
20:17 F gained dishonestly tastes sweet to a man,
21:17 loves wine and rich f will not become rich.
22:9 he has shared his f with the poor.
23:6 Do not eat the f of one who is stingy and do
27:7 hungry, even bitter f tastes sweet.
30:8 feed me only the f I need or I may feel

FOOLISH, FOOLISHLY, FOOLISHNESS
17:25 A f son is a heartache to his father and
19:13 A f son ruins his father, and a quarreling
24:9 F scheming is sinful, and a mocker is
10:8 the one who talks f will be thrown down
22:15 F is firmly attached to a child's

FOREIGNER
20:16 who makes a loan in behalf of a f.
27:13 who makes a loan in behalf of a f.

FORESIGHT
1:4 knowledge and f to the young—a wise
2:11 to your soul; f will protect you;
3:21 wisdom and f, then they will mean life
5:2 you may act with f and speak with
8:12 insight, and I acquire knowledge and f.

FOREVER
6:21 them on your heart f; hang them around
12:19 of truth lasts f, but lies last only a
27:24 for wealth is not f, nor does a crown

FORGET
2:17 and who f the covenant with her God
3:1 My son, do not f my teaching, and keep my
4:5 Do not f and do not turn away from the
31:5 they drink and f what they have decreed
31:7 person drinks and f his poverty and does

FORGIVENESS, FORGIVES
14:9 but there is f among the upright.
17:9 Whoever f an offense seeks love, but

FORTRESS
10:29 of the LORD is a f for the innocent but a

FOUNDATION
3:19 the LORD laid the f of the earth and by
8:29 He traced the f of the earth—then I
10:25 righteous person has an everlasting f.
24:3 with wisdom; its f is understanding;

FOUR
30:15 are never satisfied, f that never say, Enough!
30:18 for me, even f which I cannot understand:
30:21 to tremble, even f it cannot bear up under: a
30:24 F things on earth are small, yet they are
30:29 like a king even f that march like a king:

FRIEND
2:17 leaves the closest f of her youth
16:28 and a gossip separates the closest of f.
17:17 A f always loves, and a brother is born to
17:18 a loan in the presence of his f.
18:24 A man and his f can destroy one another,
18:24 there is a loving f who sticks closer than
19:4 but a poor person is separated from his f.

FIGHT (col 3)
19:4 Wealth adds many f, but a poor person is
19:7 much more do his f keep their distance
22:24 Do not be a f of one who has a bad temper
27:6 Wounds made by a f are intended to help,
27:9 the sweetness of a f is a fragrant forest.
27:10 Do not abandon your f or your father's
27:14 Whoever blesses his f early in the morning

FRUIT
1:31 They will eat the f of their lifestyle and
11:30 The f of the righteous is a tree of life,
11:30 tree can eat its f, and whoever protects his

FUELS
26:21 As charcoal f burning coals and wood f
26:21 the quarrelsome man f a dispute.

FUN
1:11 innocent just for f; we'll swallow them alive
1:26 calamity; I will make f of you when panic
14:9 Stubborn fools make f of guilt, but there is
15:21 Stupidity is f to the one without much sense,
17:5 Whoever makes f of a poor person insults
30:17 The eye that makes f of a father and hates to

FURY
6:34 arouses a husband's f and the husband will
11:4 help on the Day of F, but righteousness
11:23 but the hope of the wicked ends only in f.
21:14 anger, and a secret bribe calms great f.
22:8 weapon of his own f will be destroyed.
27:4 Anger is cruel and f is overwhelming, but who

FUTURE
23:18 There is indeed a f, and your hope will
24:14 it, then there is a f, and your hope will
24:20 evil person has no f, and the lamp of the
31:25 and nobility, and she smiles at the f.

GAINS
1:19 greedy for unjust g; it takes away his life.
10:2 Treasures g dishonestly profit no one, but
11:16 but ruthless men g riches.
12:24 Hardworking hands g control, but lazy hands
15:27 is greedy for unjust g brings trouble upon
16:8 a few possessions g honestly than many
16:16 much better it is to g wisdom than gold, and
16:16 than gold, and the g of understanding
19:8 A person who g sense loves himself; one who
20:17 Food g dishonestly tastes sweet to a man,
28:16 who hate unjust g will live longer.
29:23 but a humble spirit g honor.

GARLAND
1:9 are a graceful g on your head and a
4:9 you a graceful g for your head; it will

GARMENT
20:16 Hold on to the g of one who guarantees a
27:13 Hold on to the g of one who guarantees a
30:4 Who has wrapped up water in a g?
31:24 She makes linen g and sells them and

GATE
14:19 the wicked at the g of the righteous.
17:19 builds his city g high gate invites
22:22 at the city g, because the LORD will plead
24:7 fool; at the city g he does not open his
31:23 known at the city g when he sits with the

GEMS
20:15 but what precious g are the lips of

GENEROUS
11:25 A g person will be made rich, and whoever
19:6 the kindness of a g person, and everyone
22:9 Whoever is g will be blessed, for he has

GENTLE
15:1 A g answer turns away rage, but a harsh

GIFT, GIFTED
14:18 Gullible people are g with stupidity, but
18:16 A g opens doors for the giver and brings him
19:6 everyone is a friend to a man who gives g.
21:14 A g given in secret calms anger, and a
25:14 who brags about a g that he does not give.

GIRL
5:18 and enjoy the g you married when you were
9:3 out her servant g; she calls from the
27:27 keep your servant g alive.
31:15 and a share of food to her servant g.

GLAD
11:10 prosper, a city is g; when the wicked perish,
23:25 and your mother be g, and may she who gave
24:17 fall and do not feel g when they stumble, or
27:9 make the heart g, but the sweetness of a
27:11 make my heart g, so I can answer anyone
29:6 righteous person runs away from it and is g.

GLORY
17:6 and parents are the **g** of their children.
20:29 While the **g** of young men is their strength,
25:2 It is the **g** of God to hide things, but the
25:2 things, but the **g** of kings to investigate
28:12 there is great **g**, but when the wicked rise,

GLUTTON
23:21 both a drunk and a **g** will become poor, and
28:7 associates with **g** disgraces his father.

GOAT
30:31 rooster or a male **g**, and a king at the head

GOLD, GOLDEN
3:14 silver; its yield is better than fine **g**.
8:10 rather than fine **g**, because wisdom is better
11:22 Like a **g** ring in a pig's snout, so is a
16:16 to gain wisdom than **g**, and the gaining of
17:3 and the smelter for **g**, but the One who
25:11 Like **g** apples in silver settings, so is

GOOD
10:32 righteous announce **g** will, but the mouth of
11:22 woman who lacks **g** taste.
13:21 but the righteous are rewarded with **g**.
14:22 ones who are merciful and faithful plan **g**?
15:3 are everywhere, watching the evil and the **g**.
15:23 own mouth, and a timely word—oh, how **g**!
17:13 pays back evil for **g**—evil will never leave
18:5 It is not **g** to be partial toward the wicked,
18:22 wife finds something **g** and has obtained
20:23 to the LORD, and dishonest scales are no **g**.
28:21 It is not **g** to play favorites because some

GOOD-FOR-NOTHING
6:12 A **g** scoundrel is a man who has a

GOSSIP
11:13 Whoever **g** gives away secrets, but whoever
16:28 quarrels, and a **g** separates the closest of
18:8 The words of a **g** are swallowed greedily,
20:19 goes around as a **g** tells secrets; do not

GRACIOUS
3:34 the mockers, He is **g** to the humble.
11:16 A **g** woman wins respect, but ruthless men
22:11 whose speech is **g**, has a king as his

GRANDCHILDREN
13:22 leaves an inheritance to his **g**, but the
17:6 **G** are the crown of grandparents, and

GRANDPARENTS
17:6 Grandchildren are the crown of **g**, and

GRASP
1:2 given in order to **g** wisdom and discipline,
13:14 one away from the **g** of death.
14:27 one away from the **g** of death.
17:16 have a mind to **g** anything?
24:7 are beyond the **g** of a stubborn fool; at the

GRAVE
1:12 them alive like the **g**, like those in good
28:17 down to his **g**—no one should help him.
30:16 the **g** and a barren womb; a land that never

GREED, GREEDY
1:19 to everyone who is **g** for unjust gain; it
11:6 the treacherous are trapped by their own **g**.
15:27 Whoever is **g** for unjust gain brings trouble
21:26 day long he feels **g**, but a righteous person
28:25 A **g** person stirs up a fight, but whoever

GRIEF
10:1 foolish son brings **g** to his mother.
14:13 a heart can ache, and joy can end in **g**.
17:21 of a fool has **g**, and the father of a godless
17:25 father and bitter **g** to his mother.

GUARANTEE
6:1 My son, if you **g** a loan for your
11:15 Whoever **g** a stranger's loan will get
17:18 a handshake; he **g** a loan in the
20:16 of one who **g** a stranger's loan, and
22:26 among those who **g** other people's loans.
27:13 of one who **g** a stranger's loan, and

GUARD
2:8 in order to **g** those on paths of justice and
2:11 understanding will **g** you.
4:23 than anything else, **g** your heart, because
7:5 in order to **g** yourself from the adulterous
19:8 himself; one who **g** understanding finds
21:23 Whoever **g** his mouth and his tongue keeps
22:5 of him; whoever **g** himself will stay far
24:12 And won't He who **g** your soul know it?

GUILT, GUILTY
14:9 fools make fun of **g**, but there is
16:6 and faithfulness **g** is atoned for, and by the
21:8 The way of the **g** is crooked, but the
24:24 Whoever says to the **g** You are innocent"
24:25 who convict the **g** and a great blessing will

28:17 burdened with the **g** of murder will be a
30:10 he will curse you and you will be found **g**.

HAND
1:24 I stretched out my **h** to you (but no one
3:16 in wisdom's left **h** are riches and honor.
6:5 a gazelle from the **h** of the hunter and like a
6:5 like a bird from the **h** of the hunter.
6:17 a lying tongue, and **h** that kill innocent
10:4 Lazy **h** bring poverty, but hardworking **h**
12:24 Hardworking **h** gain control, but lazy **h** do
14:1 a stupid one tears it down with her own **h**.
17:16 have money in his **h** to acquire wisdom when
21:25 him, because his **h** refuse to work; all day
30:4 has gathered the wind in the palm of His **h**?
30:32 had better put your **h** over your mouth, for
31:20 She opens her **h** to the oppressed and

HANDSHAKE
6:1 a stranger with a **h**, you are trapped by
17:18 a deal with a **h**; he guarantees a loan in
22:26 make deals with a **h**, among those who

HARD
5:10 will have to work **h** in a pagan's house.
10:22 a person rich, and **h** work adds nothing to it.
14:23 In all **h** work there is always something

HARD-HEARTED
28:14 but whoever is **h** falls into disaster.

HARDWORKING
10:4 poverty, but **h** hands bring riches; he
12:24 **H** hands gain control, but lazy hands
12:27 his prey, but a **h** person becomes
13:4 the appetite of **h** people is satisfied.
21:5 The plans of a **h** person certainly lead

HARM
3:30 a man for no reason if he has done you no **h**.
12:21 No lasting **h** comes to the righteous, but
19:23 a person will rest easy without suffering **h**.

HARVEST
10:5 he who sleeps at **h** time brings shame.
10:16 is life; the **h** of the wicked is sin.
14:4 strength of an ox produces plentiful **h**.
25:13 of snow on a **h** day, so is the
26:1 and rain at **h** time, so honor is just not

HATE, HATRED
1:29 me, because they **h** knowledge and did not
5:12 will say, Oh, how I **h** discipline and how
6:16 that the LORD **h**, even seven that are
8:13 is to **h** evil; I **h** pride, arrogance, evil
8:36 all those who **h** Me love death.
10:12 **H** starts quarrels, but love covers every
10:18 Whoever conceals **h** has lying lips, and
11:15 trouble, but whoever **h** the closing of a deal
12:1 learn, but whoever **h** correction is a dumb
13:5 A righteous person **h** lying, but a wicked
13:24 to spank his son **h** him, but he who loves him
14:20 A poor person is **h** even by his neighbor, but
15:10 path; anyone who **h** a warning will die.
15:17 is love than juicy steaks where there is **h**.
15:27 family, but whoever **h** bribes will live.
25:17 too much of you and **h** you.
26:24 One filled with **h** disguises it with his
26:26 His **h** is deceitfully hidden, but his
26:28 A lying tongue **h** its victims, and a
28:16 but those who **h** unjust gain will live longer.
29:10 Bloodthirsty men **h** an innocent person, but
29:24 a thief's partner **h** his own life; he will
30:17 fun of a father and **h** to obey a mother will

HEAL, HEALING
3:8 body will have **h** and your bones will have
4:22 find them, and they **h** the whole body.
12:18 sword, but the words of the wise bring **h**.
13:17 trouble, but a dependable envoy brings **h**.

HEALTH, HEALTHY
1:12 like those in good **h** who go down to the pit.
14:30 heart makes for a **h** body, but jealousy is
16:24 to the spirit and **h** for the body.

HEAR
15:23 man is delighted to **h** an answer from his own
15:29 the wicked, but He **h** the prayer of the
20:12 The ear that **h**; the eye that sees: the LORD
22:17 Open your ear and **h** the words of the wise,

HEARTACHE
10:10 his eye causes **h**, and the one who talks
15:13 face, but with a **h** comes depression.
17:25 foolish son is a **h** to his father and

HEAVEN
3:19 by Understanding He established the **h**.
8:27 When He set up the **h** I was there.
25:3 Like the high **h** and the deep earth, so
30:4 Who has gone up to **h** and come down?

HELL
5:5 to death; her steps lead straight to **h**.
7:27 home is the way to **h**, leading down to the
9:18 that her guests are in the depths of **h**.
15:24 turn him away from **h** below.
23:14 yourself, and you will save his soul from **h**.

HELP
9:12 your wisdom will **h** you; if you mock, you
11:4 Riches are of no **h** on the Day of Fury, but
16:21 speaking sweetly **h** others learn.
27:6 are intended to **h**, but an enemy's kisses are
31:12 any good thing; she **h** him and never harms

HERO
16:32 slowly than to be a **h**, and better to be

HIGHWAY
15:19 the road of the upright is an open **h**.
16:17 The **h** of the upright turns away from evil;

HILLS
8:25 before the **h** I was born, when He had not

HIRES
26:10 so is one who **h** fools or drifters.

HOARDS
11:26 curse the one who **h** grain, but a blessing

HOME
3:33 but He blesses the **h** of the righteous.
7:11 and rebellious; her feet will not stay at **h**.
14:1 women builds up her **h**, but a stupid one tears
15:31 warning will be at **h** among the wise.
17:13 for good—evil will never leave his **h**.
19:14 **H** and wealth are inherited from fathers, but
21:9 roof than to share a **h** with a quarreling
24:15 lie in ambush at the **h** of the righteous; do
27:8 its nest, so is a man wandering from his **h**.

HONEST, HONESTY
11:18 righteousness earns **h** pay.
12:22 but those who are **h** are His delight.
13:6 protects the **h** way of life, but wickedness
14:25 An **h** witness saves lives, but one who tells
16:11 **H** balances and scales belong to the LORD;
16:13 Kings delight in **h** words, and whoever
29:14 the poor with **h**, his throne will always be

HONEY, HONEYCOMB
5:3 woman drip with **h**, and her kiss is smoother
16:24 words are like **h** from a **h**—sweet to the
24:13 because it is good; **h** that flows from the
24:13 Eat **h**, my son, because it is good; **h**
24:13 **h** that flows from the **h** tastes sweet
25:16 When you find **h**, eat only as much as you
25:27 Eating too much **h** is not good, and searching
27:7 is full despises **h**, but to one who is hungry,

HONOR, HONORABLE
3:9 **H** the LORD with your wealth and with the
3:16 in wisdom's left hand are riches and **h**.
3:35 wise will inherit **h**, but fools will bear
4:8 it will bring you **h** when you embrace it; it
8:18 I have riches and **h**, lasting wealth and
13:18 to constructive criticism will be **h**.
14:28 population is an **h** for a king, but without
14:31 kind to the needy **h** Him.
15:33 wisdom, and humility comes before **h**.
18:12 is proud, but humility comes before **h**.
20:3 It is **h** for a man to avoid a quarrel,
21:21 mercy will find life, righteousness, and **h**.
25:27 not good, and searching for **h** is not **h**.
26:8 so is giving of **h** to a fool.
27:18 and whoever protects his master is **h**.
29:23 humiliate him, but a humble spirit gains **h**.

HOPE
10:28 The **h** of the righteous leads to joy, but
11:7 the wicked person, **h** vanishes; moreover his
11:23 in good, but the **h** of the wicked ends only in
13:12 **H** delayed makes one sick at heart, but a
23:18 a future, and your **h** will never be cut off.
26:12 there is more **h** for a fool than for him.

HORSE
21:31 The **h** is made ready for the day of battle,
26:3 A whip is for the **h**, a bridle is for the

HOT
19:19 A person who has a **h** temper will pay for it;

HOTHEAD
15:18 A h stirs up a fight, but one who holds
22:24 company with a h, or you will learn his
29:22 up a fight, and a h does much wrong.
HOUSE
3:33 the LORD is on the h of the wicked, but He
5:10 you will have to work hard in a pagan's h.
6:31 must give up all the possessions in his h.
9:1 has built her h; she has carved out her
14:11 The h of the wicked will be destroyed, but
15:6 treasure is in the h of the righteous, but
15:25 LORD tears down the h of the proud, but He
21:12 considers the h of the wicked; He throws the
24:3 A h is built with wisdom; its foundation is
25:17 in your neighbor's h too often; otherwise,
HUMAN
15:11 how much more the h heart!
16:1 heart belong to h, but an answer on the
30:2 I don't even have h understanding, and I
30:12 washed from his own feces [h waste].
HUMBLE
3:34 the mockers, He is gracious to the h.
6:3 hands: Go, h yourself and pester your
11:2 shame, but wisdom remains with the h.
14:21 blessed is the one who is kind to the h.
16:19 fall; better to be h with the lowly than to
29:23 him, but a h spirit gains honor.
HUMILITY
15:33 wisdom, and h comes before honor.
18:12 is proud, but h comes before honor.
22:4 On the heels of h, that is, the fear of
HUNDRED
17:10 more than a h lashes impress a fool.
HUNGER, HUNGRY
6:30 a thief who is h when he steals to satisfy
16:26 because his h drives him on.
19:15 deep sleep, and an idle person will go h
25:21 If your enemy is h, give him some food to
27:7 but to one who is h, even bitter food
HUNTER
6:5 gazelle from the hand of the h
6:5 and like a bird from the hand of the h.
12:27 A lazy h does not catch his prey, but a
HURRY
1:16 rush to do evil and h to shed blood, for it
19:2 and a person in a h makes mistakes.
21:5 is always in a h certainly ends up in
25:8 Do not be in a h to go to court, for what
28:20 but the anyone in a h to get rich will not
28:22 stingy man is in a h to get rich, not
HUSBAND
6:34 arouses a h fury and the h will
7:19 love, for my h not home; he's gone on a
12:4 the crown of her h, but the wife who
31:11 Her h trusts her with all his heart, and
31:23 Her h is known at the city gates when he
HYPOCRISY
11:3 the upright, but h leads the treacherous

IDLE, IDLENESS
14:23 gained, but i talk leads only to poverty.
19:15 deep sleep, and an i person will go hungry.
31:27 and she does not eat the bread of i.
IGNORE
1:25 attention and you i all my advice and you
10:17 life, but whoever i a warning strays.
13:18 to the one who i discipline, but whoever
15:32 Whoever i discipline despises himself, but
28:27 but whoever i the poor receives many
IMAGINATION
18:11 and is like a high wall in his i.
IMPRESS
17:10 A scolding i a person who has
17:10 a hundred lashes i a fool.
INCOME
3:9 the first and best part of all your i.
15:6 along with the i of the wicked.
INCREASE
10:31 of the righteous i wisdom, but the
28:28 but when they perish, the righteous i.
29:2 the righteous i, the people of God
29:16 When the wicked i, crime i, but
INHERIT, INHERITANCE
3:35 The wise will i honor, but fools will bear
8:21 to give an i to those who love me and
11:29 upon his family i only wind, and that
13:22 man leaves an i to his grandchildren,
17:2 will share the i with the brothers.

19:14 and wealth are i from fathers, but a
20:21 An i quickly obtained in the beginning
28:10 the innocent will i good things.
INJUSTICE
13:11 gained through i dwindles away, but
16:8 honestly than many gained through i.
22:8 Whoever sows i will reap trouble, and
INNOCENT
1:11 hide to ambush the i just for fun; we'll
6:17 hands that kill i people; a mind devising
11:20 delighted with those whose ways are i.
17:26 To punish an i person is not good; to
18:5 depriving the i of justice.
28:10 own pit, but the i will inherit good
29:10 men hate an i person, but upright people
INSIGHT
1:4 to give i to gullible people, to give
2:3 you call out for i; if you ask aloud for
5:2 may act with foresight and speak with i.
8:12 Wisdom, live with i, and I acquire
12:8 according to his i, but whoever has a
INSTRUCTION, INSTRUCTORS
5:13 ear open to my i; I almost reached
19:27 listening to i, my son, A worthless
31:26 and on her tongue there is tender i.
INSULT
12:16 but a sensible person hides the i.
14:31 oppresses the poor i his Maker, but
17:5 of a poor person i his Maker; whoever is
18:3 also comes, and i comes along with disgrace.
INTEGRITY
2:7 those who walk in i in order to guard
2:21 and the people of i will remain in it,
11:3 I guides the upright, but hypocrisy
20:7 the basis of his i—blessed are his
28:6 person who has i than to be rich and
INTELLIGENT
17:28 he is considered i if he keeps his
24:5 strong, and an i man has strength, for
INTEREST
28:8 unfair loans and i collects them only
INTOXICATED
5:19 you; always be i with her love.
5:20 you, my son, be i with an adulterous
IRON
27:17 As i sharpens i, so one man sharpens the

JEALOUSY
6:34 out, because j arouses a husband's fury
14:30 healthy body, but j is like a bone
27:4 overwhelming, but who can stand before j?
JEWEL
3:15 more precious than j, and all your desires
8:11 is better than j, and nothing you desire
17:8 seems like a j to the one who gives it;
20:15 gold and plenty of j, but what precious
31:10 She is worth far more than j.
JOY, JOYFUL
10:28 righteous leads to j, but the eager waiting
11:10 when the wicked perish, there are songs of j.
12:20 who plan evil, but j belongs to those who
12:25 down, but an encouraging word makes him j.
14:10 bitterness, and no stranger can share its j.
14:13 heart can ache, and j can end in grief.
15:13 A j heart makes a cheerful face, but with a
17:21 and the father of a godless fool has no j.
17:22 A j heart is good medicine, but depression
JUDGE, JUDGMENT
8:16 princes rule, so do nobles and all just j.
16:10 king's lips, he cannot voice a wrong j.
20:8 on his throne to j sifts out every evil with
24:23 It is not good to show partiality as a j.
29:14 When a king j the poor with honesty, his
31:9 Speak out, j fairly, and defend the rights
JUSTICE
1:3 righteousness and j and fairness—to
2:8 those who paths of j and to watch over the
8:20 on the paths of j, to give an inheritance
13:23 person is swept away where there is no j.
17:23 accepts a bribe to corrupt the ways of j.
21:15 When j is done, the righteous are
29:4 By means of j a king builds up a country,
JUSTIFIES
17:15 Whoever j the wicked and whoever

KEEP
3:1 my teaching, and k my commands in mind,
4:4 cling to my words; k my commands so that

4:21 of these things; k them deep within your
6:20 My son, k the command of your father and
7:2 K my commands so that you may live, and k
8:32 are those who k My ways.
11:13 in spirit can k a secret.
17:28 to be wise if he k silent; he is considered
17:28 intelligent if he k his lips sealed.
19:16 He who k the law preserves his life, but
22:18 is pleasant if you k them in mind so that
22:24 temper and never k company with a hothead,
28:4 wicked, but those who k God's teaching
28:7 Whoever k God's teaching is a wise son,
29:18 are those who k God's teaching.
30:7 two things; don't k them from me before I die:
30:8 me before I die: k vanity and lies far away
31:27 She k a close eye on the conduct of her
KILL
1:32 away, the gullible k themselves; and because
6:17 and hands that k innocent people; a mind
7:26 and numerous are all those she has k.
21:25 a lazy person will k him, because his hands
KIND, KINDNESS
14:21 is the one who is k to the humble.
14:31 Maker, but whoever is k to the needy honors
19:6 try to win the k of a generous person,
24:4 knowledge, with every k of riches, both
28:8 to the one who is k to the poor.
KING
8:15 With me k reign, and rulers decree just laws.
14:28 is an honor for a k, but without people a
16:10 revelation is on a k lips, he cannot voice
16:12 is disgusting to k, because a throne is
16:13 K delight in honest words, and whoever
16:14 A k anger announces death, but a wise man
16:15 When the k is cheerful there is life, and his
19:12 The rage of a k is like the roar of a lion,
20:8 A k who sits on his throne to judge sifts out
20:26 A wise k scatters the wicked and then runs
20:28 and truth protect a k, and with mercy he
24:21 my son (fear the k as well); do not
25:2 but the glory of k to investigate them.
25:3 so the mind of k is unsearchable.
29:4 means of justice a k builds up a country,
29:14 When a k judges the poor with honesty, his
30:22 when he becomes a godless fool when
30:27 locusts have no k, yet all of them divide
30:29 that march like a k: a lion, mightiest
KISS
5:3 with honey, and her k is smoother than oil,
7:13 She grabs him and k him and brazenly says
24:26 answer is like a k on the lips.
27:6 help, but an enemy's k are too much to bear.
KNOWLEDGE
1:7 the beginning of k; wisdom and
1:22 and how long will you fools hate k?
15:7 righteous spread k, but a foolish
15:14 searches for k, but the mouth of fools
17:27 A person who has k controls his words,
19:2 A person without k is no good, and a
19:25 person and he will gain more k.
21:11 wise person is instructed, he gains k.
30:3 and I don't have k of the Holy One!

LACK
5:23 he will die for his l of discipline and
11:22 beautiful woman who l good taste.
25:28 so is a man who l self-control.
28:27 gives to the poor l nothing, but whoever
31:11 he does not l any good thing; she helps
LAMBS
27:26 on the hills; l will provide you with
LAME
25:19 a broken tooth and a l foot, so is
26:7 Like a l person's limp legs, so is a
LAMP
6:23 for the command is a l and the teaching is a
13:9 but the l of the wicked will be snuffed
20:20 and mother, his l will be snuffed out in
20:27 soul is the LORD's l; it searches his entire
21:4 heart, which are the l of the wicked, are
24:20 no future, and the l of the wicked will be
31:18 a good profit; her l burns late at night.
LAND
2:21 will live in the l and the people of
2:22 be cut off from the l and the treacherous
8:26 He had not yet made l or fields or the first
10:30 wicked will not continue to live in the l.
28:19 Whoever works his l will have plenty to eat;

30:16 and a barren womb; a l that never gets enough
31:23 gates when he sits with the elders of the l.

LAST
8:18 riches and honor, l wealth and
12:19 word of truth l forever, but lies l only
27:24 is not forever, nor does a crown always l.
28:2 knowledge will a it l a long time.

LAUGH, LAUGHTER
1:26 I too will l at your calamity; I will make
10:23 Like the l of a fool when he carries out
29:9 fool, he may rage or l, but there is no

LAW
8:15 me kings reign, and rulers decree just l.
13:13 one who fears His l will be rewarded.
19:16 He who keeps the l preserves his life, but

LAZINESS
19:15 l throws one into a deep sleep, and an

LAZY
6:6 ant, you l bum; watch its ways and become
10:4 L hands bring poverty, but hardworking
12:24 gain control, but l hands do slave labor.
12:27 A l hunter does not catch his prey, but a
13:4 A l person craves food and there is none, but
18:9 Whoever is l in his work is a brother to a
19:24 A l person puts his fork in his food; he
20:4 A l person does not plow in the fall; he
21:25 The desire of a l person will kill him,
22:13 A l person says, There's a lion outside!
24:30 I passed by a l man's field, the vineyard
26:14 its hinges, so the l person turns on his bed.
26:16 A l person thinks he is wiser than seven

LEADS
11:3 but hypocrisy l the treacherous to ruin.
11:19 As righteousness l to life, so whoever
12:26 path of the wicked l others astray.
14:23 but idle talk l only to poverty.
15:24 life for the wise l upward in order to turn
16:29 his neighbor and l him on a path that is not
19:23 fear of the LORD l to life, and such a
22:16 the rich certainly l to poverty.

LEARN
1:5 and continue to l, and an understanding
8:5 gullible people, l how to be sensible!
9:9 person and he will l more.
16:21 and speaking sweetly helps others l.
16:23 speech, and what he says helps others l.
19:25 gullible person may l a lesson; warn an
22:25 hothead, or you will l his ways and set a
24:32 I saw it and l my lesson.
30:3 and I haven't l wisdom, and I don't have

LEAVES
2:17 smooth talk, who l the closest friend of
13:22 A good man l an inheritance to his
15:10 to anyone who l the right path; anyone
28:3 a driving rain that l no food.

LENDER, LENDS
19:17 pity on the poor l to the LORD, and He
22:7 poor, and the borrower is a slave to the l.

LESSON
19:25 person may learn a l; warn an understanding
24:32 it to heart; I saw it and learned my l.

LIAR
17:4 to wicked lips; a l opens his ears to a
19:22 and it is better to be a poor man than a l.
30:6 scold you, and you will be found to be a l.

LIES
6:19 spitting out l, and a person who spreads
12:19 lasts forever, but l last only a moment.
14:25 but one who tells l is dangerous.
19:5 and one who utters l will not escape.
19:9 and one who utters l will perish.
29:12 pays attention to l, all his servants become
30:8 die: Keep vanity and l far away from me;

LIFE
3:2 will bring you long l, good years, and peace.
3:16 Long l is in wisdom's right hand; in
3:18 is a tree of l for those who take firm hold
4:10 and they will multiply the years of your l.
4:22 because they are l to those who find them,
4:23 the source of your l flows from it.
7:23 not realize that it will cost him his l.
8:35 finds Me finds l and obtains favor from the
9:11 longer, and years will be added to your l.
10:11 is a fountain of l, but the mouth of the
10:17 is on the way to l, but whoever ignores a
11:19 leads to l, so whoever pursues evil finds his
11:30 is a tree of l, and a winner of souls is wise.
12:28 is everlasting l, and along its path there
13:3 protects his own l; whoever has a big mouth

13:6 the honest way of l, but wickedness negates a
13:14 is a fountain of l to turn one away from
14:8 guides his way of l, but the stupidity of
15:4 tongue is a tree of l, but a deceitful tongue
15:24 The path of l for the wise leads upward in
16:15 cheerful there is l, and his favor is like a
16:17 whoever watches his way preserves his own l.
16:31 is a beautiful crown found in a righteous l.
18:21 has the power of l and death, and those who
19:3 a person turns his l upside down, and his
19:16 law preserves his l, but he who despises
19:20 so that you may be wise the rest of your l.
20:2 lion; whoever makes him angry forfeits his l.
21:21 and mercy will find l, righteousness, and
21:29 person's way of l is his own security.
22:4 of the LORD, come riches and honor and l.
23:12 a more disciplined and listen carefully to
29:24 hates his own l; he will not testify under
31:12 and never harms him all the days of her l.

LIFTS
14:34 Righteousness l up a nation, but sin is a

LIGHT
4:18 is like the l of dawn that becomes brighter
6:23 the teaching is a l, and the warnings from
13:9 The l of the righteous beams brightly, but

LION
19:12 like the roar of a l, but his favor is like
20:2 like the roar of a l; whoever makes him angry
22:13 says, There's a l outside!
26:13 says, There's a l out on the road!
26:13 There's a l loose in the streets!
28:1 him, but the righteous are as bold as a l.
28:15 Like a roaring l and like a prowling bear,
30:30 like a king: a l, mightiest among animals,

LIQUOR
20:1 mock; l makes them noisy; and everyone
31:4 for rulers to crave l; otherwise, they drink
31:6 Give l to the person who is perishing and

LISTEN
1:5 a wise person will l and continue to learn,
1:8 L, my son, to your father's discipline and
1:24 and you refused to l, since I stretched
5:13 correction; I didn't l to what my teachers
8:33 L to discipline and become wise.
12:15 but a person who l to advice is wise.
13:1 A wise son l to his father's discipline,
13:1 a mocker does not l to scolding.
15:31 The ear that l to a life-giving warning
15:32 but the one who l to warning gains
18:13 answer before he l is stupid and shameful.
21:28 but a man who l to advice will continue to
23:12 life and l carefully to words of knowledge.
23:19 L and be wise, and keep your mind going in
23:22 L to your father since you are his son, and
25:12 criticism is to the ear of one who l.
28:9 Whoever refuses to l to God's teaching,

LITTLE
6:10 a l sleep, just a l slumber, just a l
13:11 but whoever gathers l by l has plenty.
15:16 is better to have a l with the fear of the
24:33 a l sleep, just a l slumber, just a l

LIVE
1:33 listens to me will l without worry and will
2:21 for the upright will l in the land and the
4:4 so that you may l: Acquire wisdom!
7:2 so that you may l, and keep my teaching just
8:12 I, Wisdom, l with insight, and I acquire
9:11 of me you will l longer, and years will be
10:9 but whoever l dishonestly will be found out.
10:30 will not continue to l in the land.
14:2 Whoever l right fears the LORD, but the
15:27 his family, but whoever hates bribes will l.
19:1 a poor person who l innocently than to be
20:7 A righteous person l on the basis of his
21:9 Better to l on a corner of a roof than to
21:19 Better to l in a desert than with a
23:12 L a more disciplined life and listen
28:16 unjust gain will l longer.
28:18 Whoever l honestly will be safe, but whoever
28:18 safe, but whoever l dishonestly will fall

LIZARD
30:28 by instinct; a l you can hold in your hands,

LOAN
6:1 if you guarantee a l for your neighbor or
11:15 a stranger's l will get into trouble, but
17:18 he guarantees a l in the presence of his
20:16 a stranger's l, and hold responsible the
20:16 person who makes a l in behalf of a foreigner.
22:26 among those who guarantee other people's l.

27:13 a stranger's l, and hold responsible the
27:13 person who makes a l in behalf of a foreigner.
28:8 through unfair l and interest collects

LOCUSTS
30:27 home in the rocks; l have no king, yet all

LOOSE
2:16 from the l woman with her smooth talk,
5:20 woman and fondle a l woman's breast?
6:24 smooth talk of a l woman.
7:5 from the l woman with her smooth talk.
23:27 a deep pit, and a l woman is a narrow well;

LORD
3:5 Trust the L with all your heart, and do not
3:9 Honor the L with your wealth and with the
3:12 because the L warns the one He loves,
3:19 By Wisdom the L laid the foundation of the
5:21 clearly seen by the L, and He surveys all his
10:3 The L will not allow the righteous person to
11:1 disgusting to the L, but accurate weights are
15:3 The eyes of the L are everywhere, watching
15:25 The L tears down the house of the proud, but
16:2 are pure, but the L weighs motives.
16:3 your works to the L, and your plans will
16:4 L has made everything for His own purpose,
16:9 own journey, but the L directs his steps.
16:11 belong to the L; He made the entire set of
16:20 attention to the L word prospers, and
16:20 and blessed is the one who trusts the L.
17:3 One who purifies hearts by fire is the L.
18:10 The Name of the L is a strong tower; a
18:22 good and has obtained favor from the L.
19:14 but a sensible wife comes from the L.
19:17 poor lends to the L, and He will repay him
19:21 the advice of the L will endure.
20:12 eye that sees: the L made them both!
20:22 Wait for the L and He will save you.
20:23 disgusting to the L, and dishonest scales are
20:24 The L is the One who directs a man's steps;
20:27 soul is the L lamp; it searches his entire
21:2 is right, but the L weighs hearts.
21:3 acceptable to the L than offering a sacrifice.
21:31 of battle, but the victory belongs to the L.
22:2 this in common: the L is the Maker of them
22:12 The L eyes watch over knowledge, but He
22:23 gate, because the L will plead their case and
25:22 on his head, and the L will reward you.
28:5 those who seek the L understand everything.
28:25 whoever trusts the L prospers.
29:26 one who trusts the L is safe.
29:26 but justice for mankind comes from the L.

LOVE
1:22 you gullible people l being so gullible, and
3:12 warns the one He l, even as a father warns a
4:6 will watch over you; l wisdom and it will
8:21 to those who l me and to fill their
8:36 those who hate Me l death.
9:8 warn a wise person and he will l you.
10:12 starts quarrels, but l covers every wrong.
12:1 Whoever l discipline l to learn, but
13:24 him, but he who l his son disciplines him
15:9 the LORD, but He l the one who pursues
15:17 where there is l than juicy steaks where
16:13 and whoever speaks what is right is l.
17:9 an offense seeks l, but whoever keeps
17:17 A friend always l, and a brother is born to
17:19 Whoever l sin loves a quarrel; whoever
18:21 death, and those who l to talk will have to
19:8 who gains sense l himself; one who guards
20:13 Do not l sleep or you will end up poor;
21:17 Whoever l pleasure will become a poor man;
21:17 a poor man; whoever l wine and rich food
22:11 Whoever l a pure heart and whose speech is
27:5 Open criticism is better than unexpressed l.
29:3 man who l wisdom makes his father happy,

LOYAL, LOYALTY
19:22 L is desirable in a person, and it is
20:6 declares himself l, but who can find a

LURE
1:10 My son, if sinners l you, don't go along!

LYING
6:17 arrogant eyes, a l tongue, and hands that
10:18 conceals hatred has l lips, and whoever
12:17 honestly, but a l witness speaks deceitfully.
13:5 person hates l, but a wicked person behaves
17:7 how much less does l fit a noble person!
21:6 gather wealth by l are wasting time; they
21:28 A l witness will perish, but a man who
26:28 A l tongue hates its victims, and a

MADE
8:26 when He had not yet **m** land or fields or the
16:4 LORD has **m** everything for His own purpose,
16:11 to the LORD; He **m** the entire set of weights.
20:9 Who can say, I've **m** my heart pure; I'm
20:12 that sees: the LORD **m** them both!

MAKER
14:31 poor insults his **M**, but whoever is kind to
17:5 person insults his **M**; whoever is happy
22:2 the LORD is the **M** of them all.

MANKIND
3:4 much success in the sight of God and **m**.
8:31 His inhabited world, and delighting in **m**.
29:26 but justice for **m** comes from the LORD.
30:14 the earth and the needy from among **m**.

MARKER
22:28 an ancient boundary **m** that your ancestors
23:10 an ancient boundary **m** or enter the fields

MARRIED
5:18 enjoy the girl you **m** when you were young,
6:26 of bread, but a **m** woman hunts for your
30:23 when she gets **m** and a maid when she

MASTER
8:30 was beside Him as a **M** Craftsman.
17:2 slave will become **m** over a son who acts
25:13 those who send him: he refreshes his **m**.
27:18 protects his **m** is honored.
30:10 a slave to his **m** or he will curse you and

MEASURES
20:10 of weights and **m**—both are disgusting

MEAT
7:14 some sacrificial **m**; today I kept my vows.
9:2 has prepared her **m**; she has mixed her wine;
23:20 who eat too much **m**, because both a drunk

MEDICINE
17:22 heart is good **m**, but depression drains

MERCIFUL
11:17 A **m** man benefits himself, but a cruel man
14:22 the ones who are **m** and faithful plan good?

MERCY
3:3 Do not let **m** and truth leave you: fasten
6:34 will show no **m** when he takes revenge.
16:6 By **m** and faithfulness guilt is atoned for,
20:28 **M** and truth protect a king, and with **m** he
21:21 righteousness and **m** will find life,

MESSENGER
13:17 An undependable **m** gets into trouble, but
17:11 therefore, a cruel **m** will be sent
25:13 the trustworthy **m** to those who send him:

MILK
27:27 enough goats' **m** to feed you, to feed your
30:33 for just as churning **m** produces butter and

MISERABLE, MISERY
15:15 day for a **m** person, but a cheerful heart
23:29 Who has woe? Who has **m**?
24:22 and who knows what **m** both may bring?

MISLEADS
14:8 stupidity of fools **m** them.
16:29 A violent man **m** his neighbor and leads
28:10 Whoever **m** the upright into evil will fall

MOCK
1:22 delight in your **m**, and how long will you
3:34 When He **m** the mockers, He is gracious to
9:12 help you; if you, you alone will be held
19:28 A worthless witness **m** justice, and the mouth
20:1 Wine makes people **m**; liquor makes them
29:8 Men who **m** create an uproar in a city, but

MOCKER
1:22 how long will you **m** delight in your
3:34 When He mocks the **m**, He is gracious to the
9:7 Whoever corrects a **m** receives abuse, and
9:8 Do not warn a **m** or he will hate you; warn a
13:1 discipline, but a **m** does not listen to
14:6 A **m** searches for wisdom without finding it,
15:12 A **m** does not appreciate a warning; he will
19:25 Strike a **m** and a gullible person may learn
19:29 are set for **m** and beatings for the backs
21:11 When a **m** is punished, a gullible person
21:24 person is called a **m**; he acts with extreme
22:10 Drive out a **m**, and conflict will leave;
24:9 is sinful, and a **m** is disgusting to

MOMENT
6:15 him suddenly; in a **m** he will be crushed
7:12 One **m** she is out on the street, the next
12:19 lasts forever, but lies last only a **m**.

MONEY
2:4 it as if it were **m** and hunt for it as if it
6:35 No amount of **m** will change his mind, and

7:20 took lots of **m** with him; he won't be home
17:16 should a fool have **m** in his hand to acquire
22:27 If you have no **m** to pay back a loan why
27:26 clothing, and the **m** from the male goats will

MORTAR
27:22 stubborn fool in a **m** with a pestle, along

MOTHER
1:8 not neglect your **m** teaching, because they
4:3 father, a tender and only child of my **m**.
6:20 teaching of your **m**: fasten them on your
10:1 but a foolish son brings grief to his **m**.
15:20 happy, but a foolish child despises its **m**.
17:25 to his father and bitter grief to his **m**.
19:26 who drives away his **m** brings shame and
20:20 his father and his, his lamp will be snuffed
23:22 do not despise your **m** just because she is
23:25 father and your **m** be glad, and may she who
28:24 his father or his **m** and says, It isn't
29:15 an undisciplined child disgraces his **m**.
30:11 his father and does not bless his **m**.
30:17 and hates to obey a **m** will be plucked out
31:1 used by his **m** to discipline him.

MOTIVE
7:10 as a prostitute, with an ulterior **m**!
16:2 his ways are pure, but the LORD weighs **m**.
20:5 A **m** in a man's heart is like deep waters,

MULTIPLY
4:10 and they will **m** the years of your life.

MURDER
1:11 ambush to commit **m**; let's hide to ambush
1:18 for their own **m**; they go into hiding only
22:13 I'll be **m** in the streets!
28:17 with the guilt of **m** will be a fugitive down

NAME
7:4 sister, and give the **n** My Relative to
10:7 is blessed, but the **n** of the wicked will rot
18:10 The **N** of the LORD is a strong tower; a
22:1 A good **n** is more desirable than great wealth;
30:4 What is His **N** or the **N** of His Son?
30:9 steal and give the **N** of my God a bad

NATION
11:14 A **n** will fall when there is no direction,
14:34 lifts up a **n**, but sin is a defect in any
24:24 and condemned by **n**, but it will be a

NEEDY
14:31 is kind to the **n** honors Him.
30:14 the earth and the **n** from among mankind.
31:9 defend the rights of the oppressed and **n**.
31:20 oppressed and stretches them out to the **n**.

NEIGHBOR
6:1 a loan for your **n** or pledge yourself for
6:3 fallen into your **n** hands: Go, humble
6:3 and pester your **n**; give no sleep to your
6:29 has sex with his **n** wife; none who touch
11:9 can ruin his **n**, but the righteous are
11:12 who despises a **n** has no sense, but a
12:26 looks out for his **n**, but the path of the
14:20 hated even by his **n**, but a rich person is
14:21 despises his **n** sins, but blessed is the
16:29 man misleads his **n** and leads him on a
21:10 evil and has no consideration for his **n**.
25:8 against your **n** without a reason, and do
25:9 argument to your **n**, but do not reveal
25:17 set foot in your **n** house too often;
25:18 who gives false testimony against his **n**.
26:19 man who tricks his **n** and says, I was only
27:10 are in trouble; a **n** living nearby is
29:5 who flatters his **n** is spreading a net for

NEWS
15:30 the heart; good **n** refreshes the body.
25:25 soul, so is good **n** from far away.

NIGHT
7:9 in the evening, in the dark hours of the **n**.
31:18 a good profit; her lamp burns late at **n**.

NOBILITY, NOBLE
8:6 I am speaking about **n** things, and my lips
8:16 princes rule, so do **n** and all just judges.
17:7 does lying fit a **n** person!
17:26 good; to strike down **n** people is not right.
31:25 with strength and **n**, and she smiles at
31:29 women have done **n** work, but you have

NOISY
1:21 at the corners of **n** streets she calls out;
20:1 liquor makes them **n**; and everyone under

OATH
29:24 his own life; he will not testify under **o**.

OBEY
30:17 father and hates to **o** a mother will be

OCEAN
8:24 Before there were **o** I was born, before
8:27 the surface of the **o**, when He established
8:28 the currents in the **o**, when He set a limit

OFFENDED
18:19 An **o** brother is more resistant than a

OIL
5:3 is smoother than **o**, but in the end she is as
27:16 even pick up olive **o** with his right hand.

OLD, OLDER
20:29 the splendor of **o** people is their silver
22:6 and even when he is **o** he will not turn away
23:22 despise your mother just because she is **o**.

OPEN
4:20 to my words; **o** your ears to what I say:
5:1 my wisdom; **o** your ears to my understanding
5:13 did I keep my ear **o** to my instructors; I
18:16 A gift **o** doors for the giver and brings him
20:13 poor; keep your eyes **o** and you will have
20:19 with a person whose mouth is always **o**.
22:17 **O** your ear and hear the words of the wise,
24:7 gate he does not **o** his mouth.
27:5 **O** criticism is better than unexpressed love.
31:20 She **o** her hands to the oppressed and

OPPOSE
18:1 for himself; he **o** all sound reasoning.
28:4 God's teaching **o** them.

OPPRESS, OPPRESSOR
14:31 Whoever **o** the poor insults his Maker,
28:3 A poor man who **o** poorer people is like
29:13 A poor man and an **o** have this in common:
30:14 devouring the **o** from the earth and the
31:5 the standard of justice for all the **o**.
31:9 the rights of the **o** and needy.
31:20 her hands to the **o** and she stretches them

ORPHANS
23:10 the fields of **o**, because their Redeemer is

OUTCOME
16:33 thrown, but the LORD determines every **o**.

OVERCONFIDENT
14:16 evil, but a fool is careless and **o**.

OVERTHROW
12:7 **O** the wicked and they are no more, but

OVERTURNS
22:12 knowledge, but He **o** the words of the

OVERWHELMING
27:4 and fury is **o**, but who can stand

OX
14:4 the strength of an **o** produces plentiful

PAIN
23:35 me, but I feel no **p**; they beat me, but

PALACES
30:28 and yet it can even be found in royal **p**.

PANIC
1:26 fun of you when **p** strikes you, when panic
1:27 strikes you, when **p** strikes you like a

PARENT
17:6 grandparents, and **p** are the glory of their
17:21 The **p** of a fool has grief, and the father

PARTIAL, PARTIALITY
18:5 is not good to be **p** toward the wicked,
24:23 not good to show **p** as a judge.

PARTNER
29:24 who is a thief's **p** hates his own life; he

PATH
1:15 set foot on their **p**, because they rush to do
2:8 to guard those on **p** of justice and to watch
2:13 who abandon the **p** of righteousness to walk
2:15 of evil; their **p** are crooked, and their ways
2:19 they ever reach the **p** of life.
3:17 ways and all its **p** lead to peace.
4:14 not stray onto the **p** of the wicked nor walk
4:18 But the **p** of the righteous is like the light
4:26 walk a straight **p** and all your ways will be
7:25 not wander onto her **p**, because she has
8:20 on the **p** of justice, to give an inheritance
12:26 neighbor, but the **p** of the wicked leads
12:28 life, and along its **p** there is no eternal
15:10 leaves the right **p**; anyone who hates a
16:29 and leads him on a **p** that is not good.

PATIENCE, PATIENT
19:11 with good sense is **p**, and it is to his
25:15 With **p** you can persuade a ruler, and a

PAY
4:1 discipline, and p attention in order to gain
5:1 My son, p attention to my wisdom; open your
7:24 listen to me, and p attention to the words of
11:18 spreads righteousness earns honest p.
13:8 poor person does not p attention to threats.
13:13 God's word will p the penalty, but the one
13:18 but whoever p attention to constructive
17:4 An evildoer p attention to wicked lips; a
17:13 Whoever p back evil for good—evil will
19:19 a hot temper will p for it; if you rescue him
23:1 to eat with a ruler, p close attention to what
24:12 won't He p back everyone according to what
24:29 he treated me; I'll p him back for what he's
29:3 happy, but one who p prostitutes
29:12 If a ruler p attention to lies, all his

PEACE
3:2 bring you long life, good years, and p.
3:17 pleasant ways and all its paths lead to p.
12:20 evil, but joy belongs to those who advise p.
17:1 bread eaten in p than a family feast
29:9 but there is no p and quiet.
29:17 he will give you p of mind, and he will

PENALTY
13:13 word will pay the p, but the one who fears

PERISH
11:10 when the wicked p, there are songs of joy.
19:9 unpunished, and one who utters lies will p.
21:28 lying witness will p, but a man who listens
28:28 hide, but when they p, the righteous
31:6 the person who is p and wine to one who

PERSUADE
7:21 charms she p him; with her smooth lips
25:15 patience you can p a ruler, and a soft

PITY
19:17 has p on the poor lends to the LORD,

PLACE
11:8 person takes his p; with his talk a godless
14:26 will have a p of refuge.
21:18 will take the p of the upright.
22:28 marker that your ancestors set in p.

PLAN
3:29 Do not p to do wrong against your neighbor
6:18 devising wicked p, feet that are quick to do
10:23 carries out an evil p, so is wisdom to a
15:22 Without advice p go wrong, but with many
16:1 The p of the heart belong to humans, but an
16:3 the LORD, and your p will succeed.
16:9 A person may p his own journey, but the
19:21 Many p are in a man's heart, but the advice
21:5 The p of a hardworking person certainly lead
24:8 Anyone who p to do evil will be known as a

PLEAD
22:23 the LORD will p their case and will take the
23:11 is strong; He will p their case against you.

PLEASANT
2:10 knowledge will be p to your soul;
3:17 ways are p ways and all its paths lead to
15:26 to the LORD, but p words are pure to Him.
16:24 P words are like honey from a honeycomb
22:18 you, for it is p if you keep them in mind
23:8 and spoil your p conversation.
24:4 kind of riches, both precious and p.

PLEASING
11:1 accurate weights are p to Him.
16:7 a man's ways are p to the LORD, He makes

PLEASURE
21:17 Whoever loves p will become a poor man;

PLEDGE
6:1 your neighbor or p yourself for a stranger

PLENTY
12:11 his land will have p to eat, but the one
13:11 whoever gathers little by little has p.
20:13 and you will have p to eat.
20:15 There is gold and p of jewels, but what
28:19 rainbows will have p of nothing.

PLOT
14:17 and a man who p evil is hated.
16:27 worthless man p trouble, and his speech is
24:2 because their minds p violence, and their

PLUNDER
16:19 than to share p with the proud.

POISONOUS
23:32 strikes like a p snake.

POOR
10:15 is his strong city; poverty ruins the p.
13:7 pretends to be p but has great wealth.
13:8 his life, but the p person does not pay
13:23 When p people are able to plow, there is

14:20 A p person is hated even by his neighbor, but
14:31 oppresses the p insults his Maker, but
17:5 makes fun of a p person insults his Maker;
18:23 A p person is timid when begging, but a rich
19:4 many friends, but a p person is separated
19:7 the brothers of a p man hate him—how much
19:17 has pity on the p lends to the LORD, and He
19:22 it is better to be a p man than a liar.
21:17 will become a p man; whoever loves wine
22:2 The rich and the p have this in common: the
22:7 rules over the p, and the borrower is a slave
22:9 for he has shared his food with the p.
22:16 Oppressing the p for profit or giving to
22:22 p, because he is p or trample on the
28:3 A p man who oppresses poorer people is like
28:6 Better to be a p person who has integrity
28:8 the wealth to the one who is kind to the p.
28:27 Whoever gives to the p lacks nothing, but
28:27 whoever ignores the p receives many curses.
29:14 a king judges the p with honesty, his throne
30:9 or I may become p and steal and give the

POPULATION
14:28 A large p is an honor for a king, but

POSSESSIONS
1:13 of valuable p; we'll fill our homes
6:31 give up all the p in his house.

POUR
1:23 I will generously p out my spirit for you;

POVERTY
6:11 So your p will come upon you like a
10:4 Lazy hands bring p, but hardworking hands
14:23 gained, but idle talk leads only to p.
21:5 in a hurry certainly ends up in p.
22:16 giving to the rich certainly leads to p.
24:34 Then your p will come upon you like a
28:22 not realizing that p is about to overtake
30:8 give me either p or riches; feed me only
31:7 and forgets his p and does not remember

POWER, POWERFUL
3:27 when it is in your p to do so.
18:18 and settles issues between the p.
18:21 the tongue has the p of life and death, and
31:3 to women or your p to those who ruin kings.

PRACTICES
10:17 Whoever p discipline is on the way to

PRAISE
12:8 A man is p according to his insight, but
27:2 P should come from another person and not
27:21 is tested by the p given to him.
28:4 God's teaching p the wicked, but those
31:28 he sings her p, saying Many women have
31:30 has the fear of the LORD—she to be p!
31:31 her achievements p her at the city gates!

PRAYER
15:8 the LORD, but the p of the upright is His
15:29 but He hears the p of the righteous.
28:9 teaching, even his p is disgusting.
31:2 And what, son of my p?

PRECEDES
16:18 Pride p a disaster, and an arrogant
16:18 arrogant attitude p a fall; better to be

PRECIOUS
3:15 Wisdom is more p than jewels, and all
20:15 jewels, but what p gems are the lips of
24:4 of riches, both p and pleasant.

PRESENCE
17:18 a loan in the p of his friend.
18:16 him into the p of great people.
25:5 away from the p of a king and justice

PRESENT
25:9 P your argument to your neighbor, but do

PRESERVES
16:17 watches his way p his own life.
19:16 who keeps the law p his life, but he

PRETENDS
13:7 One person p to be rich but has nothing;
13:7 nothing; another p to be poor but has

PRICELESS
2:7 He has reserved p wisdom for upright
3:21 these things: Use p wisdom and foresight,
8:14 Advice and p wisdom are mine; I,

PRIDE
8:13 hate evil; I hate p, arrogance, evil
11:2 P comes, then comes shame, but wisdom
13:10 P produces only quarreling, but those who
16:18 P precedes a disaster, and an arrogant
21:24 is called a mocker; he acts with extreme p.
29:23 A person's p will humiliate him, but a

PRODUCE
8:19 What I p is better than gold, pure gold;
12:12 of the righteous p fruit An evil person
13:10 Pride p only quarreling, but those who
14:4 strength of an ox p plentiful harvests.
29:15 and a warning p wisdom, but an

PROFIT
3:14 for the p gained from wisdom is
3:14 is greater than the p gained from silver;
10:2 gained dishonestly p no one, but
22:16 the poor for p or giving to the rich
31:16 vineyard from the p she has earned.
31:18 is making a good p; her lamp burns late at

PROMISE
6:2 of your own mouth, caught by your own p.

PROPHETIC
29:18 Without p vision people run wild, but
30:1 son of Jakeh, his p revelation!
31:1 of King Lemuel, a p revelation, used by

PROSPER, PROSPERITY
11:10 When the righteous p, a city is glad; when
16:20 the LORD's word p, and blessed is the one
17:8 who gives it; wherever he turns he p.
21:5 lead to p, but everyone who is always
28:13 his sins does not p, but whoever confesses
28:25 a fight, but whoever trusts the LORD p.

PROSTITUTE
6:26 A p price is only a loaf of bread,
7:10 him, dressed as a p, with an ulterior
23:27 in my ways: A p is a deep pit, and a
29:3 but one who pays p wastes his wealth.

PROTECT, PROTECTION
2:11 foresight will p you; understanding will
7:2 just as you p the pupil of your eye,
13:3 controls his mouth p his own life;
13:6 Righteousness p the honest way of life,
14:3 but the wise are p by their speech.
15:25 the proud, but He p the property of the
20:28 Mercy and truth p a king, and with mercy
30:5 Shield to those who come to Him for p.

PROUD
15:25 the house of the p, but He protects the
16:19 the lowly than to share plunder with the p.
18:12 a man's heart is p, but humility comes
21:4 look and a p heart, which are the lamp of
21:24 A p, conceited person is called a mocker; he

PROVERB
1:1 The p of Solomon son of David, king of
1:6 to understand a p and a clever saying, to
10:1 The p of Solomon: A wise son makes his
25:1 also are Solomon's p which were copied by
26:7 limp legs, so is a p in the mouth of fools.
26:9 hand, so is a p in the mouth of fools.

PROVIDES
18:20 speaking ability p for his stomach; his
18:20 his talking p him a living;

PUNISH, PUNISHMENT
6:29 wife; none who touch her will escape p.
16:22 but stubborn fools p themselves with their
17:5 in distress will not escape p.
17:26 To p an innocent person is not good; to
19:29 P are set for mockers and beatings for
21:11 When a mocker is p, a gullible person
28:20 a hurry to get rich will not escape p.

PUPIL
7:2 as you protect the p of your eye,

PURE
8:19 is better than gold, p gold; what I yield is
10:20 of the righteous is p silver; the heart of
15:26 pleasant words are p to Him.
16:2 all his ways are p, but the LORD weighs
20:9 I've made my heart p; I'm cleansed from my
20:11 his deeds are p or right.
21:8 the behavior of the p is upright.
22:11 Whoever loves a p heart and whose speech is
30:12 who thinks he is p but is not washed from his

PURSUES
11:19 life, so whoever p evil finds his own
15:9 loves the one who p righteousness.
21:21 Whoever p righteousness and mercy will

QUARREL, QUARRELSOME
3:30 Do not q with a man for no reason if he
10:12 Hate starts q, but love covers every
13:10 produces only q, but those who take
16:28 man spreads q, and a gossip separates the
17:14 Starting a q is like opening a floodgate,
17:19 loves sin loves a q; whoever builds his

19:13 his father, and a **q** woman is like
20:3 a man to avoid a **q**, but any stubborn fool
21:9 a home with a **q** woman.
21:19 than with a **q** and angry woman.
22:10 will leave; **q** and abuse will stop.
26:17 who gets involved in someone else's **q**.
26:20 without gossip a **q** dies down.
26:21 fire, so the **q** man fuels a dispute.
27:15 day is like a **q** woman.

QUICK
6:18 plans, feet that are **q** to do wrong, a
29:20 met a man who is **q** to answer?

QUIET
11:12 a person who has understanding keeps **q**.
29:9 rage or laugh, but there is no peace and **q**.

RAGE
15:1 answer turns away **r**, but a harsh word stirs
19:3 down, and his heart **r** against the LORD.
19:12 The **r** of a king is like the roar of a lion,
20:2 The screaming **r** of a king is like the roar of
29:9 fool, he may **r** or laugh, but there is no

RAIN, RAINBOWS, RAINY
12:11 the one who chases **r** has no sense.
16:15 his favor is like a cloud bringing spring **r**.
25:23 north wind brings **r**, so the whispering tongue
26:1 in summertime and **r** at harvest time, so
27:15 dripping water on a **r** day is like a
28:3 is like a driving **r** that leaves no food.
28:19 but whoever chases **r** will have plenty of

RAM
7:22 slaughtered, like a **r** hobbling into captivity

RANSOM
13:8 riches are the **r** for his life, but the poor
21:18 wicked becomes a **r** for the righteous, and

RAVENS
30:17 be plucked out by **r** in the valley and eaten

REACH
2:2 letting your mind **r** for understanding
2:19 nor do they ever **r** the paths of life.
5:14 I almost **r** total ruin in the assembly and

READY
21:31 The horse is made **r** for the day of battle,
24:27 and get things **r** for yourself in the field
25:4 and a vessel is **r** for the silversmith to

REALIZE
5:6 and she doesn't **r** it.
7:23 trap, he does not **r** that it will cost him

REAP
22:8 sows injustice will **r** trouble, and this

REASON, REASONING
3:30 with a man for no **r** if he has done you no
18:1 for himself; he opposes all sound **r**.
23:29 Who has wounds for no **r**?
24:28 neighbor without a **r**, and do not deceive

RECOVERY
6:15 in a moment he will be crushed beyond **r**.

REDEEMER
23:11 because their **R** is strong; He will plead

REFINING
17:3 crucible is for **r** silver and the smelter
27:21 crucible is for **r** silver and the smelter

REFUGE
14:26 and His children will have a place of **r**.
14:32 in his death a righteous person has a **r**.

REFUSE
1:24 I called (and you **r** to listen), since I
1:30 They **r** my advice; they despised my every
13:24 He who **r** to spank his son hates him, but
21:7 away since they **r** to do what is just.
21:25 because his hands **r** to work; all day long
28:9 Whoever **r** to listen to God's teaching,

REJECT
3:11 Do not **r** the discipline of the LORD, my
10:3 He intentionally **r** the desire of the

REJOICE
2:14 from those who **r** in the deviousness of
23:15 my heart will **r** as well; my heart rejoices
23:16 as well; my heart **r** when you speak what
23:24 will certainly **r**; one who has a wise son
23:25 glad, and may she who gave birth to you **r**.
29:2 people of God **r**, but when a wicked

RELAX
4:13 discipline; do not **r** your grip on it; keep

RELIGIOUS
29:4 who confiscates **r** contributions tears it

RELY
3:5 and do not **r** on your own understanding.

REMEMBER, REMEMBRANCE
10:7 **R** of the righteous is blessed, but the
31:7 and does not **r** his trouble anymore.

REPAY
6:31 caught, he has to **r** it seven times; he must
19:17 LORD, and He will **r** him for his good deed.

REPORT
22:21 give an accurate **r** to those who send you?
25:10 you, and his evil **r** about you will never

REPUTATION
5:9 surrender your **r** to others and
30:9 and give the Name of my God a bad **r**.

RESCUE
10:2 but righteousness **r** from death.
11:8 person is **r** from trouble, and the wicked
11:9 the righteous are **r** by knowledge.
12:6 ambush, but the words of the upright **r**.
19:19 pay for it; if you **r** him you will have to
24:11 **R** captives condemned to death, and spare

RESPECT
11:16 woman wins **r**, but ruthless men gain riches.
22:1 than great wealth; **r** is better than silver

RESPONSIBLE
9:12 you mock, you alone will be held **r**.
19:18 not be the one **r** for his death.
20:16 loan, and hold **r** the person who makes
27:13 loan, and hold **r** the person who makes

REST
19:20 you may be wise the **r** of your life.
19:23 such a person will **r** easy without suffering
21:16 wise behavior will **r** in the assembly of the
26:2 a hastily spoken curse does not come to **r**.

RESULT
12:14 good things as a **r** of his speaking ability,
13:2 man eats well as a **r** of his speaking

REVEAL
24:10 in a crisis, you **r** that you are weak.
25:9 neighbor, but do not **r** another person's
26:26 wickedness will be **r** in the community.

REVELATION
16:10 When a divine **r** is on a king's lips, he
30:1 the son of Jakeh, his prophetic **r**!
31:1 a prophetic **r**, used by his mother to

REVENGE
6:34 will show no mercy when he takes **r**.

REVOLT
28:2 a country is in **r** it has many rulers, but

REWARD
10:16 The **r** of the righteous is life; the harvest
11:31 person is **r** on earth—how much more the
13:13 the one who fears His law will be **r**.
13:21 the righteous are **r** with good.
25:22 and the LORD will **r** you.
31:31 **R** her for what she has done, and let her

RICH
3:16 left hand are **r** and honor.
10:15 The **r** person's wealth is his strong city;
11:4 **R** are of no help on the Day of Fury, but
11:28 trusts in his **r** will fall, but the
13:7 pretends to be **r** but has nothing; another
13:8 A man's **r** are the ransom for his life, but
14:20 neighbor, but a **r** person is loved by many.
18:11 A **r** person's wealth is his strong city and is
18:23 when begging, but a **r** person is blunt when
21:17 loves wine and **r** food will not become **r**.
22:2 The **r** and the poor have this in common: the
22:4 of the LORD, come **r** and honor and life.
22:7 The **r** person rules over the poor, and the
22:16 or giving to the **r** certainly leads to
23:4 out getting **r**; be smart enough to stop!
24:4 with every kind of **r**, both precious and
28:6 integrity than to be **r** and double-dealing.
28:11 A **r** man is wise in his own eyes, but a poor
28:20 in a hurry to get **r** will not escape
30:8 either poverty or **r**; feed me only the

RIDDLES
1:6 the words of the wise and their **r**.

RIGHT
2:9 understand what is **r** and just and fair—
14:2 Whoever lives **r** fears the LORD, but the
21:2 he does is **r**, but the LORD weighs hearts.
23:16 my heart rejoices when you speak what is **r**.
25:11 word spoken at the **r** time.
26:1 honor is just not **r** for a fool.

RIGHTEOUS
10:11 The mouth of the **r** is a fountain of life,
10:30 The **r** will never be moved, but the
15:28 The heart of the **r** carefully considers
15:29 but He hears the prayer of the **r**.
18:10 a strong tower; a **r** person runs to it

RIGHTEOUSNESS
2:13 the paths of **r** to walk the ways of
11:6 saved by their **r**, but the
11:18 whoever spreads **r** earns honest pay.
11:19 As **r** leads to life, so whoever
13:6 **R** protects the honest way of life,
14:34 **R** lifts up a nation, but sin is a

RIGHTS
22:22 or trample on the **r** of those in distress at
31:8 speak, for the **r** of those who are doomed.
31:9 and defend the **r** of the oppressed and needy.

RISE
28:12 but when the wicked **r**, people hide themselves.
28:28 When the wicked **r**, people hide, but when they

ROAD
8:2 wayside where the **r** meet, near the gates to
9:6 start traveling the **r** to understanding!
11:5 innocent makes his **r** smooth, but the wicked
12:28 On the **r** of righteousness there is
15:19 hedge, but the **r** of the upright is an open

ROAR
19:12 a king is like the **r** of a lion, but his favor
20:2 a king is like the **r** of a lion; whoever makes

ROB
22:22 Do not **r** the poor, because he is poor or
22:23 lives of those who **r** them.
24:15 righteous; do not **r** his house, for a righteous
28:24 The one who **r** his father or his mother and

ROD
10:13 understanding, but a **r** is for the back of
26:3 the donkey, and a **r** is for the back of fools.

ROOF
21:9 on a corner of a **r** than to share a home with
25:24 on a corner of a **r** than to share a home with

ROOSTER
30:31 a strutting **r** or a male goat, and a king

ROOT
12:3 wickedness, but the **r** of the righteous cannot
12:12 evil people, but the **r** of the righteous

RUIN, RUINS
5:14 almost reached total **r** in the assembly and in
10:14 of a stubborn fool **r** comes near.
10:15 city; poverty is the poor.
10:29 the innocent but a **r** to those who are
11:3 but hypocrisy leads the treacherous to **r**.
11:9 a godless person can **r** his neighbor, but the
13:3 life; whoever has a big mouth comes to **r**.
14:28 a king, but without people a ruler is **r**.
18:7 fool's mouth is his **r**, and his lips are a
19:13 A foolish son **r** his father, and a quarreling
26:28 victims, and a flattering mouth causes **r**.
31:3 power to those who **r** kings.

RULE, RULER
8:16 With me princes **r**, so do nobles and all just
14:28 without people a **r** is ruined.
19:10 much less a slave **r** over princes.
22:7 The rich person **r** over the poor, and the
23:1 down to eat with a **r**, pay close attention to
25:15 you can persuade a **r**, and a soft tongue can
28:2 revolt it has many **r**, but only with a

RUTHLESS
11:16 wins respect, but **r** men gain riches.

SACRIFICE
13:6 wickedness negates a **s** for sin.
15:8 A **s** brought by the wicked is disgusting
21:3 to the LORD than offering a **s**.
21:27 The **s** of the wicked is disgusting,

SAFE
18:10 a righteous person runs to it and is **s**.
28:18 honestly will be **s**, but whoever lives
29:25 for him but one who trusts the LORD is **s**.

SATISFY
5:19 let her breasts **s** you; always be
6:30 when he steals to **s** his appetite; but when
6:35 bribe will not **s** him.
13:25 person eats to **s** his appetite, but the
14:14 but a good man is **s** with God's ways.
27:20 are never **s**, and a person's eyes are never **s**
30:9 or I may feel **s** and deny You and say,

SAVE
2:12 Wisdom will **s** you from the way of evil,
2:16 Wisdom will also **s** you from the adulterous
11:4 but righteousness **s** from death; the
11:6 The upright are **s** by their righteousness,
14:25 An honest witness is true, but one who tells
20:22 the LORD and He will **s** you.
23:14 and you will **s** his soul from hell.

SCALES
11:1 Dishonest s are disgusting to the LORD,
16:11 Honest balances and s belong to the LORD;
20:23 LORD, and dishonest s are no good.

SCHEME, SCHEMER
1:31 they will be stuffed with their own s.
12:2 but the LORD condemns everyone who s.
24:8 plans to do evil will be known as a s.
24:9 Foolish s is sinful, and a mocker is
30:32 yourself, or if you s evil, you had better

SCOLD
13:1 but a mocker does not listen to s.
17:10 A s impresses a person who has
30:6 words or He will s you, and you will be

SCOUNDREL
6:12 good-for-nothing s is a man who has a

SEA
8:29 set a limit for the s so the waters would not
23:34 in the middle of the s or like someone lying
30:19 ship making its way through high s;

SEARCH
2:4 if you s for it as if it were money and
11:27 eagerly seeks good s for good will, but
14:6 A mocker s for wisdom without finding it,
15:14 has understanding s for knowledge, but
20:27 LORD's lamp; it s his entire innermost

SECRET
9:17 and food eaten in s is tasty.
11:13 gossips gives away s, but whoever is
11:13 is trustworthy in spirit can keep a s.
20:19 as a gossip tells s; do not associate with
21:14 A gift given in s calms anger, and a
21:14 calms anger, and a s bribe calms great fury.
25:9 another person's s; otherwise, when he

SECRETLY
17:23 A wicked person s accepts a bribe to

SECURE, SECURELY
4:26 your ways will be s; do not lean to the
10:9 will live s, but whoever lives
11:15 hates the closing of a deal remains s.
25:5 a king and justice will make his throne s.
29:14 with honesty, his throne will always be s.

SECURITY
21:29 person's way of life is his own s.

SEEK
11:27 Whoever eagerly s good searches for good
17:9 forgives an offense s love, but whoever
18:15 the ears of the wise s knowledge.
28:5 but those who s the LORD understand
29:10 but upright people s to protect his life.
29:26 Many s an audience with a ruler, but justice

SEEMS
14:12 There is a way that s right to a man, but
16:25 There is a way that s right to a man, but
17:8 A bribe s like a jewel to the one who
18:17 to state his case s right—until his

SEE
5:21 ways are clearly s by the LORD, and He
20:12 hears; the eye that s; the LORD made them
25:7 in front of a prince whom your eyes have s.
28:11 with understanding s right through him.
31:18 with energy; she s that she is making a good

SELF-CONTROL
25:28 a wall, so is a man who lacks s.

SENSE
10:13 but a rod is for the back of one without s.
10:21 stubborn fools die because they have no s.
11:12 a neighbor has no s, but a person who has
12:11 but the one who chases rainbows has no s.
13:15 Good s brings favor, but the way of the
15:5 whoever appreciates a warning shows good s.
15:21 one without much s, but a man who has
17:18 person without good s closes a deal with a
19:8 A person who gains s loves himself; one who
19:11 A person with good s is patient, and it is

SENSIBLE
8:5 You gullible people, learn how to be s!
12:16 immediately, but a s person hides the
12:23 A s person discreetly hides knowledge,
13:16 Any s person acts with knowledge, but a
14:8 The wisdom of a s person guides his way
14:15 anything, but a s person watches his step.
14:18 stupidity, but s people are crowned with
19:14 fathers, but a s wife comes from the LORD.
22:3 A s person foresees trouble and hides
26:16 people who give a s answer.
27:12 A s person foresees trouble and hides,

SERVANT
9:3 has sent out her s girls; she calls from
14:35 delighted with a s who acts wisely, but he
27:27 and to keep your s girls alive.
29:12 to lies, all his s become wicked.
31:15 a share of food to her s girls.

SET
8:27 When He s up the heavens I was there.
8:29 the ocean, when He s a limit for the sea so
30:4 Who has s up the earth from one end to the

SEVEN
6:16 LORD hates, even s that are disgusting to
6:31 he has to repay it s times; he must give up
9:1 has carved out her s pillars; she has
24:16 person may fall s times—but he gets up
26:16 he is wiser than s people who give a
26:25 him because of the s disgusting things in

SEX
2:19 None who have s with her come back nor do
6:29 with the man who has s with his neighbor's

SHAME, SHAMEFUL
10:5 son; he who sleeps at harvest time brings s.
11:2 comes, then comes s, but wisdom remains
13:5 person behaves with s and disgrace.
13:18 Poverty and s come to the one who ignores
18:13 before he listens is stupid and s.
19:26 his mother brings s and disgrace.

SHARE
5:17 alone, so do not s them with strangers.
14:10 and no stranger can s its joy.
16:19 the lowly than to s plunder with the proud.
17:2 and he will s the inheritance with the
17:17 brother is born to s trouble.
21:9 of a roof than to s a home with a quarreling
22:9 blessed, for he has s his food with the
25:24 of a roof than to s a home with a quarreling
31:15 to her family and a s of food to her servant

SHEOL
15:11 S and Abaddon lie open before the LORD—
27:20 S and Abaddon are never satisfied, and a

SHIELD
2:7 people; He is a S for those who walk in
30:5 He is a S to those who come to Him for

SHORT, SHORT-TEMPERED
14:17 A s person acts stupid, and a man
14:29 become angry, but a s temper is the height

SHOW
6:34 the husband will s no mercy when he takes
12:16 is irritated, he s it immediately, but a
15:5 appreciates a warning s good sense.
24:23 It is not good to s partiality as a judge.

SHUTS
21:13 Whoever s his ear to the cry of the poor;

SICK, SICKNESS
13:12 delayed makes one s at heart, but a fulfilled
18:14 spirit can endure s but who can bear a

SIGHT
1:17 a net within the s of any bird.
3:4 much success in the s of God and mankind.
3:21 My son, do not lose s of these things: Use
4:21 I say: Do not lose s of these things; keep
4:25 ahead and your s be focused in front of you.
29:13 in common: the LORD gives both of them s.

SILENT
17:28 wise if he keeps s; he is considered

SILVER
3:14 gained from s; its yield is better than
8:10 my discipline, not s, and my knowledge
8:19 gold; what I yield is better than fine s.
10:20 righteous is pure s; the heart of the
16:16 of understanding should be chosen over s.
16:31 S hair is a beautiful crown found in a
17:3 is for refining s and the smelter for gold,
20:29 older people is their s hair.
25:11 golden apples in s settings, so is a word
27:21 is for refining s and the smelter for gold,

SIN, SINFUL, SINNER
1:10 My son, if s lure you, don't go along!
10:19 S is unavoidable when there is much talk, but
11:31 how much more the wicked and the s!
12:13 trapped by his own s talk, but a righteous
13:6 but wickedness negates a sacrifice for s.
14:21 his neighbor s, but blessed is the one who is
14:34 up a nation, but s is a defect in any society.
17:19 Whoever loves s loves a quarrel; whoever
20:9 my heart pure; I'm cleansed from my s?
21:4 which are the lamp of the wicked, are s.
24:9 scheming is s, and a mocker is disgusting
28:13 covers over his s does not prosper, but
29:6 To an evil man s is bait in a trap, but a

SISTER
7:4 wisdom, You are my s, and give the name My

SIX
6:16 There are s things that the LORD hates, even

SKY
23:5 itself like an eagle flying off into the s.
30:19 an eagle making its way through the s;

SLANDER, SLANDEROUS
10:18 whoever spreads s is a fool.
17:4 his ears to a s tongue.
30:10 Do not s a slave to his master or he will

SLAVE
11:29 fool becomes a s to the wise in heart.
12:9 and have a s than to act important and have
12:24 but lazy hands do s labor.
17:2 A wise s will become master over a son who
19:10 a fool, much less a s ruling over princes.
22:7 the borrower is a s to the lender.
29:19 A s cannot be disciplined with words; he
29:21 Pamper a s from childhood and later on he
30:10 Do not slander a s to his master or he will
30:22 bear up under: a s when he becomes king and

SLEEP
3:24 you lie there, your s will be sweet.
4:16 the wicked cannot s unless they do wrong,
4:16 are robbed of their s unless they make
6:4 neighbor; give no s to your eyes nor slumber
6:9 When will you get up from your s?
6:10 Just a little s, just a little slumber, just
10:5 a wise son; he who s at harvest time brings
19:15 one into a deep s, and an idle person will
20:13 Do not love s or you will end up poor; keep
24:33 Just a little s, just a little slumber, just

SLOW, SLOWLY
14:29 understanding is s to become angry, but a
16:32 Better to get angry s than to be a hero,

SLUMBER
6:4 to your eyes nor s to your eyelids;
6:10 just a little s, just a little nap.
24:33 just a little s, just a little nap.

SMALL
30:24 things on earth are s, yet they are very

SMOOTH
2:16 woman with her s talk, who leaves the
5:3 and her kiss is s than oil, but in the
6:24 woman and from the s talk of a loose woman.
11:5 makes his road s, but the wicked falls by
26:23 dross, so is s talk which covers up an

SNAKE
23:32 on it bites like a s and strikes like a
23:32 a snake and strikes like a poisonous s.
30:19 s making its way over a rock;

SNUFFED
13:9 lamp of the wicked will be s out.
20:20 his lamp will be s out in total darkness.
24:20 lamp of the wicked will be s out.

SOCIETY
14:34 a nation, but sin is a defect in any s.
23:28 she spreads unfaithfulness throughout s.

SON
1:10 My s, if sinners lure you, don't go along!
2:1 My s, if you take my words to heart and
3:1 My s, do not forget my teaching, and keep my
3:11 of the LORD, my s, nor resent His warning,
3:12 as a father warns a s in whom he delights.
3:21 My s, do not lose sight of these things: Use
5:20 Why should you, my s, be intoxicated with an
6:1 My s, if you guarantee a loan for your
15:20 A wise s makes his father happy, but a foolish
17:2 become master over a s who acts shamefully,
17:25 A foolish s is a heartache to his father and
19:18 Discipline your s while there is still hope;
23:15 My s, if you have a wise heart, my heart will
23:22 since you are his s, and do not despise your
23:24 one who has a wise s will enjoy him.
24:13 Eat honey, my s, because it is good; honey
24:21 Fear the LORD, my s (fear the king as
29:17 Correct your s and he will give you peace of
30:4 What is His Name or the Name of His S?

SONG
1:20 Wisdom sings her s in the streets; in the
8:3 wisdom sings its s: I am calling to you,

SOUL
2:10 be pleasant to your s; foresight will protect
2:18 ways lead to the s of those who died.
9:18 not know that the s of those who died are
11:30 and a winner of s is wise.
13:19 is sweet to the s, but turning from evil is
18:7 his ruin, and his lips are a trap to his s.

20:27 A person's s is the LORD's lamp; it searches
23:14 you will save his s from hell.
24:12 He who guards your s know it?
24:14 of wisdom is just like that for your s—
25:25 water to a thirsty s, so is good news from
29:17 mind, and he will bring delight to your s.

SOWS
22:8 Whoever s injustice will reap trouble, and

SPANK
13:24 He who refuses to s his son hates him, but
22:15 a child's heart; s will remove it far
23:13 a child; if you s him he will not die.
23:14 S him yourself, and you will save his soul
29:15 A s and a warning produce wisdom, but an

SPARE
24:11 to death, and s those staggering toward

SPARROW
26:2 Like a fluttering s, like a darting

SPEECH
4:24 and put deceptive s far away from your lips;
8:13 arrogance, evil behavior, and twisted s.
14:3 him, but the wise are protected by their s.
16:23 heart controls his, and when he says
16:27 trouble, and his s is like a burning fire.
17:7 Refined s is not fitting for a godless fool
22:11 heart and whose s is gracious, has a king
26:24 it with his s, but inside he holds on to

SPENDS
11:24 One person s freely and yet grows richer,

SPIRIT
1:23 pour out my s for you; I will make my words
11:13 is trustworthy in s can keep a secret.
15:4 life, but a deceitful tongue breaks the s.
16:24 sweet to the s and healthy for the body.
18:14 A man's s can endure sickness, but who can
18:14 sickness, but who can bear a broken s?
29:23 him, but a humble s gains honor.

SPLENDOR
20:29 strength, the s of older people is their

SPREAD
6:14 all the time; he s conflict.
6:19 and a person who s conflict among brothers.
10:18 lips, and whoever s slander is a fool.
11:18 wages, but whoever s righteousness earns
15:7 of the righteous s knowledge, but a foolish
16:28 An devious man s quarrels, and a gossip
23:28 in ambush; she s unfaithfulness throughout

STAND
12:3 A man cannot s firm on a foundation of
12:7 the family of the righteous continues to s.
31:28 Her children s up and bless her; her husband

STARVE
10:3 person to s, but He intentionally rejects

STAY
2:20 of good people and s on the paths of the
7:11 her feet will not s at home.
14:7 S away from a fool, because you will not
22:5 guards himself will s far away from them.

STEAKS
15:17 is love than juicy s where there is hate.

STEAL
6:30 is hungry when he s to satisfy his appetite;
30:9 may become poor and s and give the Name of

STEER
7:22 follows her, like a s on its way to be

STEP
5:5 to death; her s lead straight to hell.
5:6 path of life; her s wander and she doesn't
14:15 but a sensible person watches his s.
16:9 own journey, but the LORD directs his s.
20:24 who directs a man's s; how then can a man
29:5 a net for him to s into.

STINGY
23:6 food of one who is s and do not crave his
28:22 A s man is in a hurry to get rich, not

STIRS
15:1 but a harsh word s up anger.
15:18 A hothead s up a fight, but one who holds
28:25 A greedy person s up a fight, but whoever
29:22 An angry man s up a fight, and a hothead

STOMACH
18:20 provides for his s; his talking provides

STOP
17:14 a floodgate, so s before the argument gets
19:27 If you s listening to instruction, my son,
22:10 will leave; quarreling and abuse will s.
23:4 out getting rich; be smart enough to s!

STORE
10:14 Those who are wise s up knowledge, but by
13:22 of a sinner is s away for the righteous.

STORM
1:27 you like a violent s, and when calamity
10:25 When the s has passed, the wicked person has
25:14 dense fog or a dust s, so is the man who

STRAIGHT
4:25 let your eyes look s ahead and your sight
4:26 Carefully walk a s path and all your ways
5:5 her steps lead s to hell.
15:21 has understanding forges s ahead.
24:26 Giving a s answer is like a kiss on the

STRANGER
5:10 cruel person; or s will benefit from
5:17 alone, so do not share them with s.
6:1 yourself for a s with a handshake, you
11:15 guarantees a s loan will get into
14:10 bitterness, and no s can share its joy.
20:16 who guarantees a s loan, and from
27:2 own mouth, from a s and not from your
27:13 who guarantees a s loan, and hold

STRATEGY
24:6 for with the right s you can wage war,

STRAY
4:14 Do not s onto the path of the wicked nor
10:17 to life, but whoever ignores a warning s.
14:22 Don't those who s plan evil, while the ones

STRENGTH
5:10 benefit from your s, and you will have to
12:4 A wife with s of character is the crown
14:4 is empty, but the s of an ox produces
17:22 medicine, but depression drains one's s.
20:29 men is their s, the splendor of older
31:3 Don't give your s to women or your power
31:10 find a wife with s of character?

STRIKE
1:26 of you when panic s you, when panic
1:27 you, when panic s you like a violent storm,
1:27 and when calamity s you like a tornado,
17:26 is not good; to s down noble people is not
19:25 S a mocker and a gullible person may learn
23:32 like a snake and s like a poisonous snake.
23:35 mast, saying They s me, but I feel no

STUMBLE
4:12 hampered; even if you run, you will not s.
4:16 they make someone s, for they eat food
4:19 they do not know what makes them s.
5:23 of discipline and s around because of his
24:17 glad when they s, or the LORD will see it

STUPID, STUPIDITY
5:23 stumble around because of his great s.
9:13 The woman, S, is a loudmouth, gullible
13:16 with knowledge, but a fool displays s.
14:1 up her home, but a s one tears it down with
14:17 person acts s, and a man who plots evil is
14:18 are gifted with s, but sensible people
14:24 the s of fools is just that—s!
14:29 but a short temper is the height of s.
15:2 mouth of fools pours out a flood of s.
15:14 but the mouth of fools feeds on s.
17:12 than a fool carried away with his s.
18:13 he listens is s and shameful.
19:3 The s of a person turns his life upside
26:11 his vomit, so a fool repeats his s.
27:22 even then his s will not leave him.

SUCCEED, SUCCESS
3:4 favor and much s in the sight of God and
15:22 go wrong, but with many advisers they s.
16:3 works to the LORD, and your plans will s.

SUDDEN, SUDDENLY
3:25 Do not be afraid of s terror nor of the
6:15 will come on him s; in a moment he will
24:22 will come on them s, and who knows what
29:1 many warnings will s be broken beyond

SUFFER
13:20 but whoever associates with fools will s.
19:23 rest easy without s harm.
22:3 people go ahead and s the consequence.
27:12 but gullible people go ahead and s.

SWALLOW
1:12 for fun; we'll s them alive like the grave,
18:8 of a gossip are s greedily, and they go
19:28 of the wicked are s up trouble.
26:2 like a darting s, so a hastily spoken
26:22 of a gossip are s greedily, and they go

SWEET
3:24 as you lie there, your sleep will be s.
9:17 Stolen waters are s, and food eaten in
13:19 desire fulfilled is s to the soul, but
16:24 from a honeycomb—s to the spirit and
20:17 dishonestly tastes s to a man, but afterward

24:13 honeycomb tastes s; the knowledge of
27:7 who is hungry, even bitter food tastes s.

SWORD
5:4 as wormwood, as sharp as a two-edged s.
12:18 words stab like a s, but the words of the
25:18 Like a club and a s and a sharp arrow,
30:14 teeth are like s and whose jaws are

TABLE
9:2 she has set her t; she has sent out her

TABLET
3:3 write them on the t of your heart.
7:3 write them on the t of your heart.

TAKE
1:19 for unjust gain; it t away his life.
2:1 My son, if you t my words to heart and
3:18 of life for those who t firm hold of it
6:34 will show no mercy when he t revenge.
8:10 T my discipline, not silver and my knowledge
11:8 the wicked person t his place; with his talk
13:10 but those who t advice gain wisdom.
25:4 T dross away from silver and a vessel is

TALKS
10:8 but the one who t foolishly will be thrown
10:10 and the one who t foolishly will be thrown
19:1 than to be one who t dishonestly and is a
26:25 When he t charmingly, do not trust him

TASTES
20:17 gained dishonestly t sweet to a man, but
24:13 from the honeycomb t sweet; the knowledge
27:7 even bitter food t sweet.

TAXES
28:16 understanding t his people heavily, but

TEACHING
1:8 your mother's t, because they are a
3:1 do not forget my t, and keep my commands
4:2 taught you well; do not abandon my t.
6:20 not disregard the t of your mother:
6:23 is a lamp and the t is a light, and the
7:2 live, and keep my t just as you protect
13:14 The t of the wise is a fountain of life
28:4 abandon God's t praise the wicked, but
28:4 who keep God's t oppose them.
28:7 keeps God's t is a wise son, whoever
28:9 listen to God's t, even his prayer is
29:18 blessed are those who keep God's t.

TEACHERS
5:13 listen to what my t said to me nor did I

TEARS
14:1 but a stupid one t it down with her own
15:25 The LORD t down the house of the proud,
29:4 religious contributions t it down.

TEETH
10:26 Like vinegar to the t and like smoke to the
30:14 of person whose t are like swords and

TELLS
14:25 lives, but one who t lies is dangerous.
20:19 around as a gossip t secrets; do not
23:7 is what he does: he t you, Eat and drink,

TEMPER
14:29 angry, but a short t is the height of
15:18 one who holds his t calms disputes.
19:19 who has a hot t will pay for it; if you
22:24 one who has a bad t and never keep company

TENDER
4:3 son to my father, a t and only child of my
27:25 is removed, the t growth appears and
31:26 her tongue there is t instruction.

TERRIBLE
15:10 Discipline is a t burden to anyone who
15:15 Every day is a t day for a miserable

TERRIFIED
21:15 are delighted, but troublemakers are t.

TERROR
3:25 be afraid of sudden t nor of the

TESTIFY, TESTIMONY
24:28 Do not t against your neighbor without a
25:18 who gives false t against his neighbor.
29:24 life; he will not t under oath.

THIEF
6:30 do not despise a t who is hungry when he
29:24 Anyone who is a t partner hates his own

THINK
5:6 She doesn't even t about the path of life;
16:2 A man t all his ways are pure, but the LORD
21:2 A man t everything he does is right, but
26:5 or he will t he is wise.
26:12 you met a man who t he is wise?

26:16 A lazy person t he is wiser than seven
30:12 kind of person who t he is pure but is not
THIRSTY
25:21 eat, and if he is t, give him some water
25:25 cold water to a t soul, so is good news
THOUGHTS
1:2 understand deep t, to acquire the
12:5 The t of the righteous are just; the
15:26 The t of evil people are disgusting to
20:25 to have second t about those vows.
THREE
30:15 There are t things that are never satisfied,
30:18 T things are too wonderful for me, even four
30:21 T things cause the earth to tremble, even
30:29 There are t things that walk like a king
THRONE
16:12 to kings, because a t is established
20:8 who sits on his t to judge sifts out every
20:28 a king, and with mercy he maintains his t.
25:5 will make his t secure.
29:14 with honesty, his t will always be secure.
THROWN
10:8 foolishly will be t down headfirst.
10:10 foolishly will be t down headfirst.
14:32 A wicked person is t down by his own
16:33 The dice are t, but the LORD determines
19:15 Laziness t one into a deep sleep, and an
21:12 of the wicked; He t the wicked into
TIME
1:28 call to me at that t, but I will not answer;
6:14 evil all the t; he spreads conflict.
8:30 before Him all the t, rejoicing in His
21:6 lying are wasting t; they are looking for
25:11 so is a word spoken at the right t.
28:2 and knowledge will a it last a long t.
TIMELY
15:23 own mouth, and a t word—oh, how good!
TOMORROW
27:1 Do not brag about t, because you do not
TOOTH
25:19 Like a broken t and a lame foot, so is
TOTAL
5:14 I almost reached t ruin in the assembly and
20:20 be snuffed out in t darkness.
TOWER
18:10 LORD is a strong t; a righteous person runs
18:19 are like the locked gate of a castle t.
TRACED
8:27 When He t the horizon on the surface of the
8:29 command, when He t the foundations of the
TRAIN
22:6 T a child in the way he should go, and even
TRAMPLE
22:22 he is poor or t on the rights of those in
TRANQUIL
14:30 A t heart makes for a healthy body, but
TRAP
5:22 person will be t by his own wrongs, and he
6:2 handshake, you are t by the words of your
7:23 bird darting into a t, he does not realize
11:6 treacherous are t by their own greed.
12:12 in setting a t for other evil people, but
12:13 An evil person is t by his own sinful talk,
18:7 and his lips are a t to his soul.
20:25 It is a t for a man to say impulsively: This
29:6 sin is bait in a t, but a righteous person
TREACHEROUS
2:22 the land and the t will be torn from
11:3 leads the t to ruin.
11:6 but the t are trapped by their own
12:5 of the wicked is t; the words of the
13:2 appetite of the t craves violence.
13:15 the way of the t is always the same.
21:18 and the t will take the place of the
22:12 but He overturns the words of the t.
TREE
3:18 Wisdom is a t of life for those who take
11:30 the righteous is a t of life, and a winner of
13:12 longing is a t of life.
15:4 soothing tongue is a t of life, but a
27:18 takes care of a fig t can eat its fruit, and
TREMBLE
30:21 cause the earth to t, even four it cannot
TRICKS
26:19 so is the man who t his neighbor and
TRIUMPH
28:12 When the righteous t, there is great glory,
TROUBLE
1:27 a tornado, when t and anguish come upon

11:8 is rescued from t, and the wicked person
11:15 loan will get into t, but whoever hates
11:29 Whoever brings t upon his family inherits
12:13 but a righteous person escapes from t.
12:21 righteous, but the wicked have lots of t.
16:4 and even the wicked for the Day of T.
16:27 man plots t, and his speech is like a
19:28 the mouth of the wicked swallows up t.
21:23 and his tongue keeps himself out of t.
22:3 person foresees t and hides from it but
22:8 will reap t, and this weapon of his own
24:2 plot violence, and their lips talk t.
27:10 when you are in t; a neighbor living
31:7 not remember his t anymore.
TROUBLEMAKERS
10:29 but a ruin to those who are t.
21:15 delighted, but t are terrified.
TRUE
30:5 Every word of God has proven to be t.
TRUST, TRUSTWORTHY
3:5 T the LORD with all your heart, and do not
11:13 but whoever is t in spirit can keep a
11:28 Whoever t in his riches will fall, but the
14:5 A t witness does not lie, but a
16:20 is the one who t the LORD.
20:6 who can find a man who is really t?
21:22 down the strong defenses in which they t.
22:19 tongue, so that your t may be in the LORD.
25:13 day, so is the t messenger to those
26:25 charmingly, do not t him because of the
28:20 A t man has many blessings, but the
28:25 fight, but whoever t the LORD prospers.
28:26 Whoever t his own heart is a fool, but
29:25 but one who t the LORD is safe.
31:11 Her husband t her with all his heart, and
TRUTH
3:3 not let mercy t leave you: fasten them
8:7 mouth expresses the t, and wickedness is
12:19 The word of t lasts forever, but lies last
20:28 Mercy and t protect a king, and with mercy
22:21 the very words of t, so that you can give an
23:23 Buy t (and do not sell it), that is, buy
TWISTED
6:14 With a t mind he is devising evil all the
8:8 there is nothing t or crooked in it; all
8:13 evil behavior, and t speech.
12:8 but whoever has a t mind will be despised.
17:20 A t mind never finds happiness, and one
TWO
30:7 I've asked You for t things; don't keep them
30:15 leech has t daughters—Give! and Give!

UNDERSTANDING
3:5 and do not rely on your own u.
4:7 with all that you have: Acquire u!
8:5 You fools, get a heart that has u.
9:10 the knowledge of the Holy One is u.
UNDISCIPLINED
29:15 wisdom, but an u child disgraces his
UNFAITHFUL
25:19 confidence in an u person in a
UNFAITHFULNESS
23:28 she spreads u throughout society.
UNGRATEFUL
29:21 childhood and later on he will be u.
UNJUST
1:19 who is greedy for u gain; it takes away his
15:27 is greedy for u gain brings trouble upon
28:16 but those who hate u gain will live longer.
29:27 An u man is disgusting to righteous people,
UNPUNISHED
11:21 will not go u, but the descendants of
16:5 such a person will not go u.
19:5 will not go u, and one who utters lies
19:9 will not go u, and one who utters lies
UPRIGHT
2:21 righteous, for the u will live in the land
3:32 LORD; His intimate advice is with the u.
11:3 guides the u, but hypocrisy leads the
11:6 The u are saved by their righteousness,
11:11 blessing of the u a city is exalted, but
14:9 but there is forgiveness among the u.
14:11 the tent of the u will continue to expand.
21:18 treacherous will take the place of the u.

VANDAL
18:9 is lazy in his work is a brother to a v.
28:24 is a companion to a v.

VANISH
10:25 wicked person has v, but the righteous
11:7 person, hope v; moreover his confidence
11:7 moreover his confidence in strength v.
VEGETABLES
15:17 to have a dish of v where there is love
VICTIMS
7:26 brought down many v, and numerous are all
26:28 tongue hates its v, and a flattering mouth
VICTORY
11:14 but with many advisers there is v.
21:31 of battle, but the v belongs to the LORD.
24:6 war, and with many advisers there is v.
VINEYARD
24:30 man's field, the v belonging to a man
31:16 it; she plants a v from the profits she
VIOLENCE, VIOLENT
1:27 strikes you like a v storm, and when
3:31 Do not envy a v man, and do not choose any
4:17 and drink wine obtained through v.
10:6 the righteous, but v covers the mouth of
10:11 but the mouth of the wicked conceals v.
13:2 appetite of the treacherous craves v.
16:29 A v man misleads his neighbor and leads
21:7 The v of the wicked will drag them away
24:2 their minds plot v, and their lips talk
26:6 feet and brings v upon himself.
VIRGIN
30:19 a man making his way with a v.
VISION
29:18 Without prophetic v people run wild, but
VOICE
1:20 she raises her v; at the corners of noisy
8:1 out, and does not understanding raise its v?
16:10 lips, he cannot v a wrong judgment.
27:14 morning with a loud v—his blessing is
VOMIT
23:8 you will v up the little bit you have eaten
25:16 otherwise, you will have too much and v.
26:11 goes back to his v, so a fool repeats his
VULTURES
30:17 in the valley and eaten by young v.

WALK
2:7 Shield for those who w in integrity in order
2:13 of righteousness to w the ways of darkness,
2:20 Therefore, w in the way of good people and
4:15 it; turn away from it; and keep on w!
4:26 Carefully w a straight path and all your
4:27 or to the left; w away from evil!
6:22 When you w around, they will lead you; when
6:28 Or can anyone w on red-hot coals without
8:20 I w in the way of righteousness, on the paths
13:20 Whoever w with the wise will be wise, but
28:26 a fool, but whoever w in wisdom will survive.
WANDER
5:6 of life; her steps w and she doesn't
7:25 to her ways; do not w onto her paths,
21:16 A person who w from the way of wise
27:8 Like a bird w from its nest, so is a man
27:8 nest, so is a man w from his home.
WAR
20:18 advice, and with guidance one wages w.
24:6 you can wage w, and with many advisers
WARN, WARNING
1:23 Turn to me when I w you—I will generously
1:30 my advice; they despised my every w.
3:11 son, nor resent His w, because the LORD
3:12 because the LORD w the one He loves, even
3:12 even as a father w a son in whom he delights.
10:17 whoever ignores a w strays.
15:5 appreciates a w shows good sense.
15:10 anyone who hates a w will die.
15:12 not appreciate a w; he will not go to the
15:31 to a life-giving w will be at home among
15:32 one who listens to w gains understanding.
19:25 learn a lesson; w an understanding person
29:15 A spanking and a w produce wisdom, but
WATCH
2:8 of justice and to w over the way of His
4:6 and it will w over you; love wisdom and it
6:6 ant, you lazy bum; w its ways and become
6:22 lie down, they will w over you; and when you
14:15 a sensible person w his step.
16:17 from evil; whoever w his way preserves his
22:12 The LORD's eyes w over knowledge, but He

WATER
3:20 Knowledge the deep w were divided and the
5:15 Drink w out of your own cistern and running
5:15 cistern and running w from your own well.
5:16 Why should w flow out of your spring?
8:29 for the sea so the w would not overstep His
18:4 are like deep w; the fountain of wisdom
19:13 woman is like constantly dripping w.
20:5 is like deep w, but a person who has
25:21 give him some w to drink; for in this way
27:15 Constantly dripping w on a rainy day is like
27:19 is reflected in w, so a person is reflected
30:4 Who has wrapped up w in a garment?

WAY
1:15 follow them in their w; do not even set foot
2:8 to watch over the w of His godly ones; then
2:12 save you from the w of evil, from the man
2:13 to walk the w of darkness, from those who
2:15 crooked, and their w are devious.
2:18 to death, and her w lead to the souls of
2:20 walk in the w of good people and stay on the
3:6 In all your w acknowledge [give credit to]
3:23 go safely on your w, and you will not stub
4:14 nor walk in the w of evil people.
4:19 The w of the wicked is like deep darkness;
4:26 path and all your w will be secure; do not
5:21 For a man's w are clearly seen by the LORD,
6:6 lazy bum; watch its w and become wise:
7:27 Her home is the w to hell, leading down to the
8:20 I walk in the w of righteousness, on the paths
8:22 long ago, when His w began, before any of
8:32 to Me: Blessed are those who keep My w.
10:17 discipline is on the w to life, but whoever
10:29 The w of the LORD is a fortress for the
11:20 with those whose w are innocent.
12:15 considers his own w the right one, but a
13:6 protects the honest w of life, but wickedness
13:15 favor, but the w of the treacherous is always
14:2 is devious in his w despises Him.
14:8 person guides his w of life, but the stupidity
14:12 There is a w that seems right to a man, but
14:14 bored with its own w, but a good man is
14:14 but a good man is satisfied with God's w.
15:9 w of the wicked is disgusting to the LORD,
16:2 man thinks all his w are pure, but the LORD
16:7 When a man's w are pleasing to the LORD,
16:17 whoever watches his w preserves his own life.
16:25 There is a w that seems right to a man, but
17:23 bribe to corrupt the w of justice.
20:24 how then can a man understand his own w?
22:6 Train a child in the w he should go, and even

WEALTH, WEALTHY
10:15 The rich person's w is his strong city;
12:27 prey, but a hardworking person becomes w.
13:7 pretends to be poor but has great w.
13:11 W gained through injustice dwindles
18:11 A rich person's w is his strong city and is
19:4 W adds many friends, but a poor person
19:14 Home and w are inherited from fathers, but
21:6 Those who gather w by lying are wasting
28:8 Whoever becomes w through unfair loans

WEARY
30:1 declaration: I'm w, O God, I'm w, O God,

WEIGH
12:25 man's anxiety will w him down, but an
16:2 pure, but the LORD w motives.
21:2 right, but the LORD w hearts.
24:12 won't He who w hearts take note of it?
27:3 is heavy and sand w a lot, but annoyance

WEIGHTS
11:1 LORD, but accurate w are pleasing to Him.
16:11 to the LORD; He made the entire set of w.
20:10 double standard of w and measures—both
20:23 double standard of w is disgusting to the

WICKED
10:7 but the name of the w will rot away.
10:11 the mouth of the w conceals violence.
12:7 Overthrow the w and they are no more, but
13:9 but the lamp of the w will be snuffed out.
14:11 The house of the w will be destroyed, but
19:28 the mouth of the w swallows up trouble.
24:16 in a disaster, w people fall.
28:1 A w person flees when no one is chasing him,

WICKEDNESS
8:7 the truth, and w is disgusting to my
11:5 but the wicked falls by his own w.
12:3 a foundation of w, but the root of the
13:6 way of life, but w negates a sacrifice
18:3 When w comes, contempt also comes, and

20:30 cleanse away w; such beatings cleanse
26:26 hidden, but his w will be revealed in

WIDOW
15:25 but He protects the property of the w.

WIFE
6:29 with his neighbor's w; none who touch her
12:4 A w with strength of character is the crown
12:4 her husband, but the w who disgraces him is
18:22 He who finds a w finds something good and
19:14 but a sensible w comes from the LORD.
31:10 Who can find a w with strength of character?

WIND
11:29 inherits only w, and that stubborn fool
25:23 As the north w brings rain, so the
27:16 her can control the w; he can even pick up
30:4 Who has gathered the w in the palm of His

WINE
3:10 and your vats will overflow with fresh w.
9:2 she has mixed her w; also, she has set her
9:5 bread and drink the w I have mixed; give up
21:17 man; whoever loves w and rich food will not
23:20 who drink too much w, with those who eat too
23:30 after glass of w; who go and mix it with
23:31 Do not look at w just because it is red, just
31:4 it is not for kings to drink w,
31:6 who is perishing and w to one who feels

WINKS
6:13 dishonest mouth: he w his eye, makes a
10:10 Whoever w with his eye causes heartache,
16:30 Whoever w his eye is plotting something

WINNER
11:30 tree of life, and a w of souls is wise.

WINS
11:16 A gracious woman w respect, but ruthless men

WISDOM
1:7 of knowledge; w and discipline are despised
1:20 W sings her song in the streets; in the
3:19 By W the LORD laid the foundation of the
4:7 The beginning is w: Acquire w!
4:11 you the way of w; I have guided you along
5:1 attention to my w; open your ears to my
7:4 Say to w, You are my sister, and give the
8:12 I, W, live with insight, and I acquire
9:10 the beginning of w, and the knowledge of
24:7 Matters of w are beyond the grasp of a

WISE
1:6 the words of the w and their riddles.
3:35 The w will inherit honor, but fools will bear
10:5 in the summer is a w son; he who sleeps at
13:1 A w son listens to his father's discipline,
13:14 The teaching of the w is a fountain of life
15:20 A w son makes his father happy, but a foolish
16:23 A w man's heart controls his speech, and
20:26 A w king scatters the wicked and then runs

WITNESS
12:17 A truthful w speaks honestly, but a lying
12:17 but a lying w speaks deceitfully.
14:5 A trustworthy w does not lie, but a
14:5 but a dishonest w breathes lies.
14:25 An honest w saves lives, but one who tells
19:5 A lying w will not go unpunished, and
19:28 son, A worthless w mocks justice, and the
21:28 A lying w will perish, but a man who

WOMAN
2:16 from the adulterous w, from the loose w
9:13 The w, Stupidity, is a loudmouth, gullible
11:16 A gracious w wins respect, but ruthless men
14:1 The wisest of w builds up her home, but a
21:9 than to share a home with a quarreling w.
21:19 desert than with a quarreling and angry w.
25:24 than to share a home with a quarreling w.
27:15 on a rainy day is like a quarreling w.
30:20 of an adulterous w: She eats and wipes her
30:23 filled with food; a w who is unloved when
31:3 your strength to w or your power to those

WOMB
30:16 grave and a barren w; a land that never gets
31:2 And what, son of my w?

WONDERFUL
30:18 things are too w for me, even four which

WORK
5:10 and you will have to w hard in a pagan's
8:22 when His way began, before any of His w.
10:22 rich, and hard w adds nothing to it.
12:11 Whoever w his land will have plenty to eat,
14:23 In all hard w there is always something
16:3 Entrust your w to the LORD, and your plans
16:26 laborer's appetite w to his advantage
16:30 bites his lips has finished his evil w.

18:9 is lazy in his w is a brother to a vandal.
21:25 his hands refuse to w; all day long he feels
22:29 Do you see a man who is efficient in his w?
24:27 Prepare your w outside and get things ready
28:19 Whoever w his land will have plenty to eat;
31:13 with care and w with willing hands.
31:17 a belt and goes to w with energy; she sees
31:29 have done noble w, but you have surpassed

WORLD
8:26 land or fields or the first dust of the w.
8:31 in His inhabited w, and delighting in
17:24 a fool are looking around all over the w.

WORMWOOD
5:4 is as bitter as w, as sharp as a

WORRY
1:33 will live without w and will be free from

WORTH
31:10 She is w far more than jewels.

WORTHLESS
10:20 silver; the heart of the wicked is w.
16:27 A w man plots trouble, and his speech is
19:28 my son, A w witness mocks justice, and

WOUNDS
23:29 Who has w for no reason?
27:6 W made by a friend are intended to help,

WRITE
3:3 around your neck; w them on the tablet of
7:3 on your fingers; w them on the tablet of
22:20 Didn't I w to you previously with advice

WRONG, WRONGDOING
3:29 Do not plan to do w against your neighbor
4:17 through w and drink wine obtained
5:22 trapped by his own w, and he will be caught
10:12 starts quarrels, but love covers every w.
14:32 down by his own w, but even in his
15:22 advice plans go w, but with many advisers
16:10 he cannot voice a w judgment.
16:12 W is disgusting to kings, because a
28:24 father or his mother and says, It isn't w!
29:22 up a fight, and a hothead does much w.

YEARS
3:2 you long life, good y, and peace.
4:10 will multiply the y of your life.
5:9 the rest of your y to some cruel person;
9:11 live longer, and y will be added to your
10:27 days, but the y of the wicked are shortened.

YIELD
3:14 from silver; its y is better than fine gold.
8:19 pure gold; what I y is better than fine

YOUNG
1:4 foresight to the y—a wise person will
5:18 when you were y, a loving doe and a graceful
7:7 when I saw a y man without much sense
17:12 bear robbed of her y than a fool
20:29 While the glory of y men is their strength,
30:17 valley and eaten by y vultures.

PARALLELING
PROVERBS
WITH THE NEW TESTAMENT

The NET text of *Proverbs* has set certain words in *italics*. These words have "direct correspondence" to parallel words in the NT. However, beyond this distinction there are other words which remind one of certain NT phraseology. These additional parallels are referred to as "allusions." These allusions, along with the phenomenon of direct word correspondence, are felt by the NET team to be significant to Scriptural understanding, and thus worthy of inclusion in this booklet. By the way, "direct word correspondence" is not meant to imply a "word-for-word" parallel in all instances; it also implies a direct correspondence of *ideas*.

The following listing repeats those references which have been *italicized* in the NET text of *Proverbs* and which have already been correspondingly cross-referenced to the passages listed between the *lines* at the bottom of those same pages. To that data, the present listing now adds possible "allusions" that may tie *Proverbs* to the NT. Occasionally, NT references also are added to a passage or a group of passages previously cited back on the pages of the NET text. This indicates that the new additions may be more of an allusion than a direct correspondence cross reference.

As to *italic* inclusion within the text, to cite or not to cite—that was the question. One example may suffice to indicate the fine line between "direct correspondence" and "allusion." Consider "wisdom" speaking at Prov. 9:5! Whether "wisdom" is a mere *attribute* of God in this passage or is the *Son of God* of chapter 8, the way in which "wisdom" speaks does remind one of Jesus at the Lord's Supper:

> "Come, eat my bread
> and drink the wine I have mixed."

Readers have to decide personally *what* they think God is communicating. The following references and quotes from *Proverbs*, as coupled with NT references, permit NET readers to do this.

1:16b	"hurry to shed blood" (Rom. 3:15)
1:23b	"I will generously pour out my spirit for you" (Acts 2:17; 10:45; Rom. 5:5; Tit. 3:6)
1:24c	"I stretched out my hands to you" (Rom. 10:21)
1:25a	"you ignored all my advice" (Lk. 7:30)
1:28b	"they will look for me, but they will not find me" (Jn. 7:34)
2:4b	"hidden treasure" (Matt. 13:44; Col. 2:3)
2:6a	"the LORD gives wisdom" (Jas. 1:5)

2:21a	"for the upright will live in the land" (Matt. 5:5)
3:3c	"write them on the tablet of your heart" (2 Cor. 3:3)
3:4	"you will find favor and much success in the sight of God and mankind" (Lk. 2:52; Rom. 12:17; 2 Cor. 8:21)
3:6a	"acknowledge Him" (Jn. 17:3)
3:7a	"Do not consider yourself wise" (Rom. 12:16)
3:7b	"fear the LORD" (Matt. 10:28; Lk. 12:5; Acts 10:2,22,35; 13:16,26; Col. 3:22; 1 Pet. 2:17; Rev. 14:7)
3:9b	"the first and best part of all your income" (Mk. 12:41-44; Lk. 21:1-4; 1 Cor. 16:2)
3:11,12	"Do not reject the discipline of the LORD, my son, nor resent His warning, because the LORD warns the one He loves, even as a father warns a son in whom he delights" (Heb. 12:5,6)
3:12	"because the LORD warns the one He loves, even as a father warns a son in whom he delights" (Rev. 3:19)
3:13a	"wisdom" (Col. 2:3)
3:14b,c	"silver...gold" (1 Pet. 1:18)
3:18a	"a tree of life" (Rev. 2:7; 22:2,14,19)
3:18c	"those who cling...are blessed" (Rev. 1:3; 22:7)
3:25a	"Do not be afraid of sudden terror" (1 Pet. 3:6)
3:27a,b	"Do not hold back any good thing from those who are entitled to it" (Rom. 13:7; 16:1,2; 1 Tim. 5:18; Jas. 5:4)
3:34	"When He mocks the mockers, He is gracious to the humble" (Jas. 4:6; 1 Pet. 5:5)
4:19	"The way of the wicked is like deep darkness; they do not know what makes them stumble" (Jn. 12:35)
4:26a	"Carefully walk a straight path" (Heb. 12:13)
5:21	"For a man's ways are clearly seen by the LORD, and He surveys all his actions" (Heb. 4:13)
6:15	"That is why disaster will come on him suddenly; in a moment he will be crushed beyond recovery" (2 Pet. 2:1)
6:17c	"hands that kill innocent people" (Matt. 23:35; Jas. 5:6)
6:25a	"Do not desire her beauty in your heart" (Matt. 5:28)
7:3b	"write them on the tablet of your heart" (2 Cor. 3:3)
8:8b	"twisted or crooked" (Phil. 2:15)
8:17	"I love those who love Me; those eagerly looking for Me will find Me" (Jn. 14:21)
8:20a	"I walk in the way of righteousness" (Matt. 21:32)
8:22a,b	"The LORD already possessed Me long ago, when His way began" (Jn. 1:1-18; Col. 1:15; Rev. 3:14)
8:22c	"before any of His works" (Col. 1:17)
8:23d	"before the earth began" (Jn. 17:5)
8:30a	"I was beside Him" (Jn. 1:1-3)
8:32b	"Blessed are those who keep My ways" (Lk. 11:28)
9:2a	"prepared her meat" (Matt. 22:4,8; 26:17,19; Mk. 14:12,15,16; Lk. 14:7; 22:8,9,12,13; 1 Cor. 2:9)
9:3a	"has sent out her servant girls" (Matt. 22:3)
9:3b	"calls from the highest places in the city" (Matt. 22:9)
9:5a	"Come, eat my bread" (Matt. 26:26; Mk. 14:22; 1 Cor. 11:23,24)
9:5b	"drink the wine" (Matt. 26:27; Mk. 14:23; 1 Cor. 11:25)
9:7	"Whoever corrects a mocker receives abuse, and whoever warns a wicked person gets hurt" (Matt. 7:6)
10:9b	"whoever lives dishonestly will be found out" (Acts 13:10)

10:11a	"a fountain of life" (Jn. 4:14; Rev. 7:17; 21:6)
10:12b	"love covers every wrong" (Jas. 5:20; 1 Pet. 4:8)
10:25a	"When the storm has passed, the wicked person has vanished" (Matt. 7:27)
10:25b	"but the righteous person has an everlasting foundation" (Matt. 7:25)
11:17a	"A merciful man benefits himself" (Matt. 5:7)
11:24	"One person spends freely and yet grows richer, while another holds back what he owes and yet grows poorer" (2 Cor. 9:6; Gal. 6:7)
11:30a	"The fruit of the righteous" (Phil. 1:11)
11:30a	"a tree of life" (Rev. 2:7; 22:2,14,19)
11:30b	"a winner of souls is wise" (Jas. 5:20)
11:31	"If the righteous person is rewarded on earth—how much more the wicked and the sinner" (1 Pet. 4:18)
12:2a	"obtains favor from the LORD" (Lk. 1:30)
12:28a	"On the road of righteousness" (Matt. 21:32)
13:9b	"the lamp of the wicked will be snuffed out" (Matt. 25:8)
13:12b	"a tree of life" (Rev. 2:7; 22:2,4,19)
13:14a	"a fountain of life" (Jn. 4:14; Rev. 7:17; 21:6)
14:5a	"A trustworthy witness" (Rev. 1:5; 3:14)
14:5b	"a dishonest witness" (Acts 6:13)
14:12b	"but eventually it ends in death" (Rom. 6:21)
14:21b	"blessed is the one who is kind to the humble" (Matt. 5:7)
14:27a	"a fountain of life" (Jn. 4:14; Rev. 7:17; 21:6)
14:29a	"slow to become angry" (Jas. 1:19)
14:35a	"a servant who acts wisely" (Lk. 12:42; Matt. 24:45)
15:3a	"The eyes of the LORD are everywhere" (Heb. 4:13)
15:4a	"a tree of life" (Rev. 2:7; 22:2,14,19)
15:11a	"Abaddon" (Rev. 9:11)
16:22a	"a fountain of life" (Jn. 4:14; Rev. 7:17; 21:6)
16:27b	"his speech is like a burning fire" (Jas. 3:6)
17:3	"The crucible is for refining silver and the smelter for gold, but the One who purifies hearts by fire is the LORD" (1 Pet. 1:7)
18:4	"The words of a man's mouth are like deep waters; the fountain of wisdom is an overflowing stream" (Jn. 7:38)
19:5	"A lying witness...one who utters lies" (Acts 6:13)
19:9	"A lying witness...one who utters lies" (Acts 6:13)
19:17	"Whoever has pity on the poor lends to the LORD, and He will repay him for his good deed" (Matt. 25:40)
19:26a,b	"A son who assaults his father and who drives away his mother" (1 Tim. 1:9)
20:20	"Whoever curses his father and mother, his lamp will be snuffed out in total darkness" (Matt. 15:4; Mk. 7:10)
20:22a	"Do not say, 'I'll get even with you!'" (Rom. 12:17)
20:22b	"Wait for the LORD" (Rom. 12:19; 1 Thess. 5:15; 1 Pet. 3:9)
20:25b	"This is a holy offering!" (Mk. 7:11)
20:27	"A person's soul is the LORD's lamp; it searches his entire innermost being" (1 Cor. 2:10)
21:2	"A man thinks everything he does is right, but the LORD weighs hearts" (Lk. 16:15)
21:22b	"pulls down the strong defenses" (2 Cor. 10:4)
21:28a	"A lying witness" (Acts 6:13)
22:8a	"Whoever sows...will reap" (Gal. 6:7,8)
22:10	"Drive out a mocker and conflict will leave; quarreling and abuse will stop" (Gal. 4:30)

23:31a   "Do not look at wine" (Eph. 5:18)
24:12c   "won't He who guards your soul know it?" (Lk. 16:15)
24:12d   "won't He pay back everyone according to what he does?" (Matt. 16:27;
          Rom. 2:6; 2 Tim. 4:14; Rev. 2:23; 20:12; 22:12)
24:20b   "the lamp of the wicked will be snuffed out" (Matt. 25:8)
24:21   "Fear the LORD...fear the king" (1 Pet. 2:17)
24:29   "Do not say, 'I'll treat him like he treated me; I'll pay him back for what
          he's done to me.'" (Rom. 12:17; 1 Thess. 5:15; 1 Pet. 3:9)
25:6,7   "Do not brag about youself before a king or stand in the spot that belongs
          to notable people; because it is better to be told, 'Come up here,' than
          to be put down in front of a prince whom your eyes have seen"
          (Lk. 14:7-11)
25:21,22a "If your enemy is hungry, give him some food to eat, and if he is thirsty,
          give him some water to drink; for in this way you will heap burning
          coals on his head" (Rom. 12:20)
25:22b   "and the LORD will reward you" (Matt. 6:4,6)
26:11a   "As a dog goes back to his vomit" (2 Pet. 2:22)
27:1   "Do not brag about tomorrow, because you do not know what another
          day may bring" (Jas. 4:13-16)
27:18a   "Whoever takes care of a fig tree can eat its fruit" (2 Cor. 9:7)
27:20a   "Abaddon" (Rev. 9:11)
28:14b   "whoever is hard-hearted falls into disaster" (Rom. 2:5)
29:23   "A person's pride will humiliate him, but a humble spirit gains honor"
          (Matt. 23:12; Lk. 18:14)
30:4a   "Who has gone up to heaven and come down?" (Jn. 3:13; Rom. 10:6)
30:4e   "Son" (Jn. 3:13)
30:6a   "Do not add to His words" (Rev. 22:18)
30:8c   "feed me only the food I need" (Matt. 6:11)
31:17a   "puts on strength like a belt" (1 Pet. 1:13)

NOTES

NOTES